# A SOCIETY ADRIFT

# A Society Adrift

## Interviews and Debates, 1974–1997

Cornelius Castoriadis

Edited by Enrique Escobar, Myrto Gondicas,
and Pascal Vernay

Translated by Helen Arnold

FORDHAM UNIVERSITY PRESS

*New York* 2010

Previously published as *Une société à la dérive: Entretiens et
débats, 1974–1977*. © Éditions du Seuil, 2005.

Fordham University Press has no responsibility for the
persistence or accuracy of URLs for external or third-party
Internet websites referred to in this publication and does not
guarantee that any content on such websites is, or will
remain, accurate or appropriate.

Cet ouvrage, publié dans le cadre d'un programme d'aide à
la publication, bénéficie du soutien du Ministère des Affaires
étrangères et du Service Culturel de l'Ambassade de France
aux Etats-Unis.

This work, published as part of a program of aid for
publication, received support from the French Ministry of
Foreign Affairs and the Cultural Services of the French
Embassy in the United States.

Library of Congress Cataloging-in-Publication Data

Castoriadis, Cornelius, 1922–1997.
[Société à la dérive. English]
A society adrift : interviews and debates, 1974–1997 /
Cornelius Castoriadis ; edited by Enrique Escobar, Myrto
Gondicas, and Pascal Vernay ; translated by Helen Arnold.
p.  cm.
Includes bibliographical references.
ISBN 978–0-8232–3093–8 (cloth : alk. paper)
ISBN 978–0-8232–3094–5 (pbk. : alk. paper)
1. Political science—Philosophy. 2. Social sciences. 3. World
politics—1985–1995. 4. Economic history—1971–
5. Castoriadis, Cornelius, 1922–1997—Interviews. I. Escobar,
Enrique. II. Gondicas, Myrto. III. Vernay, Pascal. IV. Title.
JA71.C335  2010
320.01—dc22
2009030655

Printed in the United States of America
12 11 10  5 4 3 2 1
First edition

# CONTENTS

*Editors' Note to the French Edition*        vii

*Translator's Postscriptum*        xiii

## PART I. ITINERARY

The Project of Autonomy Is Not a Utopia (1992)    3

Why I Am No Longer a Marxist (1974)    11

Imaginary Significations (1982)    45

Response to Richard Rorty (1995)    69

On Wars in Europe (1992)    83

## PART II. INTERVENTIONS

On the Possibility of Creating a New Form of Society (1977)    103

What Political Parties Cannot Do (1979)    117

Present Issues for Democracy (1986)    125

These Are Bad Times (1986)    130

Do Vanguards Exist? (1987)    135

What Revolution Is (1987)    144

Neither a Historical Necessity nor Simply an "Ethical" Exigency:
    A Political and Human Exigency (1988)    151

When the East Swings to the West (1989)    156

The Market, Capitalism, and Democracy (1990)    161

"Democracy" without Citizens' Participation (1991)    166

The Gulf War: Setting Things Straight (1991)    171

Gorbachev: Neither Reform nor Backtracking (1991)    176

On War, Religion, and Politics (1991)    183

Communism, Fascism, and Emancipation (1991)    190

Ecology against the Merchants (1992)    194

The Revolutionary Potency of Ecology (1992)    197

A Society Adrift (1993)                                                    206

On Political Judgment (1995)                                           216

Neither Resignation nor Archaism (1995)                      220

A Rising Tide of Significancy? (1996)                             223

A Singular Trajectory (1997)                                          230

Chronology and Bio-Bibliography                               239

This volume contains a number of interviews and contributions to debates in the period between 1974 and 1997, given by Cornelius Castoriadis, a most versatile thinker and equally passionate political militant, economist, psychoanalyst, and philosopher. They are from the second part of his career, devoted essentially to philosophical reflection, subsequent to the experience of the group and journal *Socialisme ou Barbarie* (1948–67), but since one paper (1974) gives a detailed account of that experience, this book may be said to comprise Castoriadis' entire intellectual itinerary.[1] Readers for whom this is a first contact will, we hope, find this compendium helpful, in that it may furnish a guiding thread to find their way through a particularly dense, complex *oeuvre*. Others will find a clear, handy résumé of Castoriadis' positions, which, as he himself was well aware, do not go without saying, by far.

In particular, this book shows how he viewed two questions, the question of truth and that of life in society, as inseparable in the last analysis, and how the two intertwined in his own life. As stated in one of the texts, these are truly "endless" questions—in fact, we might have given that title to the book.

As its opening text, although not in the otherwise chronological order, we have chosen a 1992 interview in which Castoriadis briefly explains what he meant at the time by the "project of (individual and collective) autonomy," and which contains some positions he held until the end. Next, Part I contains two longer, more elaborate interviews that were most probably very attentively "reread and corrected" by the author, as the saying goes.[2]

---

1. We have added a chronology, as well as a bibliography that, although not exhaustive, will, we hope, be of use to those who wish to do further reading.

2. The same is true of some other long interviews, subsequently included in other books, and which also give an overview of his political positions, such as "The Revolutionary Exigency" (1976), in *Political and Social Writings*. vol. 3: *1961–1979;* "Une interrogation sans fin" (1979), in *Domaines de l'homme*, 2nd ed. (Paris: Seuil, 1986), 241–60; "Points Essais" (1999), 299–324; the 1993 text that gave its title to the anthology *La Montée de l'insignifiance* (The Rising Tide of Insignificancy) (Paris: Seuil, 1996), 82–102; and in the same volume, "Le délabrement de l'Occident" (1991). There are three ex-

The 1974 text contains his most complete presentation of the group and journal *Socialisme ou Barbarie* [henceforth *S. ou B.*]. It was written with sufficient distance (the group disbanded in 1967), but at a time when the issues debated were still very much present, both in the admittedly limited milieu of those well acquainted with or newly discovering the journal, and in his own work. Like the 1977 interview in Part II, it summarizes Castoriadis' views on the main issues discussed in the journal: the economic and social nature of the former "Soviet" bloc countries, the bureaucratization of society and of the workers' movement itself, the break with Marxism, the chances for an autonomous society. In the talk on "Imaginary Signifi-cations" (1982), he develops ideas that had been central to his thinking since *The Imaginary Institution of Society* (1984, 1987), and in particular the nature of the significations through which societies "hang together," those significations he called "imaginary" because they cannot be reduced to the "real" or to some "rational-functional" dimension. These questions were also the main focus of his seminars at the École des hautes études en sci-ences sociales (1980–95), intended as the basis for a work in several vol-umes under the title *La Création Humaine* (Human Creation), a project he never carried through.[3] Although the debate with Richard Rorty contains no overall exposition of the writer's positions, the issues it broaches are broad enough to merit its inclusion in this first part. The same is true of the 1992 lecture on wars in Europe. In addition to the intrinsic interest of the subject, it reminds us of the importance of the human psyche as a dimension of Castoriadis' life and work.

As we know, Castoriadis' most extensive analyses of economic and so-cial realities are the papers in *S. ou B.* and the updates in the "10/18" reprints,[4] mostly devoted to the 1945–75 period, when world leaders had

---

ceptions: the response to Richard Rorty, the 1992 lecture on wars in Europe and the last interview (1997), with Lilia Moglia, the final version of which was established by the editors of the present edition.

3. The EHESS seminars are now being published in French under that title, by the Éditions du Seuil. Now available: *Sur* Le Politique *de Platon* (1999) (partial publication of the 1985–86 course), translated into English as *On Plato's* Statesman (Stanford, Calif.: Stanford University Press, 2002); *Sujet et vérité dans le monde social-historique* (2002) (1986–87 course); *Ce qui fait la Grèce, 1. D'Homère à Héraclite* (2004) (partial publication of the 1982–83 course); and *La Cité et les lois. Ce qui fait la Grèce 2* (2008) (partial publication of the 1983–84 course).

4. Especially: "Sur la dynamique du capitalisme," *S. ou B.*, 12 (Aug.–Sept. 1953) and 13 (Jan.–March 1954); the texts "On the Contents of Socialism," *Political and Social Writings*, vol. 1: *1946–1955*, and vol. 2: *1955–1960*; *The Castoriadis Reader* (Malden, Mass., and Oxford, England: Basil Blackwell, 1997); "Modern Capitalism and Revolu-tion," in *Political and Social Writings*, vol. 2: *1955–1960*; as well as the "Author's Intro-

(partially) learned the lessons to be drawn from the awful experience of the interwar period. The developed part of that world rested on a relative balance between capitalist enterprise, the State and various political and trade union bureaucracies "representing" wage earners. While criticizing people who stuck to the idea that capitalism is undermined by a dynamic of objective contradictions, the essence of which is described in *Capital*, and asserting that more than a century of social *struggle* had led to the transformation of capitalism and the development of real capitalist *policy*, taking into account the overall, long-term interests of the system, Castoriadis insisted on demonstrating that this world is still wracked by the contradictions and irrationality inherent in *bureaucratic organization*, "a social structure in which collective activities are run by an impersonal, hierarchically organized apparatus, economically advantaged and recruited on the basis of rules it sets and applies to itself, and purportedly acting according to 'rational' criteria and methods."[5] This world was certainly not shielded from crisis, much to the contrary, but those crises did not stem from the factors and dynamic to which Marxist analysis ascribed them. The other side—both requisite and consequence—of that reality is the destruction of significations, mass irresponsibility, and above all what Castoriadis called *privatization*, retreat from the political sphere. The population "takes care of its private business, with the impression that society's business is beyond its reach."[6] Now, in the long run this trend—the absence of forces capable of countering the destructive tendencies of the system—would necessarily pave the way for a form of totally unbridled capitalism, and that is definitely what happened, increasingly clearly, after 1980. Castoriadis was far

---

duction to the 1974 English Edition" of *Modern Capitalism and Revolution. A Solidarity Book* (1974), reprinted in *Political and Social Writings*, vol. 1, where he gave his interpretation of the post-war inflationary episode (1960–70). But there is also "Technique," in *Crossroads in the Labyrinth* (Cambridge, Mass.: MIT Press; and Brighton, England: Harvester Press, 1984), and "Reflections on 'Rationality' and 'Development'" (1975) (*Thesis Eleven*, 9, 1985); "The Nature and Value of Equality," *Philosophy, Politics, Autonomy: Essays in Political Philosophy* (New York: Oxford University Press, 1991). For the later phase, see also pages 128–212 of *Devant la guerre* (Paris: Fayard, 1981); "The Crisis of Modern Society," in *Political and Social Writings*, vol. 3 (Minneapolis: University of Minnesota Press, 1993); and last, "The 'Rationality' of Capitalism," in the posthumous *Figures of the Thinkable* (Stanford, Calif.: Stanford University Press, 2007).

5. "Le mouvement révolutionnaire sous le capitalisme moderne," in *Capitalisme moderne et révolution* 2 (1979): 127. [My translation. Another version, by D. A. Curtis, is to be found as "Modern Capitalism and Revolution," in *Political and Social Writings*, vol. 2 (Minneapolis: University of Minnesota Press, 1988), 226–314.—Trans.]

6. Ibid., 48. [Same remark as above.—Trans.]

too busy with his philosophical work to write a comprehensive analysis[7] of that post-1980 society and the "counter-offensive" of the ruling strata during that phase characterized by the deliberate (and no doubt suicidal for the system, in the long run) eclipse of governments. Whence the value of the indications to be found in the texts published in Part II.

Here we have shorter interviews, occasional papers perhaps, but which as such suffice to refute the fiction that Castoriadis lost interest in political life at some point. Time in and time out, he returns to the question of democracy: to its open nature, its past and its future in the Western world. He is as vigorous as usual, not overly subtle (remember, these texts are meant for action; they are not in-depth analyses); he tends to speak simply; he certainly does not oversimplify. As a rule, when Castoriadis makes a brutal assertion it corresponds to a brutal fact, the features of which are often clearer in retrospect. The reader who has any doubts thereon has only to look at the dates of the talks, the diagnostic made at the time, and what has transpired since.

Two examples will suffice. His remarks on the withdrawal of citizens from public affairs may have seemed pessimistic in the 1970s and '80s. Today, in the major "democratic" countries, and even in those where what we call representative democracy is apparently most deeply rooted, the government sometimes "represents" only one voter out of five, and often the *majority* of the electorate refuses to partake in the life of the system. It is true that since 1995, and especially since 1999, there is no longer total passivity in developed countries. Movements have developed, the positive aspects of which Castoriadis would no doubt have appreciated. But he would also indubitably have felt that a necessary prerequisite for their success, however partial, would be that they learn the lessons to be drawn from the past century, and especially from the totalitarian experience. For after all, the drying of the sea of Aral, probably the worst ecological catastrophe of the century, or the millions of deaths from starvation—the price paid for the failure of China's "Great Leap Forward"—were not caused by the exclusive reign of the "marketplace." Nothing can be achieved, nothing can be obtained without a clear realization that the "free enterprise" imposture is not the only form of imposture, that the "free-market" dead end is not the only dead end to be feared for the future of humanity.

---

7. Although it was only at the very end of his life, knowing that he no longer had the time, that he gave up his efforts to develop an analysis of the "worldwide system of domination" and publish the volume on *The Dynamics of Capitalism*, planned to be part of the republication of his "10/18" imprint articles. However, "The 'Rationality' of Capitalism (1997) gives some indication of what the orientation of that work would have been.

Castoriadis also wondered what future there may be for a society in which people are bridled only by fear of penal sanctions. Today, after the Enron scandal and so many others, when we see the equivalent of the annual GNP of any number of fairly developed countries disappear unaccountably, you would have to be completely blind to view that as just one of the morally unpleasant sides of social life, as old as Methuselah and unrelated to the very structure of our society, or to object that the undeveloped countries are completely corrupt, and always have been, which is unquestionable, but clearly shows what is at stake here. Nothing, says Castoriadis,[8] "in 'liberal' discourse or in the 'values' of our times accounts for why—barring the threat written into the Criminal Code—a judge would not put his judgment up for bids, or a president use his position to get rich. But for the Criminal Code itself to function, *honest* judges are needed." He wrote that twenty years ago. One is tempted to say he hadn't seen anything yet (although the millions of dollars blown away during the Savings and Loans scandal in the United States or squandered by the Crédit Lyonnais were far from negligible affairs). There can be no doubt any more: We've gotten there.

For more than thirty years Castoriadis repeatedly returned to that all-important political question: the existence of a "democracy" without "democrats," continually tending to destroy the type of human being that might enable its survival, even in its present imperfect form. He drew a conclusion that almost everyone is forced to admit nowadays: Our society is adrift. True, everyone tries to draw the conclusion that this has strictly no consequences. When the problem takes on a particularly acute form, there is grave talk about an earthquake and it is said that things will never be the same again: then, when the fright is over, everyone forgets it in a hurry. (Anyone who thinks this is a caricature should look over the newspapers covering the last five years.) Our information-saturated society is also an amnesic society—and even if it weren't, every effort is made, as we have recently seen in France, to place "in good hands" all the means of preventing any criticism and if necessary erasing any memory. Everyone with any concern for the public weal should pay proper attention to these problems, however, for sooner or later their effects will be felt to the point where they will become inescapable. The invocation ad nauseam of "socialism" and the "dictatorship of the proletariat" did not prevent the real meaning behind those words from coming out into the open: to varying

---

8. See "Neither a Historical Necessity nor Simply an 'Ethical' Exigency: A Political and Human Exigency" in this volume.

degrees, they mean terror, oppression, inequality, and economic ineffi-ciency. The mechanical repetition of the catchwords "rule of law" and "market economy" cannot indefinitely replace a clear vision, not of what those words might possibly mean, but of the concrete historical realities behind them at the present time: that is, endless accumulation (in all senses of the word), destruction of the environment, withdrawal of the popula-tion from the public sphere, decomposition of the mechanisms for govern-ing our societies. In this respect, Castoriadis' position—the project of autonomy—is undoubtedly worthy of being *truly* considered. To our knowledge, such is not the case.

We have unhesitatingly corrected the occasional slips of the tongue and obvious errors in the published texts, and introduced some minor stylistic changes. We also made a few cuts (clearly indicated), to avoid the repeti-tions which are unavoidable in speech but may be tiresome when a text is read from beginning to end, and retained either the most synthetic or the most developed version of the same idea, depending on the case. However, it goes without saying that readers familiar with Castoriadis' work will recognize many of the formulations, for like many good thinkers of the past, he felt that when something is true it can be said twice, thrice, or even innumerable times. It is an understatement to say that he didn't care a bit about those almost literal repetitions and reworkings. He would not have lost a minute attempting to avoid them. But although this compen-dium is not aimed primarily at readers who are well acquainted with his work, even they may find this a useful reminder of ideas that go against the grain of what they read and hear day in and day out. Hopefully, then, this book will make some people want to read on (or again), to go to those writings in which the author's positions are developed more extensively.

Last, we wondered whether to add some notes, given the present for-getfulness, if only to tell our youngest readers about that Union de la Gauche [Union of the Left] that wanted, Rimbaud-like, to "change life," for example. On reflection, we decided to add a chronological table locat-ing the various talks in their historic context. With few exceptions, men-tioned in the text, the titles were chosen by the editors of the present volume. Our footnotes (mostly quotations or references to other writings by the same author) appear within braces {like this}. [The translator's notes are in square brackets.—Trans.]

Enrique Escobar, Myrto Gondicas,
and Pascal Vernay, editors of the French edition

Several years have gone by since this book first appeared in French, and the reader can only be struck by the relevance to the present situation of these comments by the editors. At this writing, the entire world is in the vortex of a financial and economic crisis of unprecedented scope and totally unknown consequences. Castoriadis' analysis of the consequences of what he calls "privatization" and his call for political/social commitment in the deepest sense of the word are particularly apposite in this context. It seemed worthwhile, then, to insert a previously unpublished interview, "A Rising Tide of Significancy?"—indeed, one of his last—indicating, if need be, his constant involvement on the political scene, and above all, his intention to take part again in a new collective venture ("a journal or bulletin"), having perceived a change of attitude, attested by the recent movements in France (November–December 1995). Unfortunately, that undertaking was prematurely interrupted by his death.

Helen Arnold, translator
Paris, November 2008

# A Society Adrift

# PART I

# Itinerary

# The Project of Autonomy Is Not a Utopia

*Why don't you like the term "utopia"?*

It isn't that I don't like the term; it's that the precise, original meaning of words is important to me. Utopia means something that has not existed and cannot exist. What I call the revolutionary project, the project of individual and collective autonomy (the two are inseparable) is not a utopia, but a social-historical project susceptible of being achieved, and which has never been shown to be impossible. Its achievement depends only on the lucid activity of individuals and peoples, their understanding, determination and imagination.

The term utopia has recently become fashionable again, to some extent under the influence of Ernst Bloch, a Marxist who had more or less adjusted to the East German regime, and who never criticized Stalinism and the totalitarian bureaucratic regimes. The word utopia was a sort of cover-up for him, a way of differentiating himself from "really existing socialism." Habermas took the term up again more recently, because after the total ruin of Marxism and Marxism-Leninism, it seems to legitimate some vague criticism of the current regime by talking about a utopian socialist transformation, with a whiff of "pre-Marxism." Actually, it's quite the opposite. No-one (except a neo-Kantian philosopher) can understand how it is possible to criticize what is on the basis of what cannot be. The term utopia is a mystification.

*What is the project of individual and collective autonomy?*

It is the project of a society in which all citizens have an equal, effective possibility of participating in legislating, governing, and judging, and in the last analysis, in instituting society. That state of affairs is predicated

{A talk with Jocelyn Wolff and Benjamin Quénelle, on December 28, 1992, published in the magazine *Propos* (Strasburg), no. 10 (March 1993): 34–40.}

on radical changes in the present institutions. That's what we may call the revolutionary project, with the understanding that revolution doesn't mean massacres, wanton bloodletting, the extermination of counter-revolutionaries and the taking of the Winter Palace. Clearly that state of affairs is a long way from the present system, which functions essentially non-democratically. Our regimes are falsely called democratic, whereas they are actually *liberal oligarchies*.

*How do those regimes work?*

They are liberal: they don't resort mostly to constraint but to a sort of vague semi-attachment of the population, which has finally adopted the capitalist imaginary, according to which the goal of human life is the un-limited expansion of production and consumption, so-called material well-being, and so on. The outcome is that the population is totally *privatized*. Nineteen-sixty-eight's *"métro-boulot-dodo"* ["subway, work, sleep"—an ironic slogan in May '68.—Trans.] has become *"bagnole-boulot-télé"* ["car, work, TV."—Trans.]. The population doesn't participate in political life. Voting every five or seven years for a person you don't know, on problems you don't know and that the system has taken care to prevent you from knowing—that isn't participation. But for change to occur, for there to be true self-government, of course there has to be a change in the institutions so that people can participate in managing the affairs of the community, but also and above all, there has to be a change in the attitude of individuals toward institutions and public affairs, the *res publica*, or what the Greeks called *ta koina* (the affairs of the community). Today, the domination of an oligarchy and the passivity and privatization of the people are simply the two sides of the same coin.

Let's go into a little theory, parenthetically. Abstractly speaking, in social life, viewed from a political angle, there are always three spheres. There is the *private sphere*, including people's strictly personal life; a *public sphere*, in which the decisions that apply necessarily to everyone and are publicly sanctioned are made; and a sphere we may call *public/private*, open to all but where there is no place for political power, even if exerted by the collectivity: the sphere where people discuss, publish, buy books, go to the theater, and so forth. In present-day parlance, the private sphere and the public/private sphere are confused, especially since Hannah Arendt, and that confusion pops up all the time among intellectuals, when they talk about "civil society." But the opposition between civil society and the State (which dates back to the late 18th century) is insufficient; it doesn't give us the means for conceptualizing a democratic society. To do so we need that articulation between three spheres. To revert to the vocabulary of ancient Greece, we have to distinguish between the *oikos* (the house, the private sphere), the *ekklèsia* (the assembly of the people, the public sphere) and the *agora* (the "marketplace" and meeting place, the public/private sphere). Under totalitarianism, the three spheres are completely merged. In liberal oligarchies, there is more or less clear domination of the public sphere by one part of the public/private sphere (the "marketplace," the economy) and at the same time, elimination of the truly public character of the public sphere (the private, secretive nature of today's State). Democracy is the correct articulation of those three spheres, with the public sphere becoming really public. This requires that everyone participate in the management of community affairs, which in turn requires institutions enabling people to participate and inciting them to do so. Which in turn is impossible without *effective* political equality. Here we have the true meaning of equality: society cannot make people equal in the sense that it would make everyone capable of running a 100-meter race in ten seconds, or of playing Beethoven's *Appassionata* admirably. But it can make them equal in their effective participation in every instituted power in existence in that society.

That is what the project of autonomy is, and its achievement poses considerable problems, of course. No-one can solve these all alone and in advance; only society as a whole will be able to solve them, provided it sets itself in motion. For instance, a democratic society is clearly incompatible with today's huge concentration of economic power. It is just as clearly incompatible with bureaucratic pseudo-planning. There is also the issue of workplace freedom. Citizens cannot be slaves at their workplace five or six days a week and free on political Sundays. Self-government in the sphere of work is therefore one objective: that is what I have been calling, for over forty years now, management of production by the producers. Of course that raises problems too, such as the participation of technicians and specialists. It also entails a market that is a *true market*, not like today's market, dominated by monopolies and oligopolies, or State intervention. All of these transformations assume—and go hand in hand with—an anthropological transformation of contemporary individuals.

*Individuals' culture, in other words?*

You may, if you like, call that culture. We are talking about the close, deep tie between the structure of individuals and that of the system. Nowadays, individuals are in conformity to the system and the system to individuals. If this society is to change, a radical change is needed in the interests and attitudes of human beings. The passionate desire for consumer goods must be replaced by passionate care about community affairs.

*How can that passion for political affairs come into being? How can it be encouraged?*

I don't know. But I know that it has existed in the course of history. There have been times, and even whole eras, in which people cared passionately about community affairs. They went into the streets; they made demands; they imposed a number of things. If we are living under a liberal (tolerant) regime today, it's not because that regime was granted by the dominant classes. The liberal elements of contemporary institutions are the sediments of centuries of mass struggles in the Western world, struggles that began as early as the 10th century, with the combats of the free boroughs to obtain relative self-government. Nowadays we see sluggishness, and even an atrophy of struggles, but no-one can claim that to be the definitive state of society, once and for all. The ink of Fukuyama's writings had hardly dried when history deafeningly demonstrated their imbecility.

Were the present state of apathy, depoliticization and privatization to continue, we might certainly expect some major crises. The problem of the environment, about which nothing is being done, would then surface again with an acuity we can't imagine at present, along with the problem of what is called the third world—actually three-fourths of humanity, and the problem of the decomposition of rich societies themselves. Because people's withdrawal from the political sphere, attended by the disappearance of political and social conflict, enables the economic, political and communications oligarchy to escape any control. And that produces utterly irrational and structurally corrupt regimes, as of right now.

*Doesn't the project of autonomy based on participation in the affairs of the community come up against the lethargy generated by television and the mass media?*

Present-day television serves to make people mindless. And we haven't seen anything yet, in France. Films are cut twice or three times for advertising, whereas in the United States or Australia, for example, cuts for advertising double or triple the length of films. But that isn't any "American" curse; it's the capitalist matrix, with the media dominated by advertising, and therefore by sponsors. In the French daily *Le Monde*, TV critics Frappat and Schneidermann constantly point out that the more or less interesting programs are scheduled at one A.M. For television, radio and the other modern mass media to serve democracy would require enormous changes, not only in the contents of programs but in the very structure of the media. In their present state, their material and social structure is the embodiment of a society of domination: there is one broadcasting pole, and an unlimited number of anonymous, isolated, passive receivers. The role of the media is absolutely consonant with the *spirit of the system* and contributes powerfully to generating overall mindlessness. Just think of how the Gulf War was "covered."

*Do you think the system you criticize is a modern system? Are we living in a postmodern era, or do you refuse that idea?*

I already criticized the term "postmodern" in *The World in Fragments*. Modernity lasted about two centuries, from 1750 to 1950. After that, we entered what I call the *age of generalized conformism*. Modernity meant constantly questioning the givens, in philosophy as well as in politics and art. That has practically disappeared since about 1950. The date is an arbitrary oversimplification of course, but it's at about that time that the immense creative inspiration that had fired the Western world for two centuries began to slacken, to the point of disappearing almost completely.

*You think the idea of progress no longer exists?*

The *idea* of progress still exists, of course—although it is increasingly moth-eaten. It's an imaginary signification that lasted as long as it could, and will go on as long as it can. But as an *idea*, it's fallacious. You can't talk about progress in the history of humanity, except in one field, the *ensemblist-identitary* field (what I call the *ensidic*) or, say, the logical-instrumental field.[1] The H-bomb is a progress over flint, for instance, since it can kill much more and better than flint. But there is no such thing as progress for fundamental things. There is neither progress nor regression between the Parthenon and Notre-Dame de Paris, between Plato and Kant, Bach and Wagner, the Altamira cave drawings and Picasso. But *there are* breaks: in Ancient Greece, between the 8th and the 5th century BCE, with the creation of democracy and philosophy, or in western Europe, starting in the 10th and 11th centuries, with an enormous quantity of new creations, and culminating in the modern period.

*But still and all, the concept of progress carries the idea that the fate of the next generation will be an improvement over the fate of the previous generation. Isn't that what made the proletariat embrace industrialization?*

---

1. ["By ensidic logic, I mean the logic that knows only the relationships of belonging, inclusion, implication among propositions, and the logic of first-order predicates." In *La Montée de l'Insignifiance* (Paris: Seuil, 1996).—Trans.]

Improvement according to what criteria? It's capitalism that has based all of social life on the idea that economic "improvement" is the only thing that counts—or the thing that, once achieved, would bring along all the rest, in the bargain. And Marx and Marxism followed suit. For a long time the proletariat, while fighting exploitation, didn't aim solely at "improving" its standard of living, but of course, that essentially capitalist imaginary, shared by Marxism as well, also penetrated the working class in the long run. There definitely was fantastic economic expansion under capitalism (which would have been unimaginable, even for Marx, as our hindsight shows). But as we now see, it was bought by irreversible destruction wreaked on the biosphere. And another requisite was workers' struggles for better pay and shorter working hours. That was what created constantly expanding national markets without which capitalism would have collapsed under the weight of crises of overproduction. That's also how the unemployment potentially generated by rising productivity was absorbed. Today's unemployment is due to the fact that the accelerated gains in the productivity of work since 1940 have only been attended by a very slight cut in the hours worked, as opposed to what occurred between 1840 and 1940, when the working week was reduced from 72 hours to 40. That obsession with increasing production and consumption is practically absent from other historical periods. As shown by Marshall Sahlins, among others (in his *Stone Age Economics*), people worked two or three hours a day in Paleolithic societies, and you can't even call that work in the present-day sense. Hunting, for instance, was also a collective festivity. The rest of the time people played, talked, and made love. What is called "economic progress" was obtained by transforming human beings into machines for producing and consuming.

*Can work be a pleasure?*

Certainly, provided that work is meaningful for the person who does it. And that depends both on the objects produced and on the organization of production and the worker's role in it.

*There are three million people jobless in France. How come the social system hasn't broken down?*

That's a very good question. First, there's no guarantee that the status quo will last indefinitely. Next, unemployment doesn't weigh as heavily on people, partly because there is a protective social net, which is not negligible. Above all, unemployment affects different strata and sections of the population to varying extents. Poverty is mostly shifted to some categories—local, ethnic, and so on—that are unable to protest very forcibly, and whose marginal status has often turned them into outlaws and deviants: their reaction doesn't take a collective form. I talked a little while ago about the main reason for rising unemployment: lack of a cutback in working hours in spite of higher productivity. There is another reason: that is, the relinquishing of Keynesian policies supporting overall demand—what made the postwar boom possible, to a large extent—and their replacement by an idiotic neo-liberalism, with Thatcher, Reagan, Friedman, the Chicago Boys, and so forth. We are witnessing some absolutely incredible things. For instance, Switzerland is now beginning to experience something of a rise in unemployment: in response, the federal government has reduced public spending! That's exactly what Hoover did in the United States at the beginning of the Great Depression in 1929–33, and it was Laval's policy in France (advised by Jacques Rueff) in 1932–33. You respond to deflation by more deflation. The reality of the mental decomposition of the ruling classes is far beyond what theory might reasonably have predicted.

*Do you think the ecologists or the alternative parties can embody that renewed spirit that is so terribly needed?*

The ecology movement is certainly positive as such, but the existing ecologist parties are totally shortsighted, politically speaking. They don't see that ecological problems are indissolubly linked to the broad societal problems, and they tend to turn into an environmentalist lobby.

*In conclusion, can you give us your opinion on the "right to interfere," inasmuch as you stress the importance of recognizing the otherness of the other, at the individual level, in your project of autonomy?*

The problem is a highly complex one. You know Robespierre's famous phrase: "Peoples do not like armed missionaries." No-one can deny that many third world countries are experiencing awful situations, with the failure of attempts to introduce either "socialism" or free-market capitalism. In Somalia and Ethiopia unlimited tribal conflicts are back; in India Hindus and Muslims are massacring each other; in Sudan the Islamic government is trying to force Islamic law on Christian and animist groups in the South; in Afghanistan there is bloody chaos; in some former Soviet Union republics the communists have returned to power after murdering their opponents; there are ruthless ethnic wars in the Caucasus and above all in ex-Yugoslavia, and so on. No-one can be indifferent to such monstrous doings. We think, and rightly so, that some of the significations created in and by our society and our history—respect for life and physical integrity, human rights, the separation of the political and the religious, and so on—have every right to universal validity. But it is tragically clear that those significations are rejected by some societies—or States—corresponding to maybe some four-fifths of the world population, and also that the liberal and Marxist illusions that those values would "spontaneously" spread around the world have been demolished. Can we impose them forcibly? Who will impose them, and how? Who has the moral right to impose them? The hypocrisy of Western governments in that respect is flagrant. The United States intervened militarily in Panama and in Iraq because of the specific interests at stake—never mind the nature of those—but they are against any intervention in Haiti. The case of ex-Yugoslavia is horrible, and it's right on our doorstep. There has been nothing but idle talk about it for over a year now. And still, in that case there is talk and "humanitarian aid." But if a comparable crisis were to break out between Russia and Ukraine, would there be talk about interference? At this very moment, there's a war going on in Sudan, waged by the Islamic government of the North to impose the *sharia* on the non-Muslim population in the South. For a large part, it is financed by Iran, which also backs Egyptian and North African fundamentalists. Why do we disregard the atrocities committed by the Sudanese government? Because Islam is too big a thing; there's the Middle Eastern powder keg, and oil. Human rights are systematically, cynically violated by China, Vietnam, Indonesia (with the extermination of a good part of the population of Timor), and Burma. Are we going to "interfere"? What kind of law is it that punishes little thieves and leaves the big gangsters alone? I think the "right to interfere" is a typical Kouchner slogan.[2]

*In the good or the bad sense of the term?*

In the Kouchnerian sense of the term.

---

2. [Bernard Kouchner, cofounder of the non-governmental organization "Doctors without Borders" and later of "Doctors of the World," member of the Socialist Party at the time, was the main champion of the idea of "the right to humanitarian interference." He was frequently criticized for his attraction to the mass media. Having gone through numerous changes of opinion (ranging from the Communist Party to the center at that point), he is now (in 2008) minister of foreign affairs in a right-wing government under President Nicolas Sarkozy.—Trans.]

# Why I Am No Longer a Marxist

## History of the Socialisme ou Barbarie Group

Socialisme ou Barbarie (S. ou B.) came out of a tendency formed in the summer of 1946 within the Parti Communiste Internationaliste (PCI), the French Trotskyist party. I personally had been criticizing the Trotskyist view of Stalinism since the turn of 1944–45, based on my experience of the Stalinist coup d'état in Greece, in December 1944–January 1945. According to Trotsky and the Trotskyists, the Stalinist parties in capitalist countries had sided with the bourgeois order once and for all (at least since Popular Front times and the Spanish Civil War). The Trotskyists viewed those parties as simply representing a new version of reformism, and analyzed them using the Leninist criticism of classical reformism. From that viewpoint, if ever Stalinists were to participate in a government, they would necessarily do so the way reformist parties do, and with the same objectives: that is, to save the bourgeois regime during a difficult phase in its existence. But in Greece, in 1944, that was obviously not what was happening, the CP was clearly trying to seize power and to set up its own dictatorship (which dictatorship it actually already wielded over almost the whole country during the last phase of the occupation). The December 1944 insurrection in Athens failed, but we know what happened during the same period in Yugoslavia, and then gradually, over the months, in the other Eastern European countries.

That experience in itself already showed the absurdity of the Trotskyist "tactic" of supporting the CP and "pushing it" to take power (the French

---

{An interview on January 26, 1974, with the APL (Agence de Presse Libération) group [an alternative press agency.—Trans.] based in Caen (*Basse-Normandie*). The text was entirely revised by Castoriadis and published as a supplement to the agency's "Weekly Bulletin." A mimeographed version was circulated in 1975 by the Deux Mondes bookshop in Paris. Part of the APL group later published a journal called *l'Anti-Mythes*, in Caen, in which they gave interviews of other former members of Socialisme ou Barbarie: Henri Simon (*l'Anti-Mythes*, no. 6 [Dec. 1974]), Claude Lefort (no. 14 [Nov. 1975]), and Daniel Mothé (no. 18 [Sept. 1976]). Jean-François Lyotard gave his version of the history of Socialisme ou Barbarie in *"Pierre Souyri: le marxisme qui n'a pas fini"* (*Esprit*, no. 6 [Jan. 1982]: 11–31), also published as the preface to Pierre Souyri's [untranslated] *Révolution et Contre-révolution en Chine* (Paris: Bourgois, 1982).

Trotskyist slogan was, and still is, to my knowledge, "government by the CP, SP and CGT") [the SP being the Socialist Party and the CGT the Communist-dominated trade union.—Trans.]. That tactic rested on two ideas, both equally illusory: one, that once in power, the CP would be as fragile as, say, Kerensky, and the other that the contradiction between the reasons why the masses (presumed to want a revolutionary change of regime) adhered to or supported the CP and the party's actual politics (presumed to want to preserve the bourgeois order) would explode once the CP came into power. Now, once in power the CP is anything but fragile (and if it were, we actually wouldn't be here to talk about it, since the first thing a CP does when it comes into power has always been to exterminate any revolutionaries it can get its hands on). And the "contradiction" between the CP politics and the masses' desire for a transformation doesn't explode for the good reason that the CP does effectively *transform* the regime, by expropriating the traditional bourgeoisie, creating a "planned" economy, and so on, and that it takes a while for the masses to realize clearly that they simply have a new brand of exploiters.

But that all meant taking a new look at the "Russian question" and refusing Trotsky's conception according to which the Russian bureaucracy was nothing but a parasitic, temporary social stratum that only maintained itself in power because of the unstable balance, globally speaking, between international capitalism on the one hand and the revolution on the other. Whence Trotsky's prediction that the war would cause the breakdown of the Russian bureaucracy and would necessarily lead either to an international revolution or to the victory of capitalism (which he viewed as implying the restoration of capitalism in Russia itself). That prediction, totally belied by the outcome of the war, wasn't merely journalistic; it represented a condensation of all the ins and outs of the Trotskyist conception, both on the issue of the bureaucracy and on the contemporary period.

The fact that the bureaucracy not only wasn't weakened but was in fact enormously reinforced at the end of the war, that it extended its power over all of Eastern Europe and that regimes exactly the same as the Russian one were being set up under the auspices of the CP, led unavoidably to the conclusion that it wasn't a "parasitic social stratum" but purely and simply a dominant, exploitative class—a fact corroborated on the economic and sociological levels by a fresh analysis of the Russian regime.

When I arrived in France in late 1945, the PCI was preparing the second conference of the "4th International," with the question of the USSR and Stalinism as the main item on the agenda. I participated in the preparatory discussions, and developed the ideas I have just summarized. It was during one of those discussions that I first met Claude Lefort, who was increasingly uncomfortable with the official line of the PCI. We soon discovered that our ideas were similar, and with a handful of comrades we formed a tendency within the PCI. The first texts written by the tendency began to circulate in August 1946. In 1947, during the post-war peak in the PCI's influence (with some 700 militants in France), our tendency included a few dozen comrades. But after 1947 the PCI went into one of its periodic periods of decomposition. For one thing, its right wing left it for Rousset and Sartre's Rassemblement Démocratique Révolutionnaire (RDR); for another, those militants who remained were visibly less and less capable of challenging the party's ideology and moving forward (when they managed to understand how absurd that ideology was they simply put an end to their political activity). At the same time, both current events—the 1947 strikes in France, the evolution of the Eastern European countries and the start of the cold war—and the development of our theoretical work made us realize the immense distance between Trotskyist discourse and the relevant aspects of class struggle, world history at the time and revolutionary theory itself. When you took the analysis and criticism of the experience of the Russian Revolution to their logical conclusion, it became necessary to reconsider, fundamentally, the question, "What is socialism?" That reconsideration was necessarily predicated on the idea of the autonomous action of the proletariat as the central theoretical and practical idea of the revolution and arrived at the definition of socialism as workers' management of production and the collective management of all social activities by all those who participate in them. This was all light-years from the Trotskyist conception of "nationalization" and "planning" as the central objectives of revolution, with the all-powerful party as the means of achieving them.

By the summer of 1948 we had decided to leave the PCI and were discussing the date and the way to leave when Tito broke with the Kominform. It was one of those happily coincidental events that clinch a situation. To the last man, the Trotskyists began to shout, long live Tito, long live the Yugoslavian revolution, and they wrote to the Yugoslavian CP to propose a United Front [*sic*] with them. You have to remember that until then they were writing that Yugoslavia, like the other Russian satellite countries in fact, had remained an "essentially capitalist" country. That was because the CP hadn't nationalized everything from the start, and because the government retained a few puppet ministers who weren't formally CP members (they were usually under-cover agents) and represented parties that were Stalinist creations, completely controlled by them (just as they may give us "left-wing popular progressive democratic radicals" in France some day . . .). That reasoning is so absurd that you don't know how to tackle it. What possible importance could there be in a few percent of non-nationalized production when both the bulk of it and, in fact, that percentage were declining steadily, month after month? They could see the eastern countries only in the light of the dilemma: Is there socialism (identified with nationalization etc.) or capitalism (identified with traditional private property)? But you couldn't put the question in those terms. The point was that those countries' regimes were structurally more like the Russian regime with every day that passed, that the CPs, solidly in power, were putting their men everywhere and creating a new apparatus for managing production and society, around which a new dominant social stratum of exploiters was rapidly crystallizing, and that this process not only was not incompatible with "nationalization" and "planning" but achieved its perfectly adequate form therein. Moreover, what could it mean to have a United Front between a Stalinist party in power, disposing of an army, a budget and a State, and a few dozen Trotskyists in Paris? That was the comic side. But the whole situation put the end to Trotskyism for us. When we left the PCI we formed an independent group and published the first issue of *Socialisme ou Barbarie* in March 1949.

I don't want to go into the history of the group Socialisme ou Barbarie from the beginning to the end: to do so correctly you would have to do a "case history" of it, in detail, and thoroughly scrutinize every aspect of the life of a small revolutionary organization (those aspects evacuated by the traditional conception), over an eighteen-year period, with its real and not only "ideological" everyday life, the people involved, and so forth. That would take too long, and there are more urgent things to do. I will try to simply describe some aspects, with the reminder that I was deeply, constantly implicated, and so I am not neutral, and no doubt never will be.

The history of the group can be divided into "periods," with a first phase extending from 1949 to 1953. You must remember the social, political and international context. In 1949, the cold war was in the making; in June 1950 the Korean War broke out. People were scared stiff; they perceived the situation as if the third world war were about to break out. After the great strikes in 1947 there were very few struggles in France. The miners' strike in 1948, the last major conflict of the immediate post-war period, was totally, totalitarianly controlled by the Stalinists. The immediate public of the group and the review during that period was composed of the remains of the old-style ultra-left groups: Bordiguists, council communists, a few anarchists and some offspring of the German "leftists" of the 1920s. Those groups actually split up or disappeared quite rapidly (the majority of the largest one, the Bordiguist group, joined S. ou B. in 1950). The group's activity was marked by two long debates on the "issue of the organization," which took place in rather rapid succession, the second of which produced a split (that didn't last long) with Claude Lefort and a few other comrades. From 1950 on the group was increasingly isolated; toward the end of 1952 it was down to about ten comrades, and issues of the review were meager, few and far between.

Then the scene changed, as history has the strange power to bring about. One after the other the Korean War ended, Stalin died, the workers of East Berlin revolted, France's whole public sector went on strike. The group became alive again, a number of people joined it, the content of the review was enriched, and we put it out more frequently. Daniel Mothé, who had joined the group in 1952, did very systematic work at the Renault plant, and with a group of workers there published *Tribune ouvrière*, a journal that circulated a few hundred copies inside the factory. Henri Simon, another member, played a major role in the movement of employees of a large insurance company, who set up a "council" and broke with the unions. We established other contacts with workers here and there, and had a few correspondents in the provinces. The 20th Congress of the Russian CP, Poznan, and then of course the Hungarian revolution and the Polish movement stimulated the group considerably, in that they massively corroborated our orientation, and they brought a considerable (everything is relative) increase in the circulation of the review and the number of participants in the public meetings we held in Paris. From then on, we sold at least 700 copies of the each issue of the review (and as much as 1,000 for some issues), and about a hundred non-members of the group attended our public meetings. You yourselves experienced the period after May '68, when the leftist public was quite massive. You must realize that during those years of "preaching in the desert," we held "public" meetings at the Mutualité building where there were only twenty non-members of the group.

The Algerian War began in November 1954. Guy Mollet's government (in early 1956) called a partial mobilization so as to send troops to Algeria. The recalled servicemen demonstrated, blocked the trains on which they were transported; the economy was more and more in a mess; protest movements broke out frequently. In the fall of 1957, there was a lot of agitation in the factories, and the situation was clearly unstable and open-ended. That's when we published the text "Comment lutter?" ["Ways of

Struggling."—Trans.],[1] a text that benefited enormously from discussions we held, using an initial project I had written as a starting point, with comrades in the group and others from various workplaces who weren't members of the group but came to the meetings to discuss it. But no major movement developed during the winter of 1957–58, and all of a sudden there was May 13th, and de Gaulle came into power.

Just before May 13th, the group was composed of about thirty members (regular dues-payers who participated in the meetings and in collectively decided tasks on a regular basis). The events attracted several dozen sympathizers who wanted to organize and act with us. That again raised "the issue of the organization" for the group, in practical terms this time. It was obvious that if our numbers rose to a hundred-odd we couldn't function the same way as when we were about thirty and everyone who wanted to could speak out at the group's weekly meeting. A general meeting of one hundred people almost fatally becomes a general assembly in which a few loudmouths talk and the others listen. Furthermore, that sort of meeting can't decide on practical tasks of the kind the group did. We had to "split up," then. But if you split up, you also have to come back together. How, in what forms?

The conflict over the issue of the organization, brewing since the beginning but which had never explicitly turned up again since the 1951–52 discussions, then came out into the open again. The debate actually didn't last very long and ended in September 1958 with a scission. Some comrades, whose spokesmen were Claude Lefort and Henri Simon, left S. ou B. and formed a group called Informations et liaisons ouvrières (later to become Informations et correspondance ouvrières). Their positions are formulated in Claude Lefort's paper, "Organisation et parti" [Organization and Party, untranslated.—Trans.], published in issue 26 of *Socialisme ou Barbarie*.[2] The majority rallied behind the text "Proletariat and Organization," published in issues 28 and 29.[3] In that text I was trying to go beyond the "external" criticism of the traditional organization and its activity. It wasn't merely that bolshevism set itself up as the "leadership"

---

1. Re-published in *L'Expérience du mouvement ouvrier*, 2 (Paris: UGE, "10/18," 1974).

2. Now published in Lefort's book, *Elements pour une critique de la bureaucratie* (Geneva: Droz, 1971) {partially re-published (Paris: Gallimard, "Tel")}. [Not translated.—Trans.]

3. In *Political and Social Writings*, vol. 2: *1955–1960: From the Workers' Struggle Against Bureaucracy to Revolution in the Age of Modern Capitalism* (Minneapolis: University of Minnesota Press, 1988).

and the party was subjected to an authoritarian, bureaucratic regime. In doing so, it espoused the capitalist model of organization in the broadest sense, and injected it into the working-class movement (as social democracy had, in different forms). The organization was divided into order-givers and order-takers, and it set itself up comprehensively as the leadership, the order-giver, facing the proletariat, that order-taker of the revolution. The *type of work* done by the militants was of the order-taker type. And last, but most important, the conception of revolutionary theory behind that organizational model and the type of activity it implied, as well as the content of that theory, had remained capitalist in their essence, and that was even true for Marx himself.

Correlatively to that analysis and criticism there was an effort to define the new revolutionary organization differently. We had to reject the capitalist model in every sphere and in all of its implications. That could be done, to begin with, only by taking our inspiration from what the working class had created over the last one hundred and fifty years. It went without saying, but it was also said, that the revolutionary organization couldn't be the "leadership" of the working class, but rather an instrument—one of the instruments—of the revolutionary struggle. And that it necessarily took its inspiration from those forms of organization created by the proletariat, and from their "spirit." It therefore had to adjust its structure and internal functioning to the principles underlying the organization of the soviets or workers' councils (sovereign general assemblies, as frequent as possible, and whenever a decision by the general assembly isn't possible, committees whose delegates are elected and whose mandate can always be revoked by their electors). But over and beyond changes in the type of organization, it was the traditional conception as a whole that was profoundly called into question.

## POLITICS

Let's begin with a point that played an enormous role in the 1958 split, although not explicitly so. To my way of thinking, Lefort and Simon's conceptions resulted, without saying so, in the refusal, or rejection, of the political dimension of the organization. If "political" is meant in the French CP or Trotskyist sense, we would all agree, of course. But that's obviously not what we're talking about.

The political question is the question of society as a whole, and one of the organization's tasks is to constantly maintain that question open for

the proletariat. I don't see how you can conceive of yourself as a revolutionary and think as one if you elude that question. We claim to be partisans of workers' management (or self-management, as it's called
nowadays). What does that mean, what does it imply? Let's suppose the
workers set up their own power in each factory, taken separately. There
remains the fact that the factories are all directly, intimately interdepen-
dent, and that their activities have to be unified in one way or another,
and if that isn't done in a revolutionary fashion it will inevitably be done
anyway, and in that case it will be done in bureaucratic fashion, that is, by
specialists of universality, who will start off by saying, "You go on managing your little place, that's fine; we're going to take care of the overall
coordination." Of course, if that occurred, the local "management" would
very rapidly become completely meaningless, since the question of the
integration of the different "social units" at every level (firms, towns, types
of activity, and so on) can't be solved miraculously, all by itself, and it isn't
some external, secondary aspect with potentially limited repercussions on
each unit, both in extent and in importance. It's absurd to imagine socialist, or simply self-managed factories in the context of a bureaucratic "coordination" of the economy and of society.

Second, since people are always aware of that question in one way or
another, all their personal attempts are hindered and inhibited by the fact
that they doubt their own abilities, or the objective possibility of confront-
ing that overall question of society, of social organization as such. All other
considerations aside, workers clearly cannot reach the point of "taking
power" in the factory if they haven't already envisioned, in one way or
another, however obscurely, half-consciously, or ambiguously, the question of power at the societal level. I'm not only talking about "power relations." I'm not saying that the workers' power in the factory can be
liquidated, brutally or deviously, by the bourgeoisie if it is only "power
within the factory"; that's a truism, illustrated once again by the LIP experience.[4] What I mean is that beyond a certain point, people who are struggling necessarily ask themselves, "What next, on the societal level?" If the

---

4. [In 1973, to prevent the liquidation of their factory, workers at the LIP watch-
manufacturing company occupied the premises and ran the factory themselves, with
the slogan "it's possible: we do the making and selling, we distribute the pay." The
movement, widely supported both regionally and nationally, held out for more than six
months, until the government and the confederation of industrials (CNPF) devised a
solution in which Claude Neuschwander, head of the Publicis group and member of
the left-wing, "self-management"-oriented PSU (Parti Socialiste Unifié, 1960–89)
party, took over the company in an attempt to save it, hiring back 850 workers, thus

question isn't explicitly clarified as completely as possible, that factor will necessarily hold the movement back at one point or another. It is the task of the revolutionary organization to help workers elucidate and clarify that question and to show that there is no *fatality* to the predicament according to which either the movement collapses or a central "power" separate from the masses—a bureaucracy, then—develops and you therefore return shortly thereafter to some version of the previous state of affairs. It is the task of the organization to show the feasibility of a socialist organization of society as a whole, over and beyond the factory itself.

But there is another even more important aspect of this question. The implicit or explicit rejection of the political dimension of the existence and activity of the organization, based on the precept that the organization should only express the workers' concerns *hic et nunc*, and that workers do not enter that perspective on their own *right now*, is tantamount to repeating the predicates of Lenin's position in *What Is to Be Done?*, even if that position is sharply criticized otherwise. Because that is a denial of any path or internal relation between the situation and struggles of the working class "at the moment" and the question of society as a whole. Now that path and that relation do exist, and they are of the utmost importance. They reside in the fact that some struggle in some factory, some activity of a given category of workers, some subject of "everyday" concerns may contain, and generally do potentially contain, much more than is superficially visible. They contain the seeds of opposition—implicit but comprehensive in its implications and consequences—to the established order. The idea, then, is first to uncover that signification, to clarify the elements of all those "singular" struggles, activities, and so on, which potentially contain that contestation of the established system, and which almost always remain obscure for the participants themselves. For that signification, those seeds are repressed by the entire structure of contemporary society, by the prevailing ideology, by the tireless efforts of traditional organizations and of course, by the mental assimilation of that structure by individuals; that is, the self-repression of the new significations they create not quite consciously.

---

putting an end to the movement. (For more about the PSU, see note 2 in "What Political Parties Cannot Do," page 121 in this volume.) During the following two years, devious industrial and financial maneuvers finally got the best of the firm. Some of the original occupiers then (in 1977) created a series of cooperatives. In spite of the popularity of the movement and the strikes it sparked, it did not spread, and debates on self-management rarely gave the idea its broadest meaning.—Trans.]

For instance, it's really laughable to say that the organization should circulate descriptions and accounts of exemplary struggles, and to avoid some questions: What makes those struggles exemplary, and why? And who decides they are? Now struggles are only exemplary because of that potential signification exceeding the immediate, manifest content, not only inasmuch as what occurred there is "numerically" valid for other cases but in that its implications exceed by far the apparent cause of their occurrence. An elected, revocable strike committee isn't exemplary simply because strike committees should all be elected and revocable, but also because by establishing it, and by its relations with it, the mass of strikers *breaks* with twenty-five centuries of political philosophy and creates another principle. But that's what we say, of course, and we can say so only on the basis of our overall conception. Now, not only must we shoulder overt responsibility for that overall conception, but moreover, I think it is dishonest and manipulative not to clarify it explicitly.

If that conception is accurate, it clearly also disrupts the traditional distinction between "immediacy" and "the political." But also, it shows how to go beyond traditional views on revolutionary theory and the way it is elaborated. The need for that elaboration is clear, just as it is clear that the revolutionary organization cannot and should not be an academic research institute on revolution. Theoretical activity is commanded by a prior decision on the question: *What is important?* We can answer that question only by focusing essentially on what germinates in the population and what its concerns are (which, I repeat, remain repressed). If we are to go beyond the traditional conception of theory, both as content and as a mode of activity, we must change the main lines of its concerns, the central themes of theoretical activity, for one thing, but also, and this necessarily goes hand in hand, we must change the method and the kind of elaboration. While it must not remain solely in the hands of a separate category of specialists, with all the inevitable implications, revolutionary theory can be elaborated only in a milieu in which people we may call the spokespeople of the population and those who tend to give a general turn to what the former express mix and cooperate. And it is clear that a similar circuit of cooperation and exchange must be developed between the organization as such and its surrounding milieu, and finally, the social milieu in general.

Starting in early 1959, we published a mimeographed monthly called *Pouvoir ouvrier*. Half of it was given over to a column called "Workers speak out," where we published everything we received. But it's a huge job to really give workers the possibility of speaking out. It's not enough to "give" it to them; they have to actually *take* it. It's not because you get people together and tell them, "You're free to talk and to say whatever you like; there's no taboo here, no authority, nothing that is judged trivial or unimportant a priori" that they actually speak. It's not by calling a column "Workers speak out," even less, that workers write in. People don't express themselves. All of instituted society has always been working at convincing them that what they have to say is unimportant, whereas what is important is what is known and said by politicians Giscard, Marchais or Mendès-France, or specialists in economics or politics (or more generally, pseudo-specialists in pseudo-sciences). That effort has achieved its goal, and people think, "My own concerns are hardly of any importance; they're just my own stupid little personal things; I can't talk about the big societal questions, because I'm ignorant of them." We have to destroy the effects of that effort, reverse the value signs, spread the obvious idea that all the talk filling the newspapers, the radio and TV day in and day out are of practically no importance and the concerns of ordinary people are the *only* important matter, socially speaking.

## On the Experience of ILO and ICO

After the split, Lefort and Simon founded a group and published a mimeographed journal, *ILO* (*Informations et liaisons ouvrières*). Some time later Lefort left the group and Simon continued, with a new name for the group and the journal, *ICO* (*Informations et correspondance ouvrières*). The people who founded ILO had a restrictive conception, to say the least, and I think a deeply contradictory one, of revolutionary action, asserting that the group's only real task should be collecting and recirculating information. The basis of that attitude was a particular interpretation of the idea of the autonomy of the proletariat, believed to imply a refusal to intervene and to contribute anything "foreign" to the experience of the proletariat itself. To my way of thinking, that position remains imprisoned in a conceptual framework whose other outcome is bureaucracy: We have our ideas and we impose them on people—or else, simple negation of the previous statement, on the same terrain: We have our ideas, but we don't tell them, because if we did we would be imposing them on people (and adulterating their "autonomous" evolution). Actually, the autonomous evolution of people is meaningless. People's evolution isn't "autonomous" in the absolute; it occurs in the midst of a struggle and a social dialectic in which capitalists, Stalinists, and so forth, are constantly present. The only result achieved that way would be to make the revolutionary voice the only one absent from the concert. It's one thing to condemn the conception of the party as "the leadership"; it's quite another to refuse one's own responsibilities, and to say, "Our only point of view consists of making our journal available for anyone who wants to speak out."

Need I remind you that this is my perception of things; the texts are there, anyway; they can be read by anyone who wants to. I think my criticism of the time was corroborated by the subsequent events. I would like to illustrate this more specifically using an important and still timely problem.

One implication of the position of the people who founded ILO was that it was out of the question to say clearly, firmly, that some people are members of the organization and others are not—first of all because you don't see *on what basis* to say that. Of course the quarrel around the question of membership in the organization rings somewhat sinisterly: the split between Bolsheviks and Mensheviks at the second conference of the Russian Social Democratic Labor Party was over article 1 of the statutes: Who is a member? The Bolsheviks wanted to set a strict boundary and only accept as members those people who worked under the *leadership* of an agency of the organization; the Mensheviks wanted membership for everyone who agreed with the party's program and paid dues by doing any kind of work for the party. The terms in which the question was put at the time, as well as the way the discussion went, are obviously outdated. But the question itself persists; there's no getting around it. Suppose you want to eliminate it. There is a group that came together on the basis of shared ideas; it goes puttering along, with ten or fifteen participants who are old acquaintances, who meet, and have gotten to the point of liking the smell of each other; they are isolated, with a few outside contacts; there aren't any problems. Then all of a sudden—say, after May '68—about a hundred people show up at their meeting, never mind who they are in fact, and they ask, "Is the meeting open? Can we come?" They are told, "Yes, of course." So the person who was supposed to present the agenda of the meeting says, "We had decided to talk about A, B, and C today." Shouting in the room, "What's going on here? Who's that fathead bureaucrat? Agendas are a bureaucratic invention." "But we have to decide on the table of contents of the next issue of the journal." "Why must there be a table of contents? We need an anti-journal, with an anti-table of contents." Or else, "The question of the table of contents is already decided; we'll publish the joint program of the left-wing parties; that needs to be circulated." There will be nothing else for the ten or fifteen original participants to do but steal out, while the others rightly accuse them of having deluded them by claiming that their group was "open," and go meet elsewhere, in a "closed" room.

There's no way of evacuating the problems involved here using petty, negative recipes. If some revolutionaries want to work together, that means that for as long as they agree to some extent, they are ready to take on a number of tasks together, collectively. They alone can decide what those tasks are, how they will be accomplished, and by whom. It's essential, of course, to put an end to the complete opposition between militants in the organization and a shapeless, uncommitted mass [*marais*] of sympathizers to be indoctrinated, ransomed, sold the journal and asked for addresses of potential correspondents. We have to break with that conception of the organization's milieu and of "sympathizers"; we have to break with it in our acts, by organizing meetings frequently, in which everyone is on an equal footing, invent activities that can be effectively shared. But there is no avoiding the fact that those people who have committed themselves, on an ongoing basis, to doing the work decided by the collective—the militants—are also those who make the decisions as to their orientation and activity.

If you claim to eliminate the distinction between militants, members of the organization, and the others, if you refuse to say who is a member of the group and who is not, then you avoid—in thought only—the real difficulties that arise because there are some people for whom work in a collective based on a revolutionary project is very important (it's a task that will only end with their death, for them), and there are also people who take interest in it at some point in their existence, are willing to participate partially, but for whom that activity isn't the fulcrum of their life (which makes them no less worthwhile in our eyes). The coexistence of those two categories of individuals is a fact we have to face. You don't face it by saying that the former kind of individuals doesn't exist because it shouldn't exist. That only results in hypocrisy and manipulation of another sort: those individuals, those who are militants, irrespective of what they call themselves, still exist; they do things, be it silently, and so they have some power, but that power is concealed because formally they aren't anything more than anyone else. They have de facto power, concealed by the elimination of the issue of power as an explicit issue: a disastrous situation, not only because it masks their power, but infinitely worse, because it masks *the issue of power*.

One last point, to finish the story of the 1958 split: I think that for Claude Lefort, it was overdetermined—I'm interpreting, he didn't write that at the time—by a conception already in its inception and which he only expressed, more or less, later on. I would sum it up, approximately, as follows: Your goal can't be a radical revolution; there are definitely some struggles that unsettle the established order, movements that prefigure a new societal form; we're on their side and we try to go in the same direction; but the idea that a radical transformation of society is possible, that social alienation can be overcome, is philosophically absurd. I haven't taken close interest in the evolution of ILO-ICO, but I think the subsequent break between Lefort and Simon was conditioned by that conception.

## The Interpretation of Gaullism

Between 1958 and 1961, the group S. ou B. developed quite well, numerically. There were two or three cells in Paris, and several others in the provinces, with some students and a few workers. We were almost a hundred at the end of 1960, which was quite a lot for the time. Our public meetings were well attended; the group influenced some non-negligible groups of students in Paris and some workers at the Renault plant, thanks to Mothé's work there. That evolution is tied to the struggle against the Algerian War and to the unspeakable attitude of the traditional organizations to the very end of that war.

There were no differences of opinion within the group on how to interpret Gaullism, which was on its way in. None of us ever viewed Gaullism as fascism. It was immediately interpreted as the transition to modern capitalism, with the specific features entailed by the history of the French bourgeoisie and society, as an attempt to liquidate a whole series of the previous regime's "backward" traits, such as the colonial empire of course, but also the economic and financial chaos, and even the bourgeois republic's political chaos. The article I wrote at the time advanced that interpretation, but it also stressed the inability of the French bourgeoisie, with or without de Gaulle, to arrive at a "normal," "regular" political functioning. Today—in January 1974—we can say that in one sense the political problem too has been "solved," since we have Pompidou. But we can also say that it hasn't been solved since, precisely, we have Pompidou. On the other hand, de Gaulle came to power by the defaulting of the population—by even more than that, since de Gaulle and his Constitution won a landslide victory in November 1958. We couldn't ignore the meaning of that.

## ANOTHER SPLIT

So the question arose of how to interpret the population's attitude toward politics. That interpretation had to delve into the overall evolution of all modern capitalist countries, since the same attitude was to be found everywhere. Other threads, and especially our criticism of the traditional conception of socialism, also pointed to the need for a radical reappraisal.

My attempt to pull all those threads together was written into the article "Le mouvement révolutionnaire sous le capitalisme moderne" (published in English as "Modern Capitalism and Revolution"), a first version of which began to circulate in the group in 1959, and which immediately sparked a division, since it was the crystallizing factor for the opposition of all those who, within the group, rejected a radical critical effort. There had already been other texts (such as "Sur la dynamique du capitalisme [On the Dynamics of Capitalism]," 1953–54), which implicitly rejected the conventional positions on immiseration, crises, the growing industrial reserve army, in short, everything that's supposed to be, and actually is, Marx's economic theory, as well as the classical conception of imperialism. There was also "Sur le contenu du socialisme" in 1955–58—published in English as "On the Content of Socialism"—rejecting another central Marxist idea according to which the revolution may be conceived as simply receiving capitalist technology and making it serve socialism, as well as the traditional conception of the role and content of theory (see above), which partakes of the speculative stance developed in the Western world over the last twenty-five centuries. That all flowed together, with converging consequences, until finally the quantitative was transformed into the qualitative, as comrade Mao would say. It was no longer any particular position that was challenged, but Marxism as a whole. And that naturally made Maille, Lyotard and Souyri shrink back, horrified, and elicited cries of "Castoriadis is abandoning Marxism," or "Castoriadis has turned existentialist."

That fight lasted three years. For a long while the people who called themselves, characteristically, the "anti-tendency" fought back with nothing but polemical, mutually contradictory arguments ("the workers' standard of living isn't rising"; "it is rising, but that isn't meaningful, or it doesn't mean what you say it does," and so on). It was only during the last three months before the split that they at long last produced three texts attempting to defend an incoherent version of neopaleomarxism, which their authors didn't publish, to my own personal regret.

That fight obviously soon interfered with all of the group's activities, blocking them very seriously. At the same time, a sort of polarization had developed in the tasks performed: the "anti-tendency" had increasingly taken over *Pouvoir ouvrier*, and the comrades who agreed with the line developed in "Modern Capitalism and Revolution" tended to put out the review. The former tried to turn *PO* into a sort of agitation journal around traditional themes, and we opposed that, saying they were putting out a good Trotskyist line. They criticized the unions, saying a more radical stance was needed, that this or that should be done during a strike; they couldn't resist writing an editorial whenever the government had said or done something—an aberrant attitude, for us, since it boiled down to setting oneself on the same terrain as the enemy. When we made proposals aimed at radically transforming the axes of our propaganda and our work, devoting our attention to the problems of youth and students (all of which is explicitly said in the 1960 texts, several years before Berkeley), and of women and the family, teaching and the criticism of so-called education, and even the criticism of the very existence of education, or the importance of struggles other than those of the industrial proletariat and strikes around specific demands, they laughed at us, and advanced platitudes and permanent obstruction. The theoretical and practical distance between the two sides was constantly widening. The split took place in July 1963. By a gentleman's agreement, the "anti-tendency" kept *PO* and we kept *S. ou B.*

## Suspension of the Publication of *S. ou B.* and of the Group's Activities

After the split, we published another six issues of the review (35 to 40), the last of which is dated June 1965, and the group went on functioning until the spring of 1966. During that period, the readership of the review was perhaps at a peak (about 1,000 copies of each issue sold, with public meetings drawing up to 200 people), but on the other hand, there was almost no feedback, no response in return. The readers of the review never wrote to us, or almost never; people came to the meetings and then went back home (despite our attempts to break with the academic structure of traditional meetings). The ideas circulated, no doubt, but the public behaved like a passive consumer of ideas. Second, there was an increasingly haunting problem as to the group's membership: some very young, very lively people joined, but at the same time they weren't able to function with the older members (or vice versa; it comes to the same thing). My interpretation is that those people, drawn in by personal motivations of course, like us all, were constantly expressing them in the way they behaved in the group, and given the situation the group didn't provide any ground on which those original motivations could be transformed into something else. In a sense, the group became a substitute for the family and caused the same strong ambivalence. That in turn made the "elders" react, and the group was sapped by the resulting frictions, making its functioning increasingly less collective and less coherent.

Last, the review itself raised a very serious problem, by the trend in its very character at the time. My last articles challenged the Marxist conception as a whole, and attempted to revisit the foundations of the conception of society and history, and therefore were increasingly "abstract" and "philosophical." That remained a solitary activity, not only in the writing itself, but also because the group didn't feel any need to discuss it. Other texts were published in the review (written by Mothé and Chatel, for instance), but it was unclear what held it all together. The review had become the group's main activity—and at the same time, it no longer represented a truly collective effort. It wasn't very meaningful to keep it going and to keep the group going by hook or by crook under those conditions. Those were the considerations that led me to propose the suspension of the review. During that period, one comrade kept saying, "except a grain of wheat dies." And in fact, there was new growth later.

Why didn't we try to reconstitute the group later on? Because for the time being it's enormously difficult to maintain any revolutionary activity when you try to honestly face up to real issues, without being backed by a theoretical or supposedly theoretical corpus that enables you to say "Shut up, the answer is in Marx or in Mao." The experience of all the post–May '68 groups shows the impossibility of eluding the questions of: Who are we? How do we function? Who is us and who is not us? Is there an "us"? And above all, What do we mean by "us"? That's a very important question: That "us" can be mystifying and alienating. In fact, in organizations, you don't say "us" most of the time, you say "the party," "the group," and so on. But then, that "party," that "group"—or that "us"— was defined more or less ideally, by implicit or explicit reference to a closed, defined theory. Now what I say is that this conception of theory is a mystifying phantasm. People have to get together because they share a project—the revolutionary project. You will say that this is just shifting the difficulty. I would say more: It considerably increases it. Because a project involves a dimension of perpetual, open-ended elucidation, never finished, and implies a totally different subjective *attitude* toward theorization. To sum it up: categorical rejection of the idea that a completed theory (or an indefinitely perfectible one) is possible, or that theory is sovereign, but without consenting to the idea that "anything goes" (which is what goes on just about universally nowadays by people who think they've destroyed the traditional references, and are therefore all the more in another sort of prison; the "dominant discourse" in some "anti-establishment" movements today, made of that awful hodgepodge they call Freudo-Nietzscheo-Marxism, strictly boils down to *anything goes*). Now that sort of attitude is hard to stand by—I'm not saying it's impossible. But unless enough people who share it get together, I don't see how we could set up something susceptible of staying alive and developing.

## The Break with Marxism

*Why is a break with Marxism necessary, in your opinion? How is it tied to your analysis of the situation of the working-class movement?*

That question can be broached on two levels: the theoretical content of Marxism and the way it defines the problem of theory, and the historical fate of Marxism. On the theoretical level, there is a Marxist metaphysics, a theory of history and an economic theory, all closely tied together. All three are untenable. Since Marxists view their economic theory as the cornerstone of the construction, let's begin with that.

What is economic theory for Marx? What can it say? How far can it go? Has it any limits? We know that the mature Marx's systematic theoretical elaboration, as opposed to the spirit of some sentences written when he was young, aims at establishing a sovereign, boundless theory defining the laws of the capitalist economy and demonstrating that the functioning of the latter leads inevitably to its breakdown and to a new society. Now that kind of theory is impossible in principle. To be brief, everything said in *Capital*, the theoretical elaboration it contains, is predicated on the elimination of two decisive factors in the functioning and evolution of the capitalist economy—that is, technological change and class struggle. And that's not coincidental. It is the internal necessity of that kind of theorization, since those two factors are the primary vector for the expression of historical creativity in the economic field, the outcome being that it's out of the question to establish "laws" for economic change other than in a partial, transient sense only.

The elimination of class struggle is absolutely flagrant. Marx postulates that labor power is a commodity and treats it as such in theory (based on the idea that it really *is* that under capitalism). Now in the Marxist system, as we know, a commodity has a specific exchange value, and if it is a "means of production" it also has a specific usage value. But labor power has neither a specific usage value nor a specific exchange value. It doesn't have a specific usage value: The capitalist who buys a ton of coal knows how many calories he can extract from it, given the state of technology; but when he buys an hour of labor he doesn't know how much output he can extract from it. Now Marx constantly starts from the postulate that just as the capitalist will extract as many calories as the techniques of the time allow him to (and it's true, coal is passive), in the same way he will extract as much output from the worker as the techniques of the time (the type and speed of machines, and so on) allow him to, since the worker is necessarily passive. But that's false. Marx practically never talks about the fierce fighting around output that goes on daily in industry. Only twice in the first volume of *Capital*, in different places, does he incidentally mention how workers resist pressure to increase their yield, and both times he depicts it as unavoidably doomed to failure, which means that the worker is a purely passive object of capital in production, that there is no class *struggle* in production, but rather, complete domination, unchallenged because unchallengeable, of one class over the other.

But the history of modern industry isn't merely the history of the great pitched trade union battles; it's also and above all the history that goes on eight hours a day, sixty minutes of every hour, sixty seconds per minute in production and around production. During every one of those seconds, the worker's every motion has two sides, one conforming to the imposed production norms, the other combating them. The actual output is the outcome of the struggle that goes on around it. So labor power has no specific usage value independent of that struggle and its effects. Now it's easy to see that this struggle simultaneously, decisively codetermines the exchange value of labor power. That is so not only because it codetermines the productivity of work (and thence, the unit value of the wares consumed by workers), but above all because it alone sets the actual level of wages. Wages aren't "$x$ francs an hour." That's meaningless, for the capitalist actually doesn't buy "an hour." He claims to be buying "an hour," but in reality he's buying an effective output, which effective output is, precisely, not determined, and he's going to try to determine it by introducing new machines, timekeepers, and so forth, while the workers, in turn, will try to determine it differently, by tricking the timekeepers, cheating on specifications, organizing collectively, and so on. Wages are actually a rate of exchange: so many francs for one hour's output—and the second term is undetermined. So many francs for workers who do exactly what the timekeepers say and so many francs for those workers who resist them successfully; that's not at all the same thing.

How does Marx think the exchange value of labor power is determined? *Being a commodity*, labor power, like any other commodity, is worth the "labor" it contains—that is, the labor incorporated in the "cost of producing and reproducing it," materially represented by the amount of wares a worker (or a working-class family) consumes to live and engender a new generation of workers. If we call that quantity the "standard of living" of the working class, the exchange value of labor power will depend directly on two factors and two factors only: that "standard of living" and the unit value of each of the wares of which it is composed (actually, the simple weighted multiplication of one by the other). Now that unit value of each ware is simply the reverse, broadly speaking, of the productivity of labor: The greater the latter, the less working time is incorporated in each commodity produced, and the lower its unit value is. So, *if* the standard of living of the working class remains constant, the greater productivity of labor, relentlessly sought and achieved by capitalism, means ipso facto a drop in the value of the wares composing the worker's standard of living, and therefore a reduction of the "paid part" of the working day, *whence* a rise in the rate of exploitation, assuming the working day itself remains constant.

But can we postulate that the worker's standard of living remains constant? Marx hasn't much to say about that. He says it is "determined by historical and moral factors" at each point, and goes on to postulate implicitly that it should be assumed to be constant. But that's logically arbitrary and false in reality. For the sake of convenience and as a first approximation, we can hypothesize that the worker's standard of living remains constant if we are talking about the situation of the economy over a very short period. That's absolutely impossible over one or two centuries—which is what Marxist theory of the capitalist economy is talking about. Now there has clearly been a considerable modification (a rise) in the actual standard of living of the working class over the last one hundred and fifty years. That rise was the product of workers' struggles, both the informal, implicit struggles at the point of production we talked about earlier and the open protest movements, large or small. Marx disregards those struggles, and since all the ensuing developments in *Capital* necessarily rest on that "analysis" of the determination of the exchange value of labor power as a commodity, the entire edifice is built on sand; the entire theory is conditioned by that "forgetting" of class struggle. You also have to reread the end of *Wages, Price and Profit* to convince yourself that even when Marx admits that workers' struggles affect the level of wages, he still views that effect as contingent and within a "cycle," and not susceptible of changing the basic long-term distribution of the social product as regulated by the law of value.

There's even more to it, actually. At a given point, capitalists themselves realized that an ongoing rise in the worker's standard of living was inherently necessary to the system's functioning. Because without a continuous extension of the market for consumer goods, there can't be any capitalist expansion, or at least not of the kind we now know. Of course, in some situations (such as Nazi Germany, the USSR for a long time, wartime, and so on), the system directs production essentially to producing arms, or toward accelerated accumulation, and the real standard of living of the working class is blocked or may even drop. But the "normal" long-term evolution of the system is impossible without the ongoing expansion of the market for consumer goods. And for the most part that market is made up of solvent demand, and therefore of the wages of workers and of wage-earners in general. So that if, for the sake of convenience and as a first approximation, we want to advance a postulate, it must necessarily be that there will be a stable *pace of increase* of the real income of workers over any short-term period we study. We definitely can imagine, theoretically, a hypertheory that would try to quantify the intensity of class struggle and its relationship to the level of wages, so as to integrate it in a "more general" diagram (and there actually have been some such attempts by academic economists, who use the rate of union membership as the variable representing "pressure on wages"). I won't go into that; I think that approach is fundamentally absurd.

All this goes to show that the idea of a "law of the rising rate of exploitation" is a myth. And more generally, any idea postulating a "law" determining the evolution of the distribution of the social product between capitalists and workers while disregarding class struggle is a myth. Also, the so-called "law" of the increase in the organic composition of capital is grounded in a fallacy. Since the mass of constant capital (the *quantity* of machines, raw material, etc.) increases in ratio to "variable capital" (that is, in fact, the number of workers and of hours worked), in terms of *volume*, and even more strictly, in *physical* terms, you draw the conclusion that constant capital, in terms of *value*, increases with respect to variable capital, also in terms of *value*. That's what logic calls a non sequitur. The evolution of the physical mass of constant capital doesn't say anything about the evolution of the mass of its value, since the latter is equal to the physical mass multiplied by the unit value, and the latter *decreases* as the productivity of labor increases (and there is no reason to suppose that it rises more slowly in the sector producing the means of production than in the rest of the economy). It isn't because the quantity of machines, raw material, and so on increases as compared to the number of workers that the value of constant capital increases with respect to that of variable capital. At the same time, Marx supposed that the value of variable capital declines as time goes by, for a given number of workers, according to the rising rate of exploitation—which doesn't exist, as we have seen. So you can't make any a priori statement about the evolution of the organic composition.

As for the tendency toward a "falling rate of profit," it's a perfect example of a non-problem. Maybe some day someone should write a psychoanalytic essay on why Marx and Marxists, and classical political economists before them, are so fascinated by the idea of a century-long fall in the rate of profit. Marx's equation for profit is $pl/(c+v)$ (the ratio of total surplus value—$pl$—to constant capital plus variable capital). $Pl$ depends on the number of workers employed, since surplus value is extracted exclusively from living work. The "law of the rising organic composition of capital" says that $c$ increases faster than $v$. Therefore, since $pl$ depends on $v$ only, and since $v$ increases more slowly than $c$, the numerator of the fraction should decline over time with respect to the denominator. That's the reasoning, and each element is false. We've already seen that it isn't necessarily true (and actually isn't true) that the organic composition increases. Second, Marx claims that the rate of exploitation (the ratio $pl/v$) rises over time. How do we know that that increment doesn't suffice to balance out any increase in the organic composition, or even to overcompensate for it, in which case the tendency would be toward a rising rate of profit rather than a falling rate? Last, the equation itself is meaningless, applied to this "problem": $pl/(c+v)$ doesn't represent the rate of profit over capital, but the rate of profit over the earnings (capital is only represented by $c$, which is the fraction productively consumed during the period, usually a small fraction of the capital invested in production).

Furthermore, what do we care about all that? Is it at all relevant? Let's suppose that the rate of profit does tend to fall: What of it? If we were talking about the rate of profit *on capital*, we could draw the conclusion, all else being equal (a by no means trivial postulate) that the pace of capitalist accumulation tends to slow down: So what? (Note that in actual fact what has occurred so far is more or less the opposite. Over the last two centuries, the average annual rise in capitalist production has been, say, 4 percent. How does the idea that its annual rate of increase will fall to 2 percent around the year 2175 corroborate or affect our political prospects? But we aren't even talking about the rate of profit on capital, but only the rate of profit on business activity, which has no direct connection with the pace of accumulation.)

Last of all, if we assume that the falling rate of profit exists as a tendency, why would it cease to exist in a socialist society? The reasons Marx gives for that falling rate of profit in capitalist society are technical reasons that have nothing to do with the social structure of capitalism. They boil down to the fact that there are more and more machines, raw material, and so on, for a given number of workers. Since we aren't saying that a socialist society will try to turn technological development backwards (Marx and Marxists would never say that, at any rate), that factor will always be present. It will even be greater, since the other factor susceptible of counterbalancing it under capitalism, the increased rate of exploitation, should no longer exist in a socialist society. So will there be a falling rate of overproduction (since we can no longer speak of profit) in a socialist society? And with what consequences?

Let's go on now to what I have called Marx's elimination of the technology factor. Of course, Marx had a deep perception of the constant, repeated upheaval of the capitalist society and economy introduced by the evolution of technology; he has given consummate, incomparable social-historical analyses of it. But when constructing his economic system, it's as if he forgot all that. The implicit postulate, barring which everything in *Capital* would be meaningless, is that technical progress exists (otherwise there would be no increase in the productivity of labor), but that technical progress is represented by a continuous variable. The output of the working hour is a rising, continuous function of time, and is determined by it, and that's it. If we want to go further, and consider everything Marx sees when he talks historically, concretely, about technological progress, then there is no longer something we can call the value of capital, to be treated in economic theory the way Marx treats it: that is, as something *measurable* corresponding to the accumulation of buildings, machines, mines, and so forth.

Marx's conception actually assumes that you can *measure* the value of capital, designate that miscellaneous *collection* of objects by a *number*, add up jewelry and birdseed, and that's what the theory of labor-value is for. Each machine, for example, has a value inasmuch as it incorporates past labor, which can be computed (in terms of hours or otherwise). If there isn't any technical progress at all, meaning that the same type of machine is produced and reproduced indefinitely by the same methods, then there isn't any problem: the labor (direct and indirect) effectively expended to make the machine, its "historical" cost, unambiguously measures its value.

But if there is technical progress, that means, ipso facto, a change in manufacturing methods. The machines made earlier and still running today have a different (usually higher) "historical" cost than those produced today using more efficient methods. It would be strange, though, to say they have a "greater value" (disregarding wear and so on). Logic (and the practical reality of the capitalist economy) makes us say that the value of that kind of machine will have to be defined (like any other product, actually), not by its effective "historical cost," but by its necessary present cost (in other words, the cost of its reproducibility).

If technological progress is continuous in the mathematical sense (that is, composed of infinitesimal additions), then calculation of the "value" of a machine based on the cost of its production is demonstrably salvageable, under some other fairly restrictive conditions. But if technological progress proceeds by leaps and bounds, as is actually the case, then that possibility no longer exists. What we have is not infinitesimally advancing obsolescence (technical aging) of each machine, by which its value tends imperceptibly toward zero, but the simultaneous existence of brand new machines, others still used, although outmoded, but no longer reproduced (and for which, consequently, the cost of reproducibility can no longer be meaningfully calculated), and still others which suddenly topple from being into non-being, since they were still good yesterday, but are now affected by the invention of a new machine that makes them positively and totally unprofitable, or again because the final product for which they are used has suddenly been replaced by something else, manufactured in a completely different way. Under these conditions, no measurement of capital can be meaningful over time. We can no longer say what $c$ represents in the equations and so-called laws of capitalist development, except in an absolutely "momentary" sense.

*Doesn't that call into question any discourse on the economy?*

Yes, of course.

*So the only task left for economics would be description?*

There is certainly more than that. Even sociology can do much more than merely describe. In economics, there are links, repetitions, "local," partial regularities, broad trends. Occurrences may be intelligible, provided of course we never forget that to be at all comprehensible economics must be viewed within the social-historical context. But what doesn't exist is a political economy modeled after a physical or mathematical science. And that is precisely the model Marx had in mind when he wrote *Capital*. Now that sort of model postulates the invariance and conservation of some things. In physics, "laws" are invariant relations involving parameters that are constants (the "universal constants"). There is a relation, always the same, between the pressure, volume and temperature of a gas, and a constant for perfect gases. Throughout all the modifications in a physical system, there is always "something" that is *conserved*, be it the mass-energy equation, the electric charge, or other. But in economics, what is "conserved"? And where are invariant functional relations to be found? Every attempt to define such relations (academic economics has been trying in vain for decades), sooner or later discovers that their form changes, their parameters change, even the kind of dependence on postulated "initial" or "exogenous" conditions of validity changes. I repeat, economics is full of "locally regular" sequences, and those are not incomprehensible; but it is out of the question to integrate them in an exhaustive, permanent system of invariant relations, still less to formalize them.

*You have just demonstrated why the Marxist economic theory is untenable. What makes the Marxist theory of history untenable?*

To begin with, what I have just said about the economy shows that you can't view capitalist society as conforming to the theoretical framework propounded by historical materialism (as formulated in the *Preface to a Contribution to the Critique of Political Economy*, for instance). Even less can the history of humanity prior to the bourgeois era be understood on that basis. How does it explain so-called archaic societies, for example? Those societies, on the "basis" of the same state of their productive forces and the same kind of relations within production, exhibit an incredible variety of forms of social organization and social life. One of the Marxist responses to this consists of saying: We don't care about that variety; it's only apparent; the forms of organization and ways of life are only a cover-up; the substance is the same everywhere. It doesn't matter that some societies worship totems and others don't, that some live in a matriarchal system, others in a patriarchal system; what counts is that they are all hunters or collectors. But that is tantamount to eliminating history and society, of deciding in advance that the only reality resides in the "productive forces" and all the rest is a mere epiphenomenon (so that their very existence and the varied forms it takes are then totally incomprehensible. Why on earth don't those savages just go hunting instead of going about representing things? Why, moreover, do they have representations of *different* things, since all they all do is hunt?). That also amounts to judging

the history of all of humanity with the mentality of the crudest, most brutal capitalist boss of all times: Who is so and so? He makes so much a
month. What's that tribe? They're hunters with such and such a level of
technical development. The entire history of humanity is viewed as a series
of increasingly less imperfect attempts to achieve that ultimate perfection,
the capitalist factory. Inasmuch as they haven't gotten there yet, those
poor savages are wasting their time inventing "absurdities" (Engels says
that, literally). In the last analysis, it all goes back to the "rationalist-mate-
rialist" basis of Marxist philosophy, which is only a variation on a twenty-
five-centuries-old metaphysics that's practically devoid of meaning.

But we also have to talk about the historical fate of Marxism. It's strange
to see people who call themselves Marxist or who want to "stand up for
Marx" and who stubbornly ignore that question. Could I discuss Christianity, saying, "I don't give a damn about the Inquisition; the pope is
incidental; the participation of the Catholic Church in the Spanish Civil
War, on Franco's side, was only the act of some specific priests. That's all
secondary with respect to the essence of Christianity, epitomized in such
and such part of the Gospel"? Christianity has been an institutional social
and historic reality for two thousand years. That reality is certainly complex and ambiguous, but it nonetheless has a signification I can never ignore: Christianity was and still is the religion of those in power, teaching
people that you must render unto Caesar the things that are Caesar's, and
so on. I can't act differently toward Marxism. Of course we're only talking
about one hundred and twenty years here, not two thousand, but the latter
sixty have weighed very heavily, historically speaking. The *reality* of Marxism is, first and absolutely foremost, to a shattering extent, that it is the
ideology touted by exploitative, totalitarian, oppressive regimes exerting
their power over a billion men and women. It is also the ideology of bureaucratic parties in other countries, whose goal we know to be the establishment of regimes identical to the aforementioned, and whose day-to-
day practices are an ongoing series of infamies. That hasn't been going on
for two thousand years, but it weighs two billion tons.

If you say, "Brezhnev is obviously not Marxist; he's a swindler who uses
Marx; Marx's true thinking has nothing to do with that," then we're no
longer talking about Marxism but about "Marx's true thinking." But
"Marx's true thinking" (and that remains a mysterious expression) has the
same status as the true thinking of Freud, the true thinking of Hegel, the
true thinking of Kant, and so forth. It's a great oeuvre; it's ambiguous; it's
also contradictory; there are different layers; it takes work, an enormous

amount of work, to orient oneself in it—that is, to mostly uncover questionings. Now Marx's followers continue to believe that there's a full-fledged, straightforward truth, and that it is materially deposited in his writings. Nevertheless, Marx is of course very important. We couldn't hold this conversation even for a second if we hadn't been in contact with his thinking and if we didn't live in a world influenced by it.

*Does the revolutionary project still reside in the proletariat, as Marx contends?*

What we call the revolutionary project was born in and through the struggles of workers, even before Marx's time (between 1790 and 1840 in England and France). All the relevant ideas were formed and formulated during that period: the fact of exploitation and of its conditions, the project of a radical transformation of society, of a government by the producers, for the producers, the suppression of the wage-earning class, and so on. The history of the proletariat is a basic fact and a fathomless resource. No other known exploited class has constituted itself as an active pole of society, generated a project involving such a radical transformation, acted with such daring, such heroism, accomplished the extraordinary feat of codetermining—it, the exploited class—the course of the social system, to a decisive extent. Everything that has transpired in the Western world over the last one hundred and fifty years is the outcome of working-class struggles, for a very large part. It was they that imposed wage increases, shorter working hours, access to political rights, the "true" bourgeois republic; they too that induced a certain type of technological evolution.

But at present, we have to recognize that in modern capitalist societies the proletariat is a dwindling proportion of the overall population, and by now it has become a minority in the most "developed" countries. In the United States, manual workers represent a scant quarter of the working population, and the same trend is seen in the other modern capitalist countries. Above all, for more than twenty-five years now it has no longer positioned itself as a class striving for the radical transformation of society, as in the past. So we can no longer maintain the proletariat in the role assigned to it by Marx on the basis of the idea that the capitalist process of accumulation would turn everyone into industrial workers (aside from a handful of capitalists and maybe a few supervisors). That isn't what's happening. To say that everyone, or nearly everyone, has become a wage-earner doesn't mean that everyone has become a proletarian, with the content attached to that word. To be a wage-earner is practically a universal condition in modern capitalist society; it no longer designates a "class." Obviously there are tremendous differentiations among "wage-earners," from several viewpoints. But they don't yield criteria for a class-based division. For instance, the strictly "financial" criterion of income (wages), can't really be used. If we applied it consistently on a worldwide scale, we would have to say that the least-well-paid worker in a developed capitalist country is still an exploiter of those two-thirds of humankind that live in undeveloped countries. The other dividing line among wage-earners, between order-givers and order-takers, tends to become increasingly less relevant, since there are fewer and fewer people in the pure order-giver and order-taker categories. The bureaucratic pyramid is swelling, so to speak, in the middle, with a proliferation of productive jobs done by people who can't be said to be merely executing orders.

The only criterion that remains relevant for us, when making distinctions within the mass of workers, is their attitude toward the present system. That boils down to saying that we have to altogether relinquish any "objective criteria." With the exception of a small minority at the top, the entire population is equally open—or closed—to a revolutionary perspective. A particular stratum or category may play a more important role at some point in time, but we can no longer maintain the idea that the proletariat is "the" agent of the revolutionary project. That idea has become a sort of incantation through which, first, the CP can pose as *the* party speaking "in the name" of workers, and second, the left wing and extreme left wing *"groupuscules"* can mystify themselves by telling themselves that "there are ten of us, but we're potentially the party of the proletariat," or "we *are* rightfully that proletariat that doesn't know itself yet." Also, you clearly can't simultaneously call yourself a Marxist and try to find a substitute for the proletariat in the form of third world peasants.

The privileged political status of the proletariat in Marxism was homologous with the privileged theoretical and philosophical status of the sphere of production. We have seen that the latter can't be maintained. So, symmetrically, you can't neglect the historical importance of the evolution of youth struggles, or of what is going on in the female part of the population (after all, one requisite for production is the reproduction of the species). This all bespeaks the shaky relations between the sexes and within the traditional family structure, the crisis in every authoritarian structure. These signs should be just as important for us as any others.

One last point, on the relation between that idea of the proletariat and Marxist theory. One kind of circular reasoning still very frequently heard today goes as follows: The proletariat has a special historical role, as demonstrated in Marx's work (which is true); Marx's work has a special status (of truthfulness), since it is the conscious expression of the movement of the proletariat (which class has a historically privileged status). It isn't said in that form, but it takes no more than ten minutes of Socratic questioning to bring a statement like that out of almost any Marxist. It's like: The proof that the Scriptures are true is the Revelation; and the proof that a revelation took place is that the Scriptures say so. It's a self-corroborating system. Actually, it's true that Marx's work, in its spirit and very intention, both stands and falls on the claim that the proletariat is and manifests itself as the revolutionary class about to change the world. If that isn't the case—which it isn't—then Marx's work once again becomes what it really always was: an attempt (difficult, obscure and profoundly ambiguous) to conceive society and history in the prospect of their revolutionary trans-formation—and we have to start from scratch again, on the basis of our own situation, of which Marx himself and the history of the proletariat are of course components.

## The Revolutionary Project Today

*What you were saying a bit earlier about young people, women, and so on, was like the beginning of the development of the phrase, "the revolutionary question today must be extended to every sphere of social activity, and above all to everyday life."*

Certainly. Everyday experience includes the everyday life of workers, for example. That means eight hours or more a day of work in a factory, including the kind of working conditions we know, the implicit, informal, ceaseless struggles around production. The struggle against timekeepers contains the embryo of workers' propensity to determine their own pace of work, which is of the utmost significance. But everyday experience is also what goes on at home in the evening; it's the neighborhood, people's entire life with all those neglected, overlooked aspects viewed as unimpor-tant by people who are completely obsessed by strikes, "political" events and "international" crises.

*Does that lead to Marcuse's conception of youth struggles?*

It's hard to discern Marcuse's thinking in that respect. Sometimes he talks as if he thought that revolution is out of the question, but that there are revolutionary struggles doomed to involve only a minority. It's as if he were saying: "Up with the students, up with revolting prisoners, although we know that the world can't change, essentially. So much the better if people fight back somewhere; that shows that human beings don't accept

complete servitude and mindlessness!" I for one categorically reject that
attitude and the corresponding philosophy. Sometimes you get the impression that he denies the revolutionary role of the proletariat or, more
accurately, that he denies that workers may take a revolutionary stance,
and reserves those possibilities for other categories (such as youth, and
others). That's Marx upside down: there's a negative privileged status of
the proletariat, and still a positive privileged status for some given group.
What I'm saying is that we have to get out of that way of thinking.

*What may be said about revolutionary activity today?*

First, we must break with the imperialist conception according to which
revolutionary activity is exclusively what is done by revolutionary militants. You cannot talk about revolutionary activity in the singular, of a
single kind of revolutionary activity. There are necessarily many potentially revolutionary activities in contemporary society. The activity of militants organized in a revolutionary organization is only one of the vectors
of a combat that takes many forms, in several spheres, potentially in every
sphere (if that wasn't the case, the activity of revolutionaries would be
intrinsically absurd). The activity of revolutionary militants doesn't have
any privileged status, as such; it's a component of a historical movement
that exceeds it—and must exceed it—infinitely.

*But can we still speak of a revolutionary project?*

That's something else, and perhaps our notion of a project requires clarification here. We are not talking about a "program," a series of concrete
measures that the masses would be well advised to take, were they in power
in France or in Venezuela. The revolutionary project is the historical goal
of achieving a society that would overcome alienation. By alienation, I
mean a social-historical fact (institutional heteronomy), not a metaphysical
given. In other words, it is the goal of an autonomous society, which is
not *enslaved* by its past or its own creations. I really mean "enslaved." Of
course people are always determined by their past and their own acts, but
it all depends on what is meant by "determined," and how far that determination goes. It isn't the same for a psychotic and for a "normal" or
neurotic person, nor is it the same for "traditional" societies (be they archaic or "Asian"), Greek city-states, the United States or late 18th-century
France.

What is an autonomous society? I first used the concept of autonomy, extended to society, in the sense of "collective management." I have now been led to give it a more radical content, that is no longer simply collective management (self-management), but the *ongoing, explicit self-institution of society*, meaning a state in which the community knows that its institutions are its own creation and has become able to regard them as such, to reexamine them and transform them. If you accept that idea, it defines a unified revolutionary project.

*You seem to have defined an overall* [globale] *vision as both indispensable and impossible. One also wonders whether your analysis doesn't view struggles as having a regulatory effect. The self-institution you talk about is a comprehensive project, a way of begging the question by asserting that such an overall vision* [globalité] *is viable, and that struggles result in a sort of rationality.*

I'm not saying that day-to-day struggles, as such, lead directly to addressing society as a comprehensive whole. Nonetheless, when we analyze a given struggle—workers against timekeepers, students about curriculum—we discover that whereas it challenges the capitalist system at a specific time and on a specific point, that system, irrespective of its contradictions and weaknesses, is unquestionably a "comprehensive whole" that translates here as oppressive education, there as time and motion studies, and so on. When someone refuses to be a passive object of the educational system, or of management in a factory, or of her husband, after her father, there is definitely a "positive side" to that refusal, whether she knows it or not, a *different* principle, clashing head-on with the basic principle of capitalism. My interpretation of those struggles brings me to see them as having the same, or at least a homologous, meaning. If I'm wrong then we can't talk about a revolutionary project for the present period, and we would have to fall back on positions like the one imputed to Marcuse a few minutes ago. But if I'm not wrong, those homologous meanings, precisely because their homology is to be found in different societal sectors and activities, necessarily have to do with the question of society as a whole and its reality. Of course, when speaking of society as a comprehensive whole we're talking about a problem that is only commensurate with the whole of society as an effectively active society. And that's what gives the impression of a tremendous hiatus. I think the imaginative, creative capability of society will enable it to solve problems that seem impossible to solve now, and others whose formulation we can't even imagine. If that ability doesn't exist, then that's right, there's no use in thinking about one aspect or another of the first phase of a socialist society, and no use in talking about that. Such talk is only meaningful provided it aims at shedding as much light as possible on as many issues as possible, at clearing the ground and showing that some hurdles are imaginary, whereas for some others certain kinds of solutions are already conceivable, and so forth. But all that necessarily assumes that we are talking about the *decisive activity of people* as capable of coping with the questions that will arise—and as the only ones capable of doing so.

Let's take an example. For many years now I have viewed schools not as an institution to be reformed or perfected, but as a prison to be destroyed. The "positive side" of that negation may be a conception in which the function of educating the new generations is reabsorbed in social life. (I'm fundamentally hostile to the myth of the "good savage" that has recently come back into vogue. That doesn't prevent me from observing that in this respect archaic societies show us the achievement of such "education," which is to say the absorbing of culture by the individual as he grows up, without implying the instituting of a separate sector of activity, specialized to that effect.) But the idea is not to propose a new utopia, since the focal point of that utopia will always be empty: The reabsorption of the educational function by social life will only be meaningful if people as a whole are capable of experiencing their children, and other people's children—children *in general*, then—otherwise than they do at present. That implies deep-seated transformations, not only of the organization and nature of work itself, but also of living conditions, of people's psyche, and so on—no small order, indeed. In other words, that immediately has to do with society as a comprehensive whole—and the activity and the very being of the community as capable of taking charge of it. Will society be capable of generating a coherent response to these issues? No theoretical reflection can demonstrate that it will, and less still that it will take the direction we are trying to outline. Any such "demonstration" would clearly be a contradiction in terms.

But what we do know is that *every society throughout history has been able to respond coherently to the problem of its comprehensive whole as well as to the specific aspects of that comprehensive whole.* That coherence, by the way, staggers—or rather, should stagger—every sociologist, psychoanalyst, economist, and so forth, leaving them voiceless (I say should, because they actually don't pay any attention to it). For it infinitely exceeds any conceivable analytic capacity. The individual psyche, the economic regime, social organization, the way objects are made, the spirit of the language, and so on—all that *sticks together*; it's impossible for one to exist without the others, and for that society to exist without any one of them. It's society that sets it all down; it's society that institutes itself as a comprehensive whole. What an immense enigma—and dazzling fact: There is no bungled society, nor has there ever been. There are biological monsters, psychic messes, but there aren't any bungled societies. The Chinese, the Athenians, the French and innumerable communities throughout history have always been able to institute, unknowingly, a coherent social life. To claim that a post-revolutionary society would be the only incapable one is necessarily based on the idea that the goal of an autonomous society is radically absurd, or impossible. Now until that view is "proved" (and I claim that any such "proof" is impossible, in principle), I will continue to assert that it merely expresses the practical-political-philosophical decision of the person who says so.

*What can feasibly be done at present? And what are the tasks of revolutionaries, and more specifically as intellectuals?*

The first task is to try to organize as revolutionary militants. As long as a revolutionary remains isolated, the question you raise isn't very mysterious or very interesting. Isolated individuals must try to do what they can, where they are, but there isn't any general response. The important question is, How can we overcome the problems encountered by a community of revolutionaries and which threaten its survival and development? There's nothing we can do about the rest. Workers may or may not wage battle; the women's movement may or may not grow; the high school students will continue their movement or return to the fold. But the thing we should feel responsible for is, *there are, in France, hundreds—to say the least—of people who think pretty much along the same lines as what we are discussing, about the overall issue we address* (no matter if the answers they give vary), which lines and issue are rejected by others. However, each of them feels or knows that the curses that have ravaged small revolutionary organizations haven't disappeared, and they are no more ready than before to believe that they would be able to solve the problems that would arise again were another organization to be set up.

There's only one way to know whether you can swim, and that is to get into the water. You may of course drown, but you can also choose to start with a place where you aren't out of your depth. First we should try to determine whether an embryonic organization going in the direction to which I just referred is feasible (if there are people ready to join it), and then try to define a number of points of agreement necessary and sufficient for collective activity at its outset. With shared referential issues and ideas, you can begin to put into practice the principle that the organization is constantly self-determining, with everything that implies. People must be ready to shoulder ongoing collective action of a long-term and somewhat general nature. Also, those people must agree to look at the relations among themselves, and more generally the internal problems of the organization, in connection with those raised with respect to the outside world. In other words, they must have understood and realized that a group is composed of individuals in flesh and blood, and not of pure political consciousnesses. You can solve these problems beautifully on paper, but that's useless for practice. For what determines people's real behavior within the organization—much more than their "ideas"—is their life—their personality, their concerns, their experience, the relations they develop with other people in the organization, and so forth. The effect is all the greater since a revolutionary organization doesn't act in a field involving the "objective" constraints to be found in other kinds of collective activity. In the case of productive work, for instance, be it alienated or not, there is an "objective" constraint that tends to minimize the effects of the above-mentioned factors. The same isn't true for a community that's floating somewhat in thin air, in a sense, and must extract from its own self most of what it thinks, what it wants to do, and how it wants to and should do that.

Now, if your question means: Suppose that organization does exist, what should its tasks be?, I'll obviously answer that it's up to it to define them, that they depend to a large extent on contingent, circumstantial factors. I myself think that there is an enormous amount to be done to elucidate the revolutionary conceptual framework, to denounce the falsehoods and mystifications, to spread right and justifiable ideas, relevant, meaningful and accurate information, as well as to propagate a new attitude toward ideas and theory. We need both to break the type of relation people now entertain with ideas and theory—still of an essentially religious kind—and show that that doesn't mean one can take the liberty of saying just anything. Naturally, I view it as just as essential for the organization to participate in struggles when they exist, and become their instrument, provided that participation is neither fabricated nor artificially parachuted into them. The establishment of a new relationship between revolutionaries, in the sense we want that word to have, and the social milieu, begins with being firmly convinced that the organization has as much to learn from ordinary people as they can learn from it. But again, that's meaningless if it isn't given a concrete content, and here too, a huge field of invention is open to the activity of revolutionaries.

# Imaginary Significations

*Two of the questions guiding your thinking are: What makes people stay together to constitute societies? And what makes those societies change? What makes new forms emerge?*

It's not just that people "stay" in society. People can exist only within society and through society. What is not social in human beings, in what we usually call the individual human being, is the biological substratum, the animal being, for one thing, and for another thing, that infinitely more important thing that distinguishes us radically from simple life forms, the psyche, that obscure, unfathomable, essentially *a*-social core. That core is the source of a perpetual flow of representations that are not prompted by ordinary logic; it is the locus of limitless, unachievable desires—and for those two reasons it is incapable, in itself and as such, of living. That core must be made to see reason, in every sense of the term, by the violent imposition of everything we habitually think of as "our own": language, a more or less structured logic, ways of doing things, even ways of moving around, norms, values, and so on. It is a violent imposition, not physically so, but violent because it does violence, and must do violence, to the psyche's own intrinsic tendencies. Why can't we Europeans dance some dances the way Africans do? That's not "racial"; it's social. We generally say it's "cultural": that means *social*.

An interview conducted by Michel Tréguer, broadcast on France-Culture on January 30, 1982, and published in *Création et désordre. Recherches et pensées contemporaines* (Paris: Éditions l'Originel, 1987), 65–99. That volume contains interviews given during the international symposium titled "Disorder and Order," held at Stanford University, September 14–16, 1981. Castoriadis' speech, "The Imaginary: Creation in the Social-Historical Domain," was published in *Disorder and Order*, Stanford Literature Studies 1 (Saratoga, Calif.: Anima Libri, 1984), 146–61. The symposium was preceded by another one on similar themes, held in Cerisy, France, the texts of which were published in French under the title *L'Auto-organisation. De la physique au politique* (Paris: Éditions du Seuil, 1983).

*Are you saying that what is involved in the fact that people form social groups is making the psyche see reason?*

Yes. I think that what we call the human species is a monstrous accident in biological evolution. That evolution—the creation of new species—led to the creation "at a certain point," as we say, of a being unfit for life. We are, to my knowledge, the only living beings who don't know what is edible and what isn't, what is poisonous for themselves. A sick dog will seek out the plants that soothe it, whereas we pick and eat toadstools. A dog never trips—a man trips and breaks his bones. A human being may commit suicide, or kill his fellows—for pleasure or for no reason. That being, that species so radically unfit for life would no doubt have disappeared had it not been capable, for some unknown reason, of creating a new form, a form unheard of among living creatures: that is, society—society as an institution, embodying significations and capable of conditioning peculiar specimens of the *Homo sapiens* species so that they could live, and live together, after a fashion.

So we come to the question I raised: What is it that holds a society together? But you mustn't take that as meaning a "social contract" or a "gathering up" of hypothetically preexisting "individuals." Rousseau's mythic, unreal vision of human beings, described as having lived alone and free in the woods, at great distances from one another, and who are led to "invent" language and group life is completely untenable. Those creatures would purely and simply have been unable to survive for a single minute. Rather, the sense of my question is: Given the extraordinary mass of singular institutions, tools, skills, linguistic specificities, and significations conveyed by that language as well as by all the acts of socialized human beings, how come all of that turns into a fantastically unified, coherent whole, in all those different social universes—in the social world of contemporary France, as well as that of the ancient Romans or Greeks, of the Assyrians, the Aranda, or of any other tribe? When I say institution, I take the word in the deepest, broadest sense, meaning the entire set of tools, language, skills, norms and values, and so forth.

*Everything coherent within society?*

Everything that, with or without formal sanctions, imposes ways of acting and thinking. Ways of thinking—that must always be emphasized. People think they have "their personal way of thinking." The truth is that even the most original thinker owes everything but a minute particle of what she says to society, to what she learned, her surroundings, the opinions and mood of the times, or a trivial reworking of all that, which is to say, the conclusions that may be drawn, or the underlying postulates that may be uncovered. Were we to quantify, metaphorically, the truly novel kernel in Plato, Aristotle, Kant, Hegel, Marx, or Freud, it would represent, possibly, 1 percent of what they said or wrote.

So there is this extraordinary collection of institutions thanks to which we speak one language rather than a different one; we have cars; we are familiar with them and can learn to drive them; and so on. Why are there cars? For them to exist, there have to be factories; for that there must be capital, and workers, and so forth. What holds all that together? How come there's unity to all that? By the way, that unity remains such even during a crisis or a revolution, even when two classes are engaged in a life-and-death struggle within a society. To fight to the death with someone, there must be common grounds, if only the ground. In the case of classes, or social groups, we aren't talking about the physical ground, but there must be shared stakes, in some sense, and those stakes only exist in a shared world constructed by the institution. What is the origin of that unity? We can't really answer that question, but we can delve deeper into it, with the realization that that unity itself is the outcome of the internal cohesion of interwoven meanings, or significations, pervading all of life in society, guiding and directing it: what I call the social imaginary significations. Those significations are embodied in and breathe life into specific institutions; of course I'm using the terms "embody" and "breathe life" metaphorically, since social imaginary significations are not spirits, or djinns. Let's take the example of spirits, precisely: for people who believe in them, that is a social imaginary signification, the same as the gods, or God with a capital G, or the *polis* for the ancient Greeks, or citizenship, or the nation. No-one has ever been able to see a nation under a microscope; it's something that exists only as an imaginary signification that binds together, say, all French people, who think: we are French. And over and beyond the fact that they think it explicitly, there is the fact that in some respects they partake of a same way of life, live under the same specific institutions, and so forth. In the same way, the State, or the party—or commodities, capital, money, rates of interest—or a taboo, virtue, and sin are social imaginary significations. Or again, man, woman, child, when taken not as biological categories but as social beings, are social institutions. And in each instance, in their concrete content, they are specific to each society and shaped in relation to the whole of its social imaginary significations. To take a trite example: the male chauvinist component of some cultures doesn't come out of the blue, nor is it determined by geography or the climate, any more than by the state of the productive forces: it's a particular social imaginary positioning of being-man and being-woman (which are of course complementary). The same is true of the "child," with the tremendous historical changes we have discovered thanks to the work of Ariès, among others. Present-day Polynesian, American, and French children are completely different creatures, and the cause of those differences isn't the genetic code.

Why do I call those significations "imaginary"? Because they are neither rational (they cannot be "constructed logically") nor real (they cannot be derived from things); they do not correspond to "rational ideas" any more than to natural objects. Also, because they are the outcome of what we all view as having to do with creation: that is, with the imagination, taken here not as the individual imagination but what I call the social imaginary. I call them social for the same reason: they are a creation of the social imaginary and amount to naught if they are not shared, partaken of by that anonymous, impersonal collective which is what society also always is. No-one has formulated what society is more forcefully and clearly than Balzac, at the beginning of *Tiger-eyes*, when he says, speaking of Paris: You always have your place there; you're never missing there. That's what society is. You may be a genius or a mediocrity, a hero or a criminal; you always have your place there; you're never missing there. Seconds after the death of the greatest man, life in society continues, imperturbably. As Clemenceau put it, the graveyards are full of irreplaceable men.

*And at the same time, each person, each individual is almost society as a whole, inasmuch as he reflects that entire fabric of imaginary significations.*

Absolutely, each person incorporates it and is, as I put it using a mathematical metaphor, a total part of society. Meaning that if you, I, a Polynesian, or other could be fully analyzed from that standpoint, we could reconstitute, as it were, the society to which each of us belongs and which we carry with us, so to speak.

*That coincides with the way some of today's biologists and neurophysiologists view the brain as a hologram—that is, a structure in which a small part yields the whole and the whole is present in each part.*

Yes, that's part of it. Each individual may be viewed as a social microcosm. Can a correspondence be established between the organization of society and biological structure? Yes, there is one, and a very important one, which is their closure. In both cases there is an organizational closure, an informational closure, a cognitive closure. Life forms—biological organisms—are not closed physically or energy-wise, of course; they are constantly exchanging with their environment. But in another sense they are closed into themselves: nothing that "occurs" ever exists for the organism unless it has reappropriated, reprocessed, re-elaborated it in its own way. The organism may be viewed as an entity subjected to disruptions. One class of those disruptions is not "captured" by the organism—it isn't interesting for it. Those that are captured are transformed by the organism into information. The main point is that *there is not* any heap of "information" outside of the organism, just waiting to be picked. If some disruptions become information it is because the boundary of the organism has a transforming function; it doesn't "reflect" or passively undergo influences; it is active and transforms those "movements" in the environment into information, into something that may be said (with perhaps a slight misuse of the term) to be meaningful for the organism.

*Which is to say that a message only becomes significant for the organism by surrendering to it, by fitting into its mold?*

Exactly. To take a trivial example: radio waves don't exist for terrestrial animals and didn't exist for human beings until they forged a specific prosthetic device to capture them. We create color, too. You'll say, but we don't create it out of naught. Of course, there is something "out there": radiant energy and electromagnetic waves. But those waves don't "have" any color: the stimulus becomes color by the creative action of the organism—which action cannot really be located, in fact. We can't see without an eye, of course, but the totality of the nervous system partakes in vision. And at least in the case of human beings, it's not only the totality of the nervous system in the "electromechanical" sense; it's the entire psyche and the thought processes. When we see, we think, even if we don't think about it. That's why we can see wrong—see wrong in the physical sense of the word—because thought processes are at work, whereas our thinking usually doesn't disturb other functions, such as digestion for instance. What is the analogy with society? Society, like each living species, and each living being, sets up its own world, which of course includes a representation of itself. So each society's specific imagination—its institutions and the imaginary significations carried by those institutions—determines and defines, in each instance, what that society views as information, what is mere noise, and what is nothing at all, along with the weight, relevance, and value, of any piece of information. Or, to continue to use the language of cybernetics, the information processing and response programs. In short, it is the societal institution that determines, in each instance, what is or is not real for that society. To take the example I mentioned at the colloquium: witchcraft was a reality in Salem three centuries ago; it no longer is today. Or Karl Marx's astonishing phrase: "In Greece, the Apollo of Delphi was as real a force as any other."

So we might say, to begin with, that each society contains a system for interpreting the world. But that would be insufficient: each society *is* a system for interpreting the world. Better yet, more strictly speaking, each society is the construing, actually the creation of a world that applies to it, its own world. Its identity is nothing other than that system of interpretation, or better still, of meaning-giving. For that reason, if you attack that system of interpretation, of meaning-giving, you attack it more lethally than if you attack its physical existence, and as a rule it will fight back much more savagely.

There are obviously radical differences between the closure of a society and that of a living being, and these are very instructive. For living beings, the organization of the world has a physical, material basis, which we claim to know at present, more or less, and which is its genetic heritage, having to do with its genes, with DNA. But in society, we see that features are transmitted, and are preserved, without any genetic basis. Neither the French language nor the legislation in force in France is transmitted from generation to generation on the basis of French people's specific DNA. Another major difference, very important to my way of thinking, is that for society there is no such thing as what information theory would call noise. Everything that occurs must mean something. For society, there is an imperialism of signification that suffers practically no exception. Except when the social system explicitly decides that something is meaningless. Moreover, in living beings, the processes that forge information are quite redundant: the forging or creation of information by and for living beings is never "economical"; there is considerable excess production (which actually has a function, as such: redundancy is a guarantee against mistakes and snags). But for society, it's a different matter. Here, the production and elaboration of information are taken very far, beyond any possible functional characterization, apparently extending virtually limitlessly.

I will not dwell on the impossibility of ascribing any finality whatsoever to society, aside from the preservation of its own institution which is, as we have seen, correlative to some imaginary significations that are *arbitrary* "rationally," or "reality-wise." This brings me to one last major differential feature, pertaining to what epistemology calls the question of the meta-observer. When we talk about life forms, who is speaking? Obviously not life form in itself—nor its "environment." It is a third agent, the meta-observer, who sees—or tries to see—both what is going on (or what exists) *for* the living being, from the standpoint of the living being, and "what that corresponds to" in that being's environment, beyond the boundary of the organism. So that meta-observer tries to establish a correlation between those two series, whereas he himself is not, strictly speaking, a part of one or the other. And this is true irrespective of the fact that, as I said earlier, there is nothing in experience that "determines" what *is* for a living being, since that being creates its own world, using external disturbances. Nonetheless, for each element of the world of the life form, the meta-observer can assign—ideally, at least—a correlation with an "external" element. For the sensation of color, for example, he will find a correspondence with electromagnetic vibrations of a given wavelength. Now, in the case of society, we cannot speak of a meta-observer: observers of society cannot "extricate themselves" from it. They belong to society. Society—or some societies, if you like—produces its own meta-observers, and it does so in its own way. That's why we are constantly making that both unavoidable and impossible attempt to be inside our society and to stand outside it to wonder, for instance, what reality is *outside* of our instituted world. How would a person who did not belong to our society—*or to any other society*—see the world? The question is both inevitable and insoluble. At the same time, inasmuch as that meta-observation work can be done, we discover that every society has beings that exist overwhelmingly for it without possessing any outside correlate. Society involves the wholesale creation of entities of the utmost importance for it, and for which it would be meaningless to seek any physical correlate. Take spirits, gods, God, norms, laws, sin, virtues, human rights, and so on.

I now come to what I view as an absolutely central point: the two dimensions of the institution of any society. Briefly: no society is devoid of arithmetic, and no society is devoid of myths. Parenthetically: in contemporary society arithmetic itself has become a myth, since this society lives largely in the pure fiction that everything is computable and that everything that counts can be counted. But there is more to it, and something much more important. There is no myth without arithmetic; every myth necessarily draws on the same schemata that form the basis of arithmetic, and even, explicitly, on numbers: God is One in Three persons; there are twelve gods; Buddha has a thousand and one faces, and so forth. Conversely, there is no arithmetic without myth, since arithmetic is always based on an imaginary representation of numbers, of the universe of quantity, and so on.

Arithmetic and myths are clear illustrations of the two dimensions in which the institution of society unfolds: of what I call the ensemblist-identitary dimension, on the one hand, and the specifically imaginary dimension, on the other hand. In the ensemblist-identitary dimension, the institution of society operates (acts and thinks) along the same schemata as are active in the logical-mathematical theory of sets. There are elements, classes, properties, and relations, all of which are posited as quite distinct and well-defined. The fundamental operational schema here is that of determinacy: existence, in this realm, is determinacy; for something to exist, it must be well-defined or determined. In the imaginary dimension, on the other hand, existence is signification. Significations can be spotted, but they are not fully determined. They are indefinitely interconnected through a type of relationship called referral. The signification "priest" refers me to the signification "religion," which refers me to God, and who knows what God refers me to, but certainly, among other things in any case, to the world as his creation, and therefore to sin, for example. Significations are not very distinct and well-defined; they are not interconnected by means of necessary and sufficient requisites, and cannot be reconstructed "analytically." It's vain to try to discover "atoms of signification" on the basis of which one might, by recombining them and building on them, and so on, reconstitute the universe of significations of our society or of some primitive society. Those edifices of signification cannot be reconstructed through logical operations. That is also the reason why neither social organization nor social order can be reduced to mathematical, physical or biological notions of order and organization. But the important point is not that negation but the positive assertion that the social-historical domain creates an original type of order; this is an ontological creation.

*This brings us to the second question, which is the emergence of newness in the social field. You do of course recognize that in spite of the principle of closure, positing the absolute specificity of each culture, there can nonetheless be communication between cultures, allowing us to speak about our neighbors or predecessors, for instance. But you don't think w can find any explanatory principle for the evolution of societal facts. You have just stated that: each new state of a society is an ontological creation.*

That is a highly complex question, and we must proceed in an orderly fashion. First, any attempt to derive the forms of a society from physical conditions or constant features of human beings, such as desire, be it in the Freudian sense or some other version of desire . . .

*. . . the desire to imitate, for example?*

. . . for example, yes, those attempts are sterile and actually meaningless. If you speak of a constant desire in human beings, no matter how you define it, and if you want to turn it into an "explanation" of society and history, you end up with a monstrosity, scientifically speaking: a constant cause producing variable effects. Desire definitely exists in Central Australia and Polynesia, as much as in Paris or California. Why, then, aren't the Paris area and California inhabited by primitive societies today?

The different historical creations never occur on a tabula rasa, of course—I'll come back to that in a minute. But first, just a few words about a remark made by René Thom, more or less to the effect that criticizing determinism is tantamount to advocating laziness. I think it's obvious that if any attitude is fundamentally lazy, it is really and truly determinism. What program and wish are behind the determinist's whole work? Let us find the single equation for the whole universe (let's found a theory of grand-grand unification), following which we will at last be able to sleep in peace for all eternity. If that isn't a sign of irrepressible metaphysical laziness, I don't what laziness is. To my way of thinking, on the other hand, there is always very important work to be done to uncover those conditions of social-historical creation that are in the province of the ensemblist-identitary (and therefore of determinism, of sorts) and which are partly, but always fragmentarily, incompletely, determinable. That search is truly endless, because those conditions are always immersed in something else, which totally alters the way they operate. What is more simple, clear and transparent, in appearance, than a tool, in any society? And yet, that simplicity, that bare, ostensible "utensility" of the tool, is a very recent Western conception. For a savage or a person from a traditional society, a tool is something fantastically charged. Think of Siegfried and his sword, Ulysses and his bow.

*And here too, we could reconstitute the entire social imaginary starting from the imaginary significations and representations attached to a tool, to the way it is used, its shape, and so on. . . .*

Absolutely. Take another look, for instance, at the story of how Hephaestus (Vulcan) makes Achilles' new arms in the *Iliad*. You pull at that little thing, Achilles' arms, and you unravel the whole world of the *Iliad*. Another example, in another sphere, is today's economy. One might think that in such an eminently quantifiable and computable field it would be easy to establish determinist relations linking phenomena together. But we know that is far from being the case. Economists have never succeeded in establishing the "exact science" they wanted to establish, and their forecasts are often mistaken. If the price of gas doubled tomorrow, its consumption would almost certainly decline, but by how much? And supposing the real wages of workers decreased appreciably because prices rose much faster than wages, what would happen? Would there be strikes, or something else, or nothing at all? Political economy is unable to answer that question, which has to do directly with people's activity within society. But if it cannot answer it, then everything it has to say about the determination of the wage rate turns out to be secondary, almost ridiculous. All those nice equations are seen for what they are: a formal, empty construction.

*I think Kenneth Arrow, the Nobel Prize winner in economics, says something very similar. He is very modest about economists' ability to anticipate.*

Yes, Arrow has his feet on the ground, and he states the fact clearly, saying, we don't understand because all of that is immersed in social and political conditions. But actually, that is immersed in much more: in the magma of social imaginary significations. To return to the broader problem: Whenever we think about the creation of a new societal form, or simply about some major change in our society, we must of course ask ourselves, what is there in the old [*l'ancien*] that prepared the new [*le nouveau*] in one way or another, or was tied to it? But here again, we must remember the principle of closure. Concretely, that means that the old enters into the new with the signification given it by the new, and could not enter it otherwise. Just remember, for instance, how elements and ideas, either Christian or from ancient Greece, have been constantly rediscovered, reshaped, and reinterpreted by the Western world, for centuries now, to adjust them to what are usually, foolishly, called present "needs," meaning, really, to present-day imaginary schemata. In the past there were, simply, disciplines such as history and philology that studied classical Antiquity. At present, a new, very important discipline often called historiography is developing, for research into the history of history and philology, and the interpretation of that history. The question, in other words, is how and why the ancient Greeks were believed to have some ideas in the 17th century, others in the 18th century (look at how ancient democracy was viewed at the time of the French Revolution), still others in the 19th century, and again today. At each point we must understand the new so as to comprehend what view of the old was being forged by that new development (and reciprocally, actually: an understanding of how Victorian England viewed classical Greece, for example, essentially sheds light on Victorian England).

To return to the question of the transition from one form of society to another: it's easy to see how all of the schemata set forth as truly "explanatory" are meager and empty. For example, and since there has been talk about how biological schemata may help us understand history, it is clearly impossible to apply, however vaguely, neo-Darwinian design to the evolution of societies. Take western Europe between the end of the Middle Ages and modern times: What do we see? Not a tremendous number of societal forms beginning to emerge, all of which except one would turn out to be unfit for survival, and would give way to the single fit one. We see the birth of a new form of society—ultimately to become capitalist society—with no "random variation" and no "selection" operating on the products of such random variations.

Similarly, the new principles we have discussed at this conference, such as order coming out of noise, or organization coming out of noise, are no doubt important for biology, and perhaps even for physics and cosmology, as Prigogine has implied, but I don't think they can elucidate the emergence of new social forms. Circumspection is definitely required here, for these ways of thinking, ideas, and ways of dealing with things are very recent, and we have not yet explored all their potential, by far. Perhaps they will yield a great deal more than what is presently visible: that is the hope, in any case. But still and all, I think there are some basic reasons why those ideas cannot take us much further toward an "explanation" or even toward a better understanding of the emergence of new social forms. First, as I have already said, we cannot really talk about noise with respect to society. I don't even think the term "disorder" is applicable here, in the acceptance it has for information theory and in these new conceptions, of course. When a given society views something as disorder, it is disorder from the viewpoint of its own institution, but it isn't "disorder" as defined by these new theories. It is something that has an order of its own, but which is negatively valued from the standpoint of the existing institution.

When hungry mobs marched on Versailles during the Revolution, or when, today, ten thousand young motorcyclists gather at the place de la Bastille and then ride around Paris making a lot of noise, well, that precisely is not noise, and it is not disorder. Those are orderly things, but negative from the viewpoint of the existing order. Similarly, in the 11th, 12th, and 13th centuries, when the bourgeoisie—the proto-bourgeoisie— first emerged, and formed the first free towns—all those places called Villefranche, Freiburg, Fribourg, and so on—towns that eluded, to some extent, the grip of the existing, essentially seigniorial or feudal order, that phenomenon cannot be considered noise or disorder either, except from the perspective of feudal society. But to become consistent and extensive enough to create disorder within feudal society, it must represent order in and for itself. Indeed, what we see in it is a new order, new social imaginary significations. The bourgeoisie is only bourgeoisie inasmuch as it is already creating an organization other than the feudal one in the first towns it founds. That bourgeoisie has been enormously disparaged, and I have no intention of defending it, but still and all, it must not be confused with capitalism. The proto-bourgeoisie is the first social stratum in western Europe to reconstitute a political town [*commune*], a political collectivity. For the first time since the end of the ancient *poleis*. That political community is something radically different from the Empire, royalty, the papacy or the feudal order. That imaginary signification—the collectivity as political subject—had to be re-created, and it is because it was created (re-created) that the bourgeoisie could exist as such.

The radical difference between the biological world and the social-historical world is that autonomy emerges in the latter. We can speak of the "autonomy" of life forms, as Varela does, but that is precisely what I, like Varela himself, have called "closure." A life form has its own laws, and nothing can appear in its world that is not in conformity with those laws in one way or another, cognitively speaking. Closure therefore implies that the functioning of that life form, of that subject, of that oneself, its correspondence with what may exist "outside," is governed by rules, principles, laws that are given once and for all. With the structure of a rabbit or a bacterium, all that is given once and for all for the particular species. Some changes do occur, but they occur in a way we can only view as random. But the phenomenon we have just described and its essential characteristics provide a very precise definition of what we call—or of what I call, at any rate—heteronomy in the social-historical domain. That, for example, is typically the case of primitive societies, or even traditional religious societies, where principles, rules, laws, and significations are posited as given once and for all, as inviolable, unquestioned and unquestionable. That non-questionable character is guaranteed by instituted representations which in turn are part of the institution of society: all those representations ensuring that the source of the institution—its origin, foundation and guarantor—is non-social. Since God gave the Law to Moses, for instance, no-one among the Hebrews can stand up to say, the Law is bad and unfair. If he says that, he ceases to be a Hebrew. No matter whether he is stoned or not, he exits from that society, having shattered something absolutely fundamental to Hebraic society. (Actually, no-one does that.) This situation is precisely, literally, one of heteronomy. Someone other than ourselves has set down the Law; it is not society that creates its institution; that institution is given to us or imposed on us—no matter which, actually—by our ancestors, by the gods, by God, by the Laws of History (see the *Preface to a Contribution to the Critique of Political Economy*, by that same Karl Marx mentioned earlier). That heteronomy is embedded in the heteronomous institutions of society, and primarily in the psychosocial structure of individuals themselves, for whom the idea of challenging the Law is inconceivable. This obviously gives it fantastic potency in the service of the preservation, the conservation, of the institution, whence the discourse, rediscovered by some people nowadays, and which has in fact been hanging around for at least twenty-five centuries, according to which the best and ultimately the only reliable anchor point for any institution of society is religion. That makes for sacred institutions, really, which amounts to pretty much the same thing.

The quasi totality of human societies in the quasi totality of historical periods is in this state, to the best of our knowledge. An extraordinary historical creation then occurred, first in ancient Greece, as far as we know, and was redeveloped later, with some completely new features, in western Europe starting at the end of the Middle Ages. It is historical creation that makes autonomy exist as openness rather than as closure. What does that mean? That in those societies, in ancient Greece as well as in modern Europe, a new form of the existent, of social-historical being, and even of being in general emerges: those societies themselves call into question their institution, which is to say the law presiding over their existence. This is the first time we see any being whatsoever explicitly call into question, and change through explicit action, the law presiding over its existence. Changes in the societal institution may be seen in any society, but this is something else. Some absolute monarch succeeded to some other one, and he changed a few laws; or else, with passing time, the society gradually altered its customs. But the situation is radically different in the two cases I mentioned. Here the laws are changed deliberately; questions are posed overtly: <u>Are our laws just? Are our gods true?</u> Is our representation of the world right? In other words, radical political questions as well as radical philosophical questions are raised. The philosophical question may be reformulated in the language we used earlier. Does our system for creating information based on what we "receive"—including both the "external filters," so to speak, what goes on "at the boundaries" as well as the internal procedures, categories, and so on—yield truth? The question may be posed in various ways: Is it efficient? Does it correspond to what exists (ranging from the perfectly trite to the most profound level)?

*It's not clear to me how that question can be raised, since you said a while ago that even the notions of reality and of truth are inside the closure.*

You're absolutely right in asking that, since it is the very question of truth and reality that you are raising, just as those societies raise it. For a primitive, reality and the truth of its representation are unquestioned; she may think, for instance, that what she saw in a dream actually happened—that's a very common idea—and therefore say, last night I was in such and such a place; or else, some tree in the jungle is inhabited by such and such a spirit, and consequently some things must be done or avoided, and so forth. All those inherited representations correspond to truth and reality for her and are never questioned. The break that occurred in Greece and began again in western Europe resides in the fact that inherited representations, and ultimately the very notions of truth and reality, were questioned. They were questioned concretely at first. By Thales, for instance, who wondered whether everything in the myths or in Hesiod's *Theogony* was true, and also, might there be one single element from which the world was shaped? But then, immediately, that question redoubles in intensity; it folds back on itself and that other question arises—and here we have the true beginning of philosophy as reflexivity—what are truth and reality, actually? Now these questions did not exist, were not raised before, not in that way. In heteronomous societies, what is true is what conforms to the established modes of representation.

*What characterizes those societies, including ours, then, is the fracturing of that closure. But by definition, what is outside the closure is beyond the sphere of language, so that becomes a confrontation with something no longer nameable.*

That becomes overture to what may be called infinite, limitless interrogation. Society's representations are therefore called into question, along with the law itself—meaning that the question of justice emerges. That is also one of those questions for which there can be no single answer, once and for all. It would clearly be illusory and mystifying to claim that we could find a system of laws such that the underlying political question would never again have to be raised.

Let me go back again to that unending question of truth. We must understand one extremely simple thing: that is, the question of what part of what we think comes from "us" and what comes from the "object" is ultimately undecidable. I say ultimately because there is obviously an infinity of more or less trivial domains in which that decision can be made. Speaking about someone who is colorblind, for instance, I can say that if he inverts red and green, or if he only sees gray, the cause is his peculiar "subjective" structure, his specific makeup, his retina or I don't know what, and it is not the thing seen. At a less elementary level, it is often possible to legitimately assert that some theoretical construction is due exclusively to the ideological prejudices, or to put it more abstractly, to the mental framework of its constructor. All that must always be cleared up; but it's worth noting, because quite paradoxical, that this not only doesn't eliminate the question of truth, but assumes it to be soluble and solved, and several times over. First, there is of course the assertion: the theory T is a pure product of ideology. That assertion contends to be true, and not to be ideological itself. Next, for it to be true, it has to proceed by a comparison between T and "the true state of affairs," which is therefore assumed to be accessible *without any theory* or by virtue of "the only true theory." But once that has been cleared up, there always remains the ultimate question, which we cannot, in good faith, evacuate: Are we imposing our schemata—or new schemata—on a new layer of reality, or have we encountered something indicating that some schemata actually do correspond to something beyond our comprehension? It is always both. Were that not the case we would either be in an endless solipsistic aporia (everything we say is merely the elaboration of our "subjective structures," at the limit), or a pure, coherent, collective delusion. Or else we would claim to be pure mirrors, and even less than that, for even a mirror contributes, by its very structure, to the appearing-thus of the image (for example, advocates of what is known as the theory of "reflection" have never explained how they know we are not spherical mirrors). So the question of the ultimate origin of our knowledge is undecidable forever—that is, the principle of undecidability of the origin.

Let's return to the discussion on the creation of autonomy. Calling into question the institution of society, the representation of the world and the social imaginary significations it bears is tantamount to creating what we call democracy and philosophy. Starting with that break with the absolute closure prevailing until then, a society develops which contains the seeds of autonomy—that is, of an *explicit* self-institution of society. That goes hand in hand with the creation of individuals capable of a degree of autonomy, as well—that is, capable of questioning both the social law and their own selves, of questioning their own norms. That calling into question struggles with and against the old order, the heteronomous order. That struggle isn't over now, by a long shot, but that's another story. But still and all, we must remember that it is historical creation, the emerging of societies and individuals containing the effective seeds of autonomy, that conditions the possibility of our having the present theoretical discussion, for example, something that would be inconceivable in a different historical context. But also and above all, it conditions the possibility of true political action, action aimed at establishing a society explicitly self-instituting to an extent far greater than ancient Greek society or European societies, which would therefore represent another rupture in history, a rupture as great as the two I have just mentioned.

*Let's look at a few questions, for the sake of clarification. Can we say that the emerging of new societal forms involves mechanisms of creation that will always be beyond the explainable?*

Yes. When there is creation, that means I can approach its requisites, understand some of the dimensions in which it unfolded, but I cannot explain it in the traditional sense of the term. That would be a contradiction in terms.

*That would imply, ultimately, that history involves something irreducible, something indifferent to everything we can say about the laws of history?*

Absolutely. There are of course laws of, and impossibilities for, history: they are numerous and trivial. Many examples come to mind immediately. No society can ever institute itself in such a way that all of its participants are obliged to fast 365 days a year, or even for two months. Also: no society can institute itself in such a way that it totally inhibits heterosexual desire, and if it did so nonetheless it would be unobservable within a generation. But those are truisms. If I delve deeper, I find that some regularities do exist, but they are not "laws" in the proper, honest sense science gives to the word "law."

*Second question: Let us return to what we were saying about Greece, the origins of democracy, followed by its rebirth in Europe. How is it that in both cases, the societies this produced did not comport themselves quite like the others, and in particular, they devoured a great many other societies very violently, through Christianity and conversion, and later through colonial conquests, and finally through everything we are witnessing nowadays?*

First of all, we must not forget the answer to the previous question: we can elucidate a great many things, but we are not looking for an explanation. Second: Greek society did not particularly distinguish itself from other known societies by its violence; and even European society is far from having a monopoly on violence exerted on other societies (look at Islam, for instance). But the new, fascinating fact is that that society, that social-historical universe, succeeded in imposing itself on the entire planet. That is, it created the first effective universalization of history; it succeeded in creating history as effectively universal. Before that there were peoples who extended their empire to varying extents, but never did they exert a truly worldwide ascendancy. The European universe did. Why?

It's an enormous question, for which I don't claim to have the answer, but some elements do provide clarification. The first: through that break with inherited representation, in Greece, and through what we call the birth of rational thinking, a tremendous development took place, an extraordinary, unprecedented unfurling of the ensemblist-identitary dimension, which is to say of logic, mathematics, science, and the application of all that knowledge to technology. That yielded a whole series of previously nonexistent tools for power. Second, modern Europe is Christian, or has to do with Christianity. With Christianity we have the historical appearance of the idea of an all-powerful being (subject), and of that power as a pole. For the Greeks (and I think that is one of the reasons why they were able to create what they did), human beings are mortal beings in a very deep sense: there is nothing to be expected from another life (if it exists, it is worse than the present one). Moreover, the gods themselves are subjected to impersonal laws, and above all to an ultimate, absolutely irreducible being-thus of being. Even Plato's God in the *Timaeus*, for example, doesn't create matter and cannot create a rational world *except* "inasmuch as possible," as much as the being-thus of matter permits. I don't want to discuss the God of the Hebrews, but we do observe that he is not really a creator (or all-powerful, which is just about the same thing), but a shaper, and at any rate he does not possess the rational instrument forged by the Greeks. When the Christian God is created (as a social imaginary signification), he certainly seems, theoretically, to be all-powerful and a creator (he is depicted as such in the Nicene Creed, at any rate). Here we have a subjective pole of absolute (personal) power. And that pole was supposed to possess rationality (a fact that creates other problems, which cannot be discussed here)—at least on paper it was (seeing that both the Greek and the Latin Fathers of the Church had plundered Greek philosophy). In fact, from the standpoint that interests us, that God remained inactive for about ten centuries or more. In a sense, he was only reactivated just in time to be (definitively?) retired, not by the bourgeoisie we were talking about earlier, but by capitalism—in, let's say, the 17th century—with the emergence of a new social imaginary signification, the fundamental characteristic and the soul of capitalism: the unlimited expansion of "rational" mastery. At the outset this appeared as the unlimited expansion, or the tendency toward the unlimited expansion of productive forces—what Marx saw so clearly—and rapidly became the "rationalization" of all social life—what Max Weber saw very clearly, too. Because there are not just the productive forces: "rational" mastery had to be established over the lives of citizens, including family life, children's education, communication and information, and so on. It's that Europe, the Europe of capitalism, that really took over the planet.

The desire or thirst for might—the desire for an unlimited extension of power—has certainly been there for much longer. There had also been conquerors before, wanting to dominate the world, and who actually did succeed in dominating part of it for a while. But with capitalism, for the first time, this tendency toward the unlimited extension of might, or of mastery, encountered the appropriate, adequate instruments: "rational" instruments. Capitalism discovered, right there in front of it, readily available, that incalculably powerful instrument represented by the enormous development of ensemblist-identitary logic in the form of "rational reason," science, and the productive, manipulative and military applications of science (which, in some sense, is what it took from the Greeks), and then in turn developed it, fantastically. At the same time it inherited those other phantasms (Christian, in this case) of an all-powerful subject, and a world thoroughly "rational" because it was forged by an all-powerful rational subject, and is therefore also asymptotically re-masterable by subjects who asymptotically increase their rationality and their potency as well. It also, simultaneously, twisted those significations in some decisive ways. This illustrates what we were saying earlier, that the old enters the new, but with the signification given it by the new. We need not go into the way it twisted its Christian heritage. But let's look at another facet, less obvious at first glance, the legacy of Greek reason. Take mathematics, for instance: Pythagoras was not the only one for whom numbers convey something of the sacred order of being; all Greek mathematicians believed that mathematics correspond, in some sense, to *phusis*, to a "nature" of what is. Now, at the "noble" level, that no longer exists in modern, scientific mathematics, and at the "vulgar" level, numbers as well as geometric figures have taken on a highly instrumental character—look at Marx's very accurate allusions to the reasoned application of science to industry. This builds up an unprecedented material potency—and not only material, which brings us to another, even more difficult problem. There is the power of fascination, exerted even on uncolonized, unconquered peoples, one quite visible after World War II, including, and in fact especially, following decolonization. People everywhere, more or less, began to ape the capitalist way of life and organization, and those poor people were aping it while in dire poverty. So capitalism was able to exert direct violence, based on technical and economic development, which isn't very mysterious, but also that other violence, exerted through fascination, through the pure and simple representation of that advanced capitalist society, acting as universal model. The combination of the two led to the universal victory of capitalism, for the time being—a Pyrrhic victory in one sense, without even mentioning the people dying of hunger in the third world, since that third world is a third world inasmuch, precisely, as it has not assimilated capitalism.

Before we end this discussion, I would like to return to the political project of an autonomous society, to say a few words about an issue linked to the previous one, about which I have been concerned for many years now. I don't think people will ever mobilize to change society, particularly under the conditions of modern capitalism, and to establish an autonomous society, for the sole end of having an autonomous society. They will truly, effectively, want autonomy when they see it as the vehicle, the requisite, almost the accompaniment, however indispensable, of something substantial they view as invaluable and really want to accomplish, and which is unattainable in the present world. But that means that new values will have to emerge in social-historical life.

*Yes, otherwise they will always be fighting for values belonging to the previous state. There will be nothing new until something else develops.*

That is very accurately formulated. That's what happened with the Marxist distortion of the working-class movement, which came to mean, let's fight to be able to consume enough, at last, either through higher wages within capitalist society, or in future societies which will be societies with material abundance. Of course, abundance was said to be the requisite for something different, but actually, people remained stuck on what is capitalism's central imaginary signification, which claims that Good is more production, more things, more programming, more "rational" (obviously pseudo-rational, really) mastery.

*There remains the question of political action. If a new, yet unborn society will develop a new system of social imaginary significations irreducible to those of the previous one, then we are unable to construe that future, unborn society using our present-day conceptual framework; and conversely, once it is born we will no longer be able to conceive of our present state without using the new system of imaginary significations. In* Devant la guerre *you describe, precisely, the development of something new, of a new society coming into being before our eyes, in the Soviet Union, and the terms you use to describe it are quite terrifying, showing the development of a system entirely structured around military strength and the idea of conquest. Should we surrender to total pessimism, then, or can we uncover some bases for action, nonetheless?*

Those are evidently wide-ranging questions. I wrote *Devant la guerre* both because I am deeply convinced that my analysis is correct, and to galvanize people accordingly. You know, for a long time I was very concerned with the problem of Russia, with the bureaucratization that followed the 1917 Revolution, with what has been called totalitarianism. The fact is that, once those questions were more or less settled for me, and once I had written a great deal about them, I resumed my work in philosophy, then in psychoanalysis, and didn't really attend to them much for ten or fifteen years. So that the invasion of Afghanistan, which in itself didn't surprise me—I had always expected that sort of action from Russia—did act as a catalyst, nevertheless. It caused a great many elements that had been silently accumulating in my mind to precipitate, and to begin with, the question of how a society could put together such enormous military might when everything non-military is in such awful shape. That led me to the analyses you read in *Devant la guerre*, especially in chapter 4, which may be summed up in a single statement: when totalitarianism, or what I had called total, totalitarian bureaucratic capitalism, stays in power for sixty years, it ceases to be the classical totalitarianism described by someone like

Hannah Arendt for Nazism and for the Stalinism of the heroic period if I dare call it that (more accurately, the delirious period) of the great massacres and the great purges. It has changed, clearly, and in Russia it has turned into something radically new, what I call a stratocracy. People find that idea somewhat difficult to accept—that's evident in the criticisms of my book—for here too, they can't face up to the new thing and accept it. As soon as something new appears, they try to reduce it to some known categories. If you talk about a stratocracy, they ask, but why aren't the field marshals governing? They are thinking of Bonaparte, the Latin American generals, the praetorians, and so forth. Now in fact, a new kind of regime has been created there, a new and effectively terrifying kind of society. I myself would call it monstrous, in that it is destructive of significations. That is its fine edge, as well as what holds it together. That seems paradoxical, but that's the way it is.

*Precisely, in the last chapter of your book, you show how language no longer functions and how even something like beauty is affected.*

Yes, those points are perhaps the most important ones for me. Language is reduced to a pure code for communication, reduced to the transmission of orders, instructions, and signals. Beauty too—art, that is—works as a fantastic discriminant. Here indeed is the first society in history that not only does not create any beauty, but in which what I call an assertive hatred of the beautiful prevails. They find beauty unbearable, for reasons I try to sketch in that chapter 4 of the book, and this isn't true only in Russia; the same thing may be found in communist parties all over the world. Here we have a monstrous creation, whereas we were expecting creations of another sort as an outcome of the global society of the 20th century. We expected an evolution that would flow out of the revolutionary working-class movement, as was the case, in a sense, for the women's movement, the youth movement, the ecology movement, leading to the transformation of society toward what I call an autonomous society.

As for today's political problem, there is the general angle from which you rightly broached it a while ago, and the specific angle from which we are forced to tackle it at present. For a new society to be born, in effect, there must be, at the same time and in a same movement, the occurrence of new significations—I mean of new values, new norms, new ways of bestowing meaning on things, on relations between human beings, and on our life in general. What is the picture, in this respect, for contemporary society? Let's set Russia aside for the moment, along with that nightmare

of a third world war hanging over our heads, but without forgetting it in
the discussion. The situation is a contradictory one. On the one hand we
have a series of attempts to set up new ways of life. Such attempts have
always begun with protests against the present state of affairs. That was
true of the workers' movement, and it still is; when workers fight the pace
of production, their working conditions on an assembly line or a production line in a factory, they are fighting against the capitalist productive
logic in which a human being must simply be a nut and bolt in the machine, an object that functions within production and is of no interest in
any other respect. But that has also been the signification of the women's
movement. That movement is much broader and deeper than the explicit,
organized movements we have witnessed over the last ten or twenty years.
By the women's movement I mean what began during the last third of the
19th century, and thanks to which women began to be able to get a higher
education, change their relations with their husband and children, acquire
political rights, and so on. It was a very important, very diffuse movement:
the names we can link to it, names of individuals or of visible, locatable
and datable movements, are a fraction of the thing. The truly important
part, the one that really changed the society in which we live, was the
anonymous part. The same is true for youth. What did these movements,
be it the working-class, women's, youth, or ecology movement, express?
What are they still expressing? I think they all come under the same heading, with the same signification: movements toward and for autonomy.
These are attempts by different categories of people, aimed at no longer
being subjected to the institution of society as it is imposed on them, and
at modifying it. The institution of the family has already been modified,
in fact, by the joint effect of the women's movement and the youth movement (the two are actually closely linked, in a subconscious, subterranean
way). Ultimately, fifty years later, there have also been formal modifications in the written law, in the Civil Code, and so on. But that is an effect,
a side effect. The effective reality of the family as institution, for example,
if we compare today's family with what it was in 1880, in France or in
Victorian England—the two are not terribly different; maybe there was
more adultery going on in France—that reality has been profoundly modified. That modification process is far from finished, in fact. But what direction is it taking? Obviously, the direction of greater autonomy for women,
but also for the younger generation, including children. Now not only are
those modifications still in process, but they have also created new problems, and of course they necessarily created them, and could never merely
stop at modifying the family institution. That is easy to see, since those

modifications of the family institution soon call into question all sorts of other aspects of the life of the societal institution, including women's work, education, housing, and so forth. So there is this process of creating new norms, or at any rate of challenging and destroying the old norms, which tends, at the same time, toward a positive creation.

But we also observe—and that's the tragedy of contemporary times— the reverse trend. That reverse is not, as might be thought traditionally, a fascist movement. There isn't any fascism in Western societies (I mean any major fascist movement, or any historical chances for any such movement). There aren't even any "reactionaries": no-one dares to, or wants to be called reactionary; everyone is for progress, and is therefore progressive; since that progress is always more of the same, it's the mere preservation, at the deepest level, of what already exists. The true negative side is what I have been calling the privatization of individuals for over twenty years now. People abandon the collective spheres; they fall back on their individual or micro-familial existences, and don't care about anything beyond the very narrow circle of their personal interests. That trend is encouraged by the dominant strata: not that there is any conspiracy, of course, but there is the whole dynamic of the system. That's what consumer society is about: buy a new car, the latest model, and shut up. Even the so-called sexual liberation is partially that. You want sex? OK, here, we'll give you sex, all the porn you like, and that's it. The same is true for the economy, but it's also true for politics. That's what the bureaucratization pervading public life expresses. Trust us experts; we are technicians; we are the party that defends your interests. We are the President you elected, the government you put in power; so trust us and let us take care of things: you'll see, at the end of four or seven years. That all encourages apathy in people; it destroys public space as a space for collective activity through which people attempt to take charge of their own fate. You can see it in France, in the United States, in all of the Western countries (and the others too, in fact). Now, if we take that trend only, independent of the risk of war, and set up a sort of ideal type for the possible, and even probable future, where does that lead us? To widespread bureaucratization of society, but a soft bureaucratization, without terror or Gulags. Quite simply, people would be brought to do what the regime, those in power, the dominant strata demand that they do, simply manipulated by the dynamics of preservation and consumption, by the media, by the bureaucratic agencies that manage the various spheres of social life, and so forth.

So there are these two contradictory trends. The point is not to be optimistic or pessimistic about that situation: it is to make things clear, to try to help people to act, to fight, to go beyond that apathy. Now that apathy, or rather that lack of interest for true public affairs, for political affairs, sometimes shows up in most unexpected ways, donning the appearance of the exact opposite. For example, we have the prospect of a conflict between the two superpowers, with the risk of a nuclear war. That has triggered all those pacifist, neutralist movements, especially in Germany. Now most of the slogans, the political orientations and underlying attitudes connected with these movements seem to be totally unaware of what is really at stake, and lead to politically untenable conclusions. Like the slogan: a denuclearized Europe, from Poland to Portugal. Aside from its many other implicit absurdities, that slogan is a biological one, not a political one. It means, in so many words, we, Europeans are for our own survival, and if the Americans and Russians want to nuke each other, that's their problem. There isn't an ounce of politics in that, or, in fact, of humanity or internationalism, or a grain of realism. And of course it's a repellent slogan for both the American and the Russian populations. In spite of the grandiloquent rhetoric that goes along with it, its meaning is: I, ordinary little European, want to survive, and the others can die, if they like. That, again, is a slogan showing "privatization at the international level."

There is no doubt, however, that the threat of war produces a psychological and political jolt. People become aware that their fate, their fate in the most material, most direct sense, their survival, is in the hands of bureaucratic apparatuses, both in the Kremlin and in Washington: deeply irrational apparatuses, each pursuing its own interests and plans for domination (or for the defense of the existing domination), which plans have nothing to do with the interests of humankind. That threat jolts Western societies. Couldn't that jolt lead to the development of something other than mere survival reactions? Couldn't this situation be an incitement, a starting point, for a true anti-war movement, one which is *therefore also* against the *conditions* producing war?

# Response to Richard Rorty

I would like to begin by saying that having to respond to Richard Rorty's talk sets me in a very awkward position.[1] First of all because I have real affection for him, and at the same time I disagree totally with what he has to say, which doesn't put me in an easy position. Second, I absolutely cannot identify with that sovereign "us," or that breast-beating "us" he uses in his talk when designating intellectuals, and those of you who are at all familiar with my writings will understand what I mean. Third, and above all, because his exposé, however affable in appearance, calls everything into question. It raises all sorts of issues, with assumptions about the nature of philosophy and the history of humankind that he obviously could not have defended seriously in three-quarters of an hour—actually there cannot be any foundation in this sort of discussion—but which refer to what he has written elsewhere. There would not be much sense for me to respond with a symmetrical series of assertions based on my own previous statements and writings. Listeners would only be faced with the pure opposition between two series of theses. So I have chosen to focus on a few points that I see as strategic, as they say, or perhaps which particularly irritated my political and philosophical leanings.

The first is the conception of history combated by Rorty—and also by Ernesto Laclau, as far as I understand, since I haven't read his book.[2] That

---

{Lecture delivered on May 31, 1995, at the Collège international de philosophie in response to a talk by Richard Rorty.}

1. [Rorty's main writings include *Philosophy and the Mirror of Nature* (Princeton: Princeton University Press, 1979), *Contingency, Irony and Solidarity* (Cambridge: Cambridge University Press, 1989), *Achieving Our Country: Leftist Thought in Twentieth Century America* (Cambridge, Mass.: Harvard University Press, 1998). *Essays on Heidegger and Others: Philosophical Papers II* (Cambridge: Cambridge University Press, 1991) contains a study on Castoriadis: "Unger, Castoriadis and the Romance of a National Future."—Trans.]

2. {Ernesto Laclau, a specialist of political philosophy of Argentinean origin, is professor at the University of Essex. His main work, in English, written with Chantal

conception, according to which the history of humankind is a path toward salvation, was and still is an absurdity, irrespective of the form given to that salvation by Hegel, Marx, the Fathers of the Church or Augustine. Parenthetically, neither Plato nor Aristotle ever thought we were promised a glorious future, and I'm not saying that to exclude them from any denunciation of philosophers. We know very well when, where and how that story—those positions we are now discovering the need to combat—began. We also know that the most accomplished version of all that is to be found in the Hegelian system. In the vulgar version of the latter, history simply *goes somewhere* [*a un sens*].³ So Sartre accused Camus of not seeing that history goes in a direction—it goes to . . . Bagnolet, Porte-des-Lilas, I forget which subway station. For the only reading of the system I view as worthy of the name, history *is meaning*, history is *logos*, history is a moment in the self-achievement of Mind. However—and I think some people realized this a long time ago—those expressions are absurd. History has no more sense/direction and has no more meaning than "the gravitational field weighs fourteen kilos." It is within the gravitational field that something can weigh fourteen kilos. Likewise, history is the field in and through which meaning emerges, created by human beings. It is absurd, linguistically absurd, to try to give meaning to a field in and through which meaning emerges.

Now, while that attempt, which originates, effectively, with the Hebrew position and is continued by the Christians, is definitely not Greek, it should be clear that it is nothing but the realization, in the historical field, of a much broader philosophical proposition, which is that *being is meaning*. And the Greeks of the decadent period—that is, Plato and Aristotle—did share that position. According to Plato, beyond Ideas, beyond essences, there is Good, the source of Being; and even Aristotle's hierarchy of *phusis*, however imperfect, has a meaning or is meaning, and is enamored of the supreme meaning which is meaning reflecting itself, thought thinking itself. Whence philosophy, originally created to overthrow theology and the instituted religious imaginary, the idea that truth comes from elsewhere, is itself transformed by means of that postulate of being as meaning into a sort of theology claiming to offer human beings a comprehensive meaning guaranteeing satisfactory answers on three levels: representation, affect and practice or intention: or, what is true, what is good,

---

Mouffe, is *Hegemony and Socialist Strategy* (London: Verso, 1985; 2nd ed., 2001).} [Also, among others: *Politics and Ideology in Marxist Theory: Capitalism, Fascism, Populism* (London: Verso, 1979).—Trans.]

    3. [In French, *a un sens:* that is, possesses both direction and meaning—Trans.]

what must be done. We recognize Plato's *agathon* here: the good, the desirable, and at the same time what should be willed. That fallacy persisted up to Heidegger.

So I repeat, vehemently: being is not meaning; being has no meaning. There is, simply, a dimension of being, of total being, in which limited meaning is to be found. That is what I call ensemblist-identitary meaning: the "ensidic." The sum of two goats and two goats, or of two tables and two tables will always be four goats and four tables. In the case of ice cubes, after a half hour there will no longer be ice cubes, but water, and we'll then have to resort to a more complicated law of transformation to find an equivalence between the ice cubes and water. Beyond that limited meaning, none of us has ever proved that total being [*l'étant global*] has what we call meaning. It is very amusing to see someone like Heidegger accuse earlier philosophers of not looking for the *Sinn des Seins* [the meaning of being.—Trans.], without ever wondering what that *Sinn des Seins* might be, aside from the interpretation of the term *Sein* in the philosophical idiom (which begins with Aristotle). Also: in what language could that *Sinn des Seins* ever be enunciated?

To conclude on this first point. Rorty quoted Laclau as saying that the thesis of the end of history is true in the sense that history is beginning now. It's good to see that Laclau seems to understand what history has always been. But the main, and obvious point remains: that history has never been and will never be apprehensible. Nature itself is not apprehensible; so how and why should history, which presupposes the existence of nature, be? And if we are talking about complexity, history's complexity is necessarily infinitely greater. Why? Because what I call the creativity of beings in general manifests itself in history through the freedom of human beings, the initial indetermination of their psyche and even the indetermination of conscious individuals.

I now come to what I consider some totally erroneous statements about philosophy. I absolutely do not agree with the idea that philosophy is a series of narrations. Aristotle's *Metaphysics* is not a narration, any more than the *Critique of Pure Reason*. That is like a not very legitimate mix-up of what some philosophies of history have claimed to be and what philosophy itself is: an attempt to elucidate what is given. Likewise, I don't see what Laclau has in mind when he tells us that we can now have a conception more materialist than Marx's own. Why should we have a materialist conception, and why more or less than Marx? I don't know what the term materialism means; I don't know what the term idealism means; those are totally meaningless metaphysical terms, and we should have ceased to base our discussions on them long ago. If what is meant by materialist is "rid of some imaginary, or psychological, conceptions," very well, I agree, but why call that materialism? Materialism, as we know it in the history of philosophy, Marx included of course, is nothing but an imaginary representation of the substance or the inmost depths of beings as *matter*. But what does that mean? Think of poor Lenin's desperate attempts, in *Materialism and Empiro-Criticism*: to start with, matter is solid bits of objects, sawdust, for instance. But what is to be made of electrons, and all those elementary particles that make the concept of matter practically impossible to grasp? Lenin then falls back on energy. So, what is energy? If what is meant is that the important thing in *Saint Matthew's Passion* is that energy is required to compose and perform it, thanks a lot, but that doesn't help much. Energy is required, of course, but in quite a metaphoric sense: that's not where the essence of the *Passion* lies.

Next, I am totally opposed to the way Rorty reduces twenty-five centuries of the history of humankind to the story of the history of philosophy. The history of humankind is not the history of the mistakes made by Plato, Descartes, Hegel, Kant, and so forth. Here, precisely, lies the vice of Hegel, Heidegger and Habermas—the three Hs, if you like, or four with Husserl when he talks about European humanity—who replace effective history by the history of ideas. Which then reminds us of poor old Marx. . . . Ideas are in fact not a reflection of history, either, even if they partake of it. They very often prevail in the acts of people in our so-called advanced societies (I hate that expression), because they increasingly occupy the dominant social imaginary as well as the critical social imaginary. The Greeks didn't set up their cities and begin to fight for democracy because some Greek equivalent of Rousseau spoke up and told them, "The general will. . . ." They constituted themselves as democratic communities, and it was in those democratic communities that philosophy as the questioning of the given institution of society became possible.

Likewise, if the West has lived under a relatively liberal regime for the last two centuries, it is not because some philosopher wrote one thing or another. In that particular history, the philosophy of the Enlightenment, for example, was merely the expression, and not the reflection or the sublimation, of those parts of a new imaginary that had developed in the effective life of society and was to explode in real life with the American Revolution, the French Revolution, and the English workers' movement in the early 1800s. All those popular struggles disappear in the history of ideas as told by Hegel, Heidegger and even Habermas. Where do the 20th century's monstrous totalitarian regimes come from? One may of course claim it was Lenin who created totalitarianism. Lenin does seem to represent a specific time in the history of the second International—of the Marxist movement, that is. But what was that movement? Just one of the currents, and ultimately a sort of confiscation, of something much broader, the labor movement. Which was not invented by Plato, Aristotle or Rousseau, but was created by workers themselves, in their struggles, their demands, always susceptible of criticism and reappraisal, but the essence of which was fundamentally right. Now without those victories of the working class, capitalism and "liberal" contemporary society would not be what they are. What would they be? I have no idea. Perhaps a sort of Japanese-style capitalism. The recent remarks by [then] prime minister Edith Cresson about the Japanese can't make me abandon what I have been saying for years, since I first became familiar with Japan: beneath the institutional veneer imported, practically unaltered, from America, Japan is still the same traditional, feudal-imperial country. Except that the old courtiers have been replaced by the state and entrepreneurial bureaucracies, as well as by the political oligarchy of the Liberal-democratic party, the only one to have governed until now. And if Western society has not taken that path, it is because for over a century, up to and including 1936[4] and even later, people never stopped fighting, going on strike, getting shot. The labor movement enabled Marxism to exist in history, not the reverse, even if that movement seems to be petering out nowadays, as I have been thinking and writing since 1960.

No longer can a project for the transformation of society give the proletarian messiah the privileged, sovereign role assigned to it by Marx in his historical theology. There is no messiah, and the proletariat has no privilege. More generally, the poor as such have no privileged political role. They may be a subversive class—but subversive in what direction?—just as well as be the easiest prey for Stalinist or Nazi demagogues. According to Marx, the proletariat had a role not only because of its pauperization and dire poverty, but owing to the new modes of socialization imposed by the capitalist factory. The proletariat then comprised a new class of men, with other reflexes, other social behavior, who tended to organize themselves for the satisfaction of their demands. This shows, by the way, how much Jean-Paul Sartre understood Marx and Marxism, as usual, when he, like Fanon, wanted to transpose the role of the proletariat to third world

---

4. [In France, "1936" is short for the Popular Front, a massive, broad-based social movement leading to the government headed by Léon Blum and which won a series of measures including the 40-hour week and paid vacations.—Trans.]

peasants. Maybe those peasants will save the world, I don't know, and we don't see it coming. At any rate, we can't force them into that Marxist model of both negative and positive socialization in opposition to capital, one which, above all, sets up new forms of social coexistence, of "togetherness," in modern parlance. It is that latter element that makes the working-class movement so important.

On the question of politics, I wish to take a firm stand against the idea that the goal of politics is to reduce poverty, and ultimately to achieve happiness. That's even a very dangerous idea—I beg Rorty's pardon. If, indeed, the aim of politics was to make people happy, it would suffice to vote laws declaring universal happiness through something or other, John Cage's music, the repeated reading of the *Upanishad*, some sexual practice, or other. But all that belongs to the private sphere, to intimacy, and it is perfectly illegitimate to deal with it in the *agora*, in the public/private sphere, and more still in the *ekklèsia*, the public/public sphere. That would be a perfectly totalitarian position. After all, the rulers of communist countries were ready to make people happy against their will. The object of politics is not happiness; the object of politics is freedom. From that standpoint, the dilemma raised by Rorty—the creation of a poverty-free society or of a good society for Socrates, or for the modern Socrates we supposedly are—is a false dilemma in my eyes. Maybe no society would be good for Socrates, or for me, in fact, if I dare be so presumptuous. I don't know what a good society is. What I want is a *free* society. And the fact is that Socrates lived in a free *polis*—with freedom for free, adult males—where he was able to have discussions in the *agora*, to refute the sophists, unsettle the young men who thought they knew everything and who knew nothing. That lasted seventy years. Then, in 399, a political conjunction forced him to drink poison hemlock. But a society in which there can be a Socrates is a free society.

Rorty suggests that we introduce the word "greed" in our political vocabulary, since it designates an essential social reality not to be easily dismissed. I have nothing against that, of course: an unfree society ruled by the greediest would indeed reduce everyone else to dire poverty. That is true, and from that standpoint there is no dilemma opposing a society that is ideal for the intellectual and one in which poverty can be combated. We must go further, then. Why should poverty be reduced or eliminated? I won't go into the purely emotional aspect of the question, not that I look down on it, but it can hardly be questioned. Except if we look at extreme cases of indifference to others—take Nietzsche, for example, he thought it perfectly acceptable to massacre one's fellow beings if one is a superior person with a will to power. . . . That puts an end to discussion. Other than that, poverty must be eliminated quite simply because it turns people into slaves and prevents them from being real citizens of their community. Obviously the minimum for material well-being varies. It definitely won't be fourteen TV sets or cars per home, but it may be seven acres or seventy for a farmer in a predominantly peasant society. Without that material basis, people are obsessed with hunger and poverty and are unable to go beyond them, to think freely.

In opposition to an overall political project, some people propose improvement of the system by what the English call piecemeal reforms. But obviously, any politician, reformist or conservative, who takes partial, local measures without an overall view of the entire system will necessarily accumulate errors. That is actually what has been going on for quite a while now. The latest French example, directly responsible for my late arrival today, is the lowered age of retirement. Eight years ago it seemed evident that that was a highly social measure. So today there is concern about balancing the retirement fund budgets, and talk about higher contributions, raising the age that had previously been lowered. . . . And the workers, fearing for the rights they won, or their privileges, whatever you want to call them, go on strike. Another way of looking at that same problem of society viewed as a comprehensive whole, in which everything holds together, more or less well, is to stress how flexible or rigid it is, with the awareness that we are talking about a creation of that particular society. Primitive tribes are very rigid, whereas modern societies are much more flexible, at least in appearance. But be it the degree of interdependence of the elements or their rigidity with respect to the totality, it is always society that institutes itself as a comprehensive whole. And it wasn't any totalitarian thinkers who decided that, who postulated that comprehensive whole. Society as a totality came first, and one hundred thousand years later philosophers such as Plato in the second book of the *Republic* observed that those farmers, shopkeepers, and soldiers all formed a community that held together, that education was fundamental in maintaining that coherence. And precisely, that modicum of coherence without which society could not exist evidences the fact that society is a comprehensive whole, one neither conceived nor posited by anyone. But if that comprehensive whole is not taken into consideration, it cannot even be reformed correctly.

Take the example of capitalism. Capitalism has nothing to do with the big bad wolf, nor is it reducible to the reign of the marketplace—more about that later. Capitalism is an institution of society whose central imaginary signification is the unlimited expansion of rational mastery—pseudo-mastery, and pseudo-rational. That is why it may very well adjust to the absence of private property. What matters is the "masters and possessors of nature," including human nature, since they are beginning to play around with the human genome. Now, it is clear that such capitalism is increasingly less compatible with those few freedoms imposed on the system by past struggles. Whence the unavoidable question: Can this system reproduce itself indefinitely, if only anthropologically speaking? The point is not at all to prophesy catastrophe, Marx-wise. But when Richard Rorty teaches, does he act as a good *Homo capitalisticus?* Certainly not, otherwise he would play hooky from his courses as long and as often as he could without jeopardizing his salary. Now I not only postulate, but I know he doesn't do that; he tries to do his best, day in, day out. There is no room for that attitude—always doing one's best without expecting any material benefit from it—in the capitalist imaginary construction. Whence, in fact, the present ethical void one hears about. In this respect, capitalism survives by depleting the anthropological reserves built up during the previous millennia. Just as it survives by depleting the reserves of natural resources.

Present-day ideas represent a tremendous regression, from this viewpoint. Take Habermas, for instance, when he writes, with a calm that amazes me, that "the revolutionary changes presently culminating before our eyes contain an unequivocal lesson: that complex societies cannot reproduce themselves if they do not leave intact the self-regulatory logic of the free-market economy."[5] I don't have time here for an exhaustive enumeration of the absurdities contained in that sentence. To be brief: the market is not capitalism; capitalism is not the market. Read a good handbook of political economy, or Marx for that matter, using a little conceptual precision. Before capitalism, commodities were simply produced within, through, and for a marketplace. Which has been known, then, for five thousand years—to the Babylonians, the Phoenicians, and later the Greeks, and so on. But it wasn't a capitalist marketplace. The capitalist marketplace was not born spontaneously; it was imposed in that form in our modern societies—go back to Karl Polanyi[6]; he corroborates that. As for the logic of self-regulation of the free-market economy, either Habermas is living in a dream world or he has been completely taken in by the

---

5. {In a recent paper on the 1989 events in Eastern Europe: Jürgen Habermas, *Kleine politische Schriften VII* (Frankfurt am Main: Suhrkamp Verlag, 1990).}

6. {Karl Polanyi, *The Great Transformation* (Boston, Mass.: Beacon Press, 2001).}

German equivalents of [that French apologist of economic neo-liberalism] Guy Sornan. The self-regulation of the marketplace is an imposture. That was demonstrated once and for all in the 1930s, by Keynes and some perfectly academic economists. Half of the gross national product of our modern economies transits by the budgets of the State, local communities, and social security, which tax one activity, subsidize another, decide on expenditures, plan for facilities. How can that not affect the "free" functioning of the marketplace? How can any such budget be economically neutral? That doesn't mean there shouldn't be any marketplace. As I myself wrote in 1957 in "On the Content of Socialism,"[7] an autonomous society needs a *true marketplace*; that is to say, one dominated by consumers. Nor does it mean that today's capitalist pseudo-marketplace doesn't function infinitely more efficiently than the absurd, totalitarian pseudo-planning to be found in Eastern European countries. That's obvious.

I will conclude with a few words on the role of "intellectuals," to use that term in spite of the somewhat dangerous generalization. They are usually the object of two reproaches. For one, that they set themselves apart and judge society from outside, on the basis of their knowledge or their philosophical system. That starts with Plato, of course. He had seen the Ideas, and from them could infer the good society; but not all philosophers took that stance, not Descartes for instance. The second reproach is that they worship reality. That attitude, not to be found in Plato or Aristotle, is flagrant in the Stoics and is enormously amplified throughout the Christian period. Reality is holy and sacred, and cannot be called into question. That enormous privilege granted to what exists is found in Kant, clearly so in Hegel, and also in Marx. He would refuse this formulation of the question, of course, but why is the proletarian revolution a good thing? Because it will take place. And what about Nietzsche's *Übermensch*? Because he too will come into being. Then he adds, "[T]he future is innocent." But what does that mean, if not that reality is what it is and there is no judging it. What saddens me is that the same attitude is behind Richard Rorty's critical discourse: "Here we are, free-market capitalism has won, so. . . ." But so what? So nothing at all. Free-market capitalism has won; that's it. That's a mere statement of fact from which no political conclusion can be drawn. But it does demand that we do some thinking about

7. the Content of Socialism," in *Political and Social Writings*, vol. 2: *1955–1960: From the Workers' Struggle Against Bureaucracy to Revolution in the Age of Modern Capitalism*, trans. and ed. David Ames Curtis (Minneapolis: University of Minnesota Press, 1988).

what has happened. Why did the Russian Revolution take the course it did? Why is the labor movement falling apart? What forces are opposed to the present state of society? Why was Marx a dreamer when he talked about abolishing money, commodities, and so on? There is no other political conclusion to be drawn from capitalism's present triumph. Except, again, if you belong to the religion of *credo in unam sanctam realitatem*.

The true function of an intellectual, in my opinion, is obviously not to be the vanguard of society, but to call into question what is instituted, to interrogate and criticize what is. Not for the pure pleasure of criticizing, but because without a distance from what is instituted, there simply is no thinking. There is repetition of what is instituted, a commentary on the Civil Code, the *Summa Theologica*, the Hegelian system, and so forth. The condition for thinking, strictly speaking, with a modicum of originality, is standing at a distance, which is possible only if you have *einen kritischen Standpunkt gewonnen*, as the Germans say: you have gained a critical standpoint on what is. And that is not exclusively the task of the philosopher, who writes and thinks, but also and above all of the great artist. The reason why masterpieces are so important in our society (as was already the case with tragedy, in ancient Greece) is not only because the community identifies with them, any more than because they create new forms—that was Kant's theory, accurate but insufficient, in the third *Critique*—it's because in their own way they question social existence and, ultimately, all of human existence. At that level, Sophocles, Shakespeare and Kafka converge: beyond the mere esthetic pleasure, their works are politically and educationally important. Because tragedy told the Athenian *dèmos*: you are mortal and run the risk of falling into hubris, which will lead you to ruin, while Shakespeare tells the Elizabethan public: we are but poor actors running around on the stage, waiting for our role to be over in this life, which is nothing but a tale told by an idiot. . . .

Sometimes the question is asked: What would you intellectuals do if it befell you to govern? The answer to that is twofold: it will never befall us to govern; and if, by some unlikely chance, we did acquire some shreds of power, we would simply no longer be intellectuals. We would be philosophers, ministers, impostors, I don't know; call it what you like. . . . The intellectual's only role, to my way of thinking, is to set forth ideas, make proposals, support a project. I, for one, see the core of that project as: the power belongs to the people, the *dèmos*, and it is up to it to show that it can—or can't—seize that power so as to wield it—or have it confiscated.

One last remark. I don't want to joke about serious things, but a little while ago I heard Chantal Mouffe tell us that "we must fight the bureaucratization of the State apparatus." We must fight the militarization of the army as well, then, and the medicalization of medicine. To fight the bureaucratization of the State apparatus is like fighting the vegetal nature of plants. The State is always, necessarily, bureaucratic. Otherwise we have the Athenian *dèmos*, the Boston town hall in 1770, and so on, and that is no longer a State. Last, I would like to thank Heinz Wismann for reminding us that at the start of the 1989 events, Habermas stated that they corroborated what he had always written. It's most interesting to hear that, when you know that the distinctive feature of the Frankfurt school, its ongoing claim to fame, is that it carefully avoided any criticism of the concrete embodiments of Marxism, and even of Marxism as such. It talked a lot about the West, but practically not a word about the East.

## Discussion

[*Inaudible question*]

You're saying that happiness is what individuals can demand of the State, and I don't even understand what that might possibly mean. What can I ask of the State? That Odette de Crécy love me? That some woman make me happy? How can I expect that kind of happiness from the State? And after that, you talk about freedom as some little, internal thing. That kind of freedom has nothing to do with the effective freedom I am talking about, and which depends on the body politic and enables individuals to achieve their own autonomy. That involves not only those freedoms we know and enjoy thanks to the struggles of our forefathers, but also a great many other things. And first, education. I don't understand that sort of blindness to what those damned Greeks already knew: that individuals become essentially what society makes of them, and that the "making" mostly takes the form of education. It's not because he is an education maniac that Plato devotes whole books to it, and Aristotle too, and all the major thinkers from Locke to Rousseau: it's because *that* is where tomorrow's citizens are shaped. It is with them that democracy may develop, or again degenerate into bureaucracy.

When I educate someone, I solve a paradox: by encroaching on his potential autonomy I enable him to achieve effective autonomy. Education, irrespective of the system that provides it, including in the United States, is necessarily a public affair, in the broad sense. Even if, admittedly, private capital does much of it today. I have never had TV in my home, but after one year of school my daughter had soaked up as much advertising and stupid programs as her friends who had been watching it since they were born. Another, *a contrario* example of the all-powerful role of education in achieving autonomy: in the academic writings of some Muslim students, quotation is tantamount to proof. You can read some amazing papers in which the argumentation boils down to an accumulation of texts by some author or another. It's clearly not their fault, because that's what their religion has always taught them, as it taught Latin and orthodox Greek thinkers throughout the Middle Ages, actually. All you have to do is quote: the more you quote, the better you prove. All traditional societies have taught their children to think the way their parents, their ancestors, the whole tribe, thought before them. And despite the breaches opened in Western societies since the 18th century, that is still true to this day. Regardless of what liberal hypocrites claim, French public schools still mold children in a particular way; they are not neutral. Which, in itself, is absolutely not reprehensible. That doesn't violate children's freedom, because as soon as you raise and educate a child, you "violate" him, in some sense; and the whole question is then, to what end? If it is to help him rid himself of restraining influences, we arrive at the squaring of the circle for education; that is a political task. It is one vital aspect of the politics of freedom.

A second point on which I am once again strongly opposed to Rorty is when he claims that philosophy, as an activity, no longer has any reason to exist. It's the same old story: the old Hegelian-Nietzschean-Heideggerian song. But it's still as far off-key, since it forgets the immense, lasting need for the elucidation of society, history, and nature—an elucidation that scientists as such don't provide.

Speaking about intellectuals, I said a while ago that their role was to criticize what is instituted. That is *my* definition, but if we are talking about politics, meaning the reinstitution of society and not the mere art of the possible, I don't see what other role they might play. Now, intellectuals weren't invented either in Greece or in the West. There have been mandarins in China for two thousand five hundred years, Brahman priests and great grammarians in India, and so on. They were all extraordinarily subtle, deep thinkers, but they all partook purely and simply in the preservation of the system. That's also true of Thomas Aquinas: regardless of the conflicts and differences between theologians over several centuries, the Christian faith remained absolutely unshakable, and it was within those shackles that Thomas worked, trying to involve Aristotle, but never mind. Free thought is a critical act. Yet, for tens of thousands of years no-one anywhere thought freely. We forget that because in our historical provincialism, now that we are settled on the good side of that conquest, we think it goes without saying. That freedom of thought is mainly exerted through philosophy, which sets the existing institutions at a distance and criticizes them. But that is only one aspect of philosophical reflection, the second being the elucidation of what is. Why should we elucidate what is? I know in advance that Rorty won't like my answer: *for no reason*. It is a purely gratuitous activity. It isn't even for the honor of the human mind, as has been claimed.[8] We just want to understand. And that serves no purpose, as Ms. Thatcher said when she cut funding for universities—and too bad for basic research, we'll steal it from those idiots who pay for it, and we'll sell them our industrial applications. Why not? But basic research isn't done for any potential industrial applications. And even less is philosophy done for its political or other implications. One philosophizes because once the idiotic certainties of everyday life have vacillated, you can't do otherwise. That goes far beyond politics. The same is true of great art, the masterpieces I mentioned: *Macbeth*, *Oedipus*, and so on, are infinitely more than a mere challenge to the established order. What is needed here is a long talk about the imagination and the imaginary. The imaginary isn't the production of images; it is the *creation of a human world*, and not only at the level of the individual psyche, but in the social-historical field. There obviously is an imaginary of democracy. By the same token, social and individual autonomy are social imaginary significations—what else could they be? A mathematical concept?

*That depends on what is understood by imaginary. A regulatory idea is not necessarily a social imaginary. . . .*

Not if you give it a Platonic-Kantian status, of course. But we are not concerned with what goes on in the heavens of the Ideas, or at the transcendental level. We are talking about democracy as a real movement in history, leaving traces, institutions, significations, through which we are or should be free and equal. A social-historically effective regulatory idea cannot be anything but a social imaginary signification.

A last word on Rorty's response: "If we were to take power, we would not know what to do with it." First of all, the issue is framed wrongly: it is not for us to take power. Above all, intellectuals are obviously and primarily citizens, who, like other citizens, can have ideas. Were I given a

---

8. {By C. G. Jacobi, in a letter to Legendre dated July 2, 1830: mathematician Jean Dieudonné borrowed the expression for the title of his book *L'Honneur de l'esprit humain* (Paris: Hachette, 1987).}

platform on which to speak, I would propose that the people set up another kind of democracy, based on a constitution of about fifteen points—remembering that a constitution is nothing without the active consent of citizens. I would defend my positions, my *doxa*, with all the resources of debating, including rhetoric. But I would be acting as a citizen, then, not starting from a vision of Ideas or from a conception of the essence of politics. Now, if the other citizens are convinced and take power, and if they end up committing atrocities, then it will be my duty, like Socrates during the Arginusae trial, like Zola during the Dreyfus affair, to stand up and tell them: you are monsters and imbeciles. And if I don't do that, I am not worthy of existing.

# On Wars in Europe

"On wars in Europe": it is true that wars have been waged on our continent—like the others, in fact—for three thousand years at the least, and probably much more, since prehistoric skeletons showing marks of violent death are still being discovered, deaths that it is hard to ascribe exclusively to "private" quarrels. But as you know, we are presently faced with the situation in the Balkans, in the former Yugoslavia, one which may well occur again elsewhere. So the question seems extremely timely once more, but we mustn't forget it is also an eternal question, since we have here a feature encountered—unfortunately, but it's a fact—in practically *all* human societies. It is precisely for that reason, however apparently paradoxical, that it seems almost impossible to develop an overall theory of war or to have a general conception of the causes and processes leading to war, one which does not boil down to trivia or to statements so broad— such as Freud made—that they leave us completely helpless, both theoretically and practically. When we think about war, we don't simply want to know whether there is a death instinct that incites people to kill each other. They killed each other between 1914 and 1918, but not between 1918 and 1939. Oh, they did kill each other in Spain then, for example, but not on the same scale. Following which came that unprecedented furious outburst, given the technical means, between 1939 and 1945. But since then—we are talking about Europe only, of course—we are breaking the 1871–1914 record of a period without any open warfare, aside from those

---

{Lecture and debate organized on February 13, 1992, by the planned parenthood center Aimer à l'ULB [Loving at the Free University of Brussels] of the Université libre de Bruxelles. The subtitle was "The Relations between Unconscious Processes, the Outburst of Nationalist Fury and New Forms of Political Organization." We have used Castoriadis' transcript of a recording, with occasional use of the recording itself and of the author's handwritten notes to complete the text. Castoriadis returned to this theme at a conference in Brussels on February 24, 1994, organized by the commission of personnel of the European Communities.}

*83*

poor Balkans. Is the death instinct dormant during those periods? Why are there explosions, followed by lulls? War is a universal, then, throughout every period in history, and irrespective of the social and economic regime, the technology, the kinship system, or other, so that the problem seems almost more difficult than, say, domination of one social stratum over the others within a society (even if the two are certainly linked). Because we can find societies, primitive tribes, in which there is no such domination, and where the "power" of the "chief" is reduced to a mere ritual, but we cannot find any society devoid of war. That is the dreadful reality, to which we will return at the end of this short talk.

The problem may be subdivided into two actually linked, closely intertwined questions. First, what social processes shared by all these kinds of societies, by all those forms of regimes, periodically lead to wars (even if the periodicity is quite relative)? Second, what subconscious mechanisms or mental processes, in the deepest sense of the term, lead men who live in a particular society or regime to kill each other? Let's take the most flagrant case: 1914. The socialist parties were against the war; they said so in international meetings, proclaiming that the working class would respond to the war by a general strike, and so on. A day or two before the war broke out, Jaurès is assassinated in Paris. We can't make the dead speak, and no one knows what Jaurès would have done. Let's say he probably would have opposed the war. But several days later the socialist parties, with few exceptions, all voted to fund the war and sided with "national unity" in each and every country. Those very soldiers, half—or a third, or a fourth, it doesn't matter—of whom belonged to trade unions and socialist parties were then shouting "*À Berlin*" or "*Nach Paris.*" They knew they would be killed, and for something that was not "personally" important for them. They were swept away by the crowd, or whatever, but that movement of the crowd wasn't merely a passing fever. They spent four years in the trenches. There were few acts of mutiny. Of course they were "forced" to stay; desertion was punished by death; there was discipline; and so forth. But as everyone has always known, and La Boétie, Hobbes and Rosa Luxemburg all said: no military rule can hold if the army revolts. That, in fact, is what happened in Russia (setting aside what transpired afterwards); having fought for three years and accepted hundreds of thousands of deaths, the soldiers refused to go on fighting, the front collapsed and the Petrograd government followed suit. So there is that second question: Why the hell do people accept to kill and get killed for things that aren't important to them "personally," at least at first glance? Then, how do those two things get linked together: that is, the social processes leading to war with the processes within societies that produce individuals capable of killing and being killed in a war? Parenthetically, here too we see how the idea of a death instinct is enigmatic. The death instinct Freud talks about, with respect to war, is more elaborated; it has already become a tendency to destroy other people. But in any war, soldiers know that they themselves have a fifty-fifty chance of being killed; and yet they go with it. I repeat, discipline and fear of punishment are insufficient explanations. So there is the problem of the link between those subjective mechanisms and some social processes, or mechanisms, if you like, that produce war. Now, I really don't want to upset you, but *none* of the conceptions advanced so far hold water, in my opinion, at least on the first facet of this question.

We can make short shrift of the "demographic" theories of war as a bloodletting the human race administers to itself to combat overpopulation and the exhaustion of natural resources. Were that true, a few hundred atomic bombs would already have been exploded around the planet to eliminate the surplus population that has developed over the last fifty years. The same is true of economic "explanations." You can't possibly find any true "economic causes" at work in the endless fighting between city-states in antiquity, and especially among the Greek *poleis*, where the job of being a citizen consisted, for a large part, in warring against the neighboring *poleis*. The same is true in Rome and in Italic city-states in general, as well as in the feudal domains of the Middle Ages. What "economic" reasons pushed those feudal lords, with few exceptions, and the kings of the same period or later, to war almost constantly?

Another factor may be advanced: power as such. A country, a monarch, or an oligarchy—let's say the Venetian aristocracy—makes war or wars to extend its sphere of power, and by the same token its "benefits" (although it's difficult to imagine Alexander setting out to conquer Asia with Darius' treasures as his main goal). But that power: Whose power is it? The monarch's or the strategist's. Take Napoleon with his madness: you can understand his behavior up to about 1808. But the war against Spain is aberrant, from his own viewpoint, and the war with Russia is folly. Let's say that Napoleon is crazed with war and inebriated with power. But there are also five hundred thousand Frenchmen who follow him and get killed shouting "Long live the Emperor!" Where is *their* power? (Of course, there is an imaginary participation, both in the ordinary and the deep sense of the term.) If we want to find a "rational explanation" of war at all costs, the only wars that lend themselves more or less to one are those caused by expeditions for taking another tribe's women, like the "Rape of the Sabine Women." A bunch of men who have no women attack another band, a well-settled tribe, kill the men and take the women. This achieves a social goal (the society they form is able to reproduce itself and continue) and at the same time satisfies the sexual drives of some individuals. But that represents only a tiny proportion of known wars, not the majority.

Let's set the question in the broader context of the nature of society, of a social unit, as I see it. It is a group of human beings defined by the fact—making it *one* society—that there is *one* overall institution of society, a social imaginary holding that society together and through which those individuals belong to it. There are several aspects here. In the world as viewed by Hebrew society, the stars are lights put there by God for the beauty of the sky or as manifestations of his glory; for the ancient Greeks those same stars are gods; and for us they are masses of hydrogen transformed into helium by thermonuclear reactions. We could go on and on: the same is true for trees, rivers, individuals, society, and so on. In each instance, each society has a world of its own, qualified by three vectors (which in fact have their equivalent in the individual psyche): a representational vector (Yahweh created the world some six thousand years ago, but no earlier, etc.), the cognitive component of each society's world, accounting for the being-thus of the world in general and of the social world; an emotional vector, with a class or group of affects created by that society (for instance, *faith* in the Christian sense of the word, does not exist prior to Christianity); last, there is a *Trieb*, a drive, an instinct, or thrust of society, tied to that representation of the world and those affects. What drive? Let's take the example of the society in which we live: the idea, as you, being inside it, are well aware, is to produce and consume more and more, to achieve some power or semblance of power (and possibly, to be seen on TV). If we take Roman society, from one point on the drive was toward territorial expansion: the *pomerium* was not enough, the Latium was not enough, central Italy was not enough, the Italian peninsula was not enough, and so on and on. Had a true Christian society existed—which it never really did—there would have been a drive having to do with God and the worship of God. In the Middle Ages people actually did believe we were on earth to worship God as best we could, and should build even taller cathedrals, convert still more peoples, and so forth.

At the same time, there is a *social production* of individuals. Starting with the raw material of the psyche brought into the world at birth by each being, society must forge beings who speak, acknowledge the existence of other people, do not behave as if they were the center of the world (although each one is for herself, as we all are, always) and as if other people were nothing but pure and simple objects of their desires, but who comply with a social law, with norms and values. In other words, during this long, painful socialization process they abandon—unwittingly, in fact—their deepest drives and desires. They never completely abandon them, actually, the proof being that they dream of transgressions and sometimes really do transgress social norms. But still and all, they do abandon them, on the whole, in their real behavior. For that to take place, society must provide substitutes for them. Those are, first, social significations: God, the *polis*, the unlimited expansion of mastery, the building of socialism, and so on. That is, signification, meaning, and social objects to invest. They must also be provided with social identities they may don, like so many roles to be played. But they don't play; they believe in them; they believe they are good civil servants, good educators and good spouses. All those roles, with which individuals can and must identify, barring which they simply cannot exist socially, are offered them by society in accordance with their position and the circumstances. Even today, in the almost infinite range of roles open to people, there are always some roles offered or forced on those who refuse to play the game: being a hooligan or a deviant is still a social role. Also, and this is certainly one of the most mysterious aspects of the whole business, this all must create a tie, a feeling of belonging to the concrete community involved. There is a socially instituted name, a social answer to the question: Who are we? We are human beings, not animals, civilized people, not barbarians, possibly Christians and not Muslim infidels, or else Muslims and not Christian infidels. But at the same time, behind those abstract determinants, there is an imaginary signification of that *us*, without which the community cannot exist (and disregard for this fact constitutes one of the many aberrations of contemporary pseudo-individualism), the content of which, viewed within the history of societies, is obviously *arbitrary*. But if the contents of that institution of an *us* are both eminently variable and eminently arbitrary, the need for that reference to an *us* is neither. That reference, both as idea and as concrete community, belongs to that kind of being that may and must be called a *for-itself* [*pour soi*], in philosophical parlance. Society, unlike a living being or the human psyche, is certainly *not* an organism, but it is, still and all, a *being-for-itself*. It always creates its own world, with a particular way of being affected, and a thrust toward. . . . It defends itself by defending its being-thus, its own world. It has boundaries, not necessarily geographic ones, but even more important imaginary boundaries, for those are what determine whether ideas, representations, and behavior coming from outside will be metabolized, rejected, or, in extreme cases, will finally turn out to be lethal for the existing institution of society. Society has thrusts, or drives, then, the first of which tends toward its preservation. Every institution, be it an archaic one, the Athenian or Roman lawmakers, absolute monarchy or so-called modern democracies, tends to persevere in its being, to preserve itself. The preservation of an institution, as well as of the entire institution of a society, is the only meaning we can give to the idea of conservation, of self-preservation of society. It is incomparably more relevant than the notion of the conservation of the individuals actually living in it.

So there is something like a self-preserving system here, with self-defense including defense against internal disturbances, of course. But this does not suffice to provide an "overall explanation" of the fact of war. Self-preservation might perhaps explain why 50 percent of societies defend themselves, but not why the other 50 percent attack them. It is true that in many cases—in some of the main ones—there is no knowing which one "attacked" and which was "defending itself." Thucydides already saw that when, speaking of the origins of the Peloponnesian war, he said it had certainly been started by the Lacedaemonians, but that was because they increasingly feared the constant expansion of the Athenian empire. A similar spiral may be described for World War I, as well as for the "Cold War", between 1947 and 1985. But if you think for a minute, you realize that the development of that sort of situation already postulates "at the beginning" an expansionist thrust by one of the adversaries, along with the other party's firm resolve to resist, so that "attack" and "defense" are generally equally present in both camps. The wars waged because a society fights to the end to defend its vital creations imply the existence of another society that cannot tolerate the existence of the former. In all the other cases, the immense majority, war takes place for stakes radically different from the pure and simple preservation of one of the two societies.

Let's dwell a bit on what may seem to be a self-feeding dialectic of attack/defense. Clearly, as far back in history as we go, we find societies engaged in rivalry, suspicion, the prospect of an attack: in short, we find them immersed in a world in which war is an essential feature. That in itself suffices as an objection to the "theory" explaining war by some universal causal factor. But there is more. Periodically—but not "regularly"— that process feeds itself, and is renewed by some non-homogeneous factors. Mesopotamian city-states and kingdoms fight each other, expand, then collapse or are conquered by others. That happened to Egypt in the times of the Pharaohs, as far back as we know. Then came the Medes and the Persians, who established an immense empire: not content with that, led by Cambyses, they attacked Egypt. Why Egypt? Herodotus says Cambyses was mad. But he doesn't say that about Darius, who went after the Scythes, then the Greeks. Why did Darius want to expand to the west, at all costs? That ultimately backfired on him. But the Greeks, having conquered the Persian Empire, immediately began to war among themselves, and that lasted one hundred fifty years! I'll skip Alexander, the Diadochi, the Romans and their Empire, the Byzantine Empire, to arrive at the 7th century of our era, when an extraordinary phenomenon occurred: the expansion of Islam. A religious explosion, but at the same time an explosion of warring, leading to the conversion or colonization of the conquered peoples. There were no Arabs in Egypt, or in North Africa or Mesopotamia, or even in Palestine and Syria in the 6th century. By the 8th century all those countries were Islamized and "Arabized." Were the reasons economic or even power-linked? No, it was mostly to "spread the faith of the Prophet." In other words, to spread a new institution of society, centered on the new religion, which transformed 6th-century tribal Arab society and breathed a conquering *thrust* into it (Muslims would say, a divine mission; that is not for us to discuss). This lasted for a while, then subsided in the 10th century. The immense Arabic-Islamic empire fell prey to internal divisions, and so on. But the Byzantines thought they still had "rights" over the territories that were theirs a few centuries earlier, and so we have centuries of conflict on the eastern border of the Byzantine Empire. Then, toward the end of the 11th century, monks, popes, underemployed lords and some deviants appear in the Western world, proclaiming the need to liberate Christianity's holy places at all costs. The Crusades began (in the meanwhile the Turks, originally Seljukian, and later Ottoman, had replaced the Arabs, whom they had more or less subjugated), and for the next nine centuries the Mediterranean Sea and the Balkans became the fluctuating borders of a war between Christianity and Islam (which soon ceased to be purely "religious," in fact, as shown by both the alliance of François 1st with the Turks and the Crimean war).

Note the analogies with the present situation in Yugoslavia. The Serbs say, without Kosovo Serbia is no longer Serbia, or, the Bosnian Muslims have no right to be in "our country." Now, Kosovo—which really is the historic birthplace of the Serbs—is mostly inhabited by Albanese Muslims. Never mind: the Serbs were there *long ago*. Throughout those long centuries of war, each community created its *us* in accordance with what it viewed as its "history." Most of the time an imaginary history, in the tritest sense of the term: fictitious, fabricated, yarns people "spin," leaving out everything that would be "offensive" for the nation, according to the national imaginary. Victories are acclaimed, defeats minimized, ascribed to various betrayals or unfortunate accidents, or at any rate viewed as demonstrating how barbarian and beastly the enemies are, and so on. It is thought normal that Paris have an Austerlitz station and avenues called Wagram, Iéna, and so on, but no Waterloo or Trafalgar square. London has those. Seen from France, the history of the Napoleonic wars is primarily one victory after another, with an unfortunate end because of the Saxons' betrayal in Leipzig and Grouchy's inertia at Waterloo. Seen from England, it is the history of stubborn, heroic resistance to Napoleon, the tyrant, with a fittingly triumphant end on the Mont-Saint-Jean plateau. Viewed from Greece, the whole of Near Eastern history boils down to how the Greeks, who should have been the rulers of Alexander's empire, at the very least, were reduced to their present borders; whereas for the Turks, the main enigma in that history is, why aren't the Turks still in front of Vienna, in Algeria and in Mesopotamia? That, inevitably, is the stance of a true nationalist. A generally incomprehensible one, actually, for contemporary "Western" Europeans, since the question has been *more or less* "settled" (we all know the exceptions) for centuries in Western Europe, and people no longer have that attitude about the territorial limits of "their" nation. But looking toward Central and Eastern Europe, including the Balkans, we find borders that have not been stabilized. People there have not come to admit that henceforth that's the way it is, whether they like it or not. What we are seeing in Yugoslavia today is exactly that: We were there before, so we should be there now. We are the true owners of that land. Likewise, if you take the same view in Palestine, there is clearly no reason for the conflict to end, ever. Who was there "before"? "Before" what? The Turks, the Arabs, the Francs, the Byzantines, the Romans, the Greeks, the Persians, the Egyptians, the Hebrews . . . ? Maybe we should find another land for both the Israelis and the Palestinians, and give Palestine back to the descendants of Neanderthal man (we'll end up finding some), since there is proof that Neanderthal man inhabited the land one hundred thousand years ago. But that of course would be blasphemy to both parties.

Clearly the historical argument can lead only to ongoing warfare. One quite respectable principle might theoretically get us out of those impasses: the will of the groups presently occupying a given territory. Although for that principle to be applied, one would have to accept that present borders be left as they are. But as they are *when*? The Turks invaded Cyprus in 1974 and settled Turkish people from Anatolia there. If a referendum were conducted *today* in the part of the island occupied by the Turks, the "will of the population" would certainly be the creation of an independent Turkish State or its inclusion in Turkey. The same thing would occur in Yugoslavia for the territories conquered by the Serbs since 1989.

Why does history follow this repetitive course? Because one of the main dimensions that make up a community, a given concrete society, is that so-called collective memory. To call that memory selective would be ludicrous: it is *totally arbitrary*. The historical facts are difficult enough to establish, their meaning infinitely more so. The "judgments" applied to them are usually hardly meaningful, and those pseudo-judgments generally reflect nothing but prejudices (and they are feasible, gnoseologically speaking, only on the basis of innumerable prejudices). A few years ago, Colonel Gaddafi stated in an interview that had there not been an unfortunate historical accident with Charles Martel in Poitiers, Islam would be the religion of present-day Europe. That is a perfectly plausible view, motivated in this instance by his wish that such had been the case. To find it laughable one would need to have a symmetric, equally "arbitrary" prejudice according to which the present version of European history is perfectly satisfactory, at least for that episode. To be able to laugh, one would have to clearly assert the "inferiority" of Islamic religion and civilization to Catholic Christianity.

I repeat, these are not exclusive, or even characteristic, features of the modern period. That imaginary memory is necessarily constituent of any collective identity—as much so as a fabricated, conscious pseudo-"memory" is constituent of what we call personal identity, as psychoanalysis shows. That collective pseudo-"memory" is to be found in different forms (starting with the myths of origin, the legends of founding heroes, and so on) in every society, however archaic. But it is a fact that the nation-state, that specific modern-day creation, has taken it to unprecedented heights (the question of what makes for the originality of that form in comparison with other, apparently similar ones such as the Chinese Empire, etc., cannot be discussed here). That form was created in Europe—in France, England, Spain, and so on—and we have transmitted it to the rest of the world, causing the constitution of completely artificial "nation-states," as in Africa, where we find a genuine *in vivo* experiment in the *ex nihilo* fabrication of a "national consciousness"—in the Central African Republic, for instance. What is a national consciousness for the Central African Republic? There is of course absolutely no value judgment involved in what I'm saying. But it is not because there have been nation-states in Europe that they must exist everywhere, or that it is a good thing for them to. For African peoples to be independent, that's one thing; but why should they be independent in the form of the nation-state? You will say, *in the contemporary world* no community can be "independent," or "sovereign" if you prefer, without taking that form. But that obviously is not true, even in the framework of the existing institution of global society. The Ottoman sultan was sovereign and had dealings with the Western powers, although his empire comprised a mosaic of ethnic groups capable of hating and looking down on each other but which nonetheless coexisted for five centuries. It would be inaccurate, then, to try to derive the inevitability of the nation-state form from the "real necessities" of international life. But it is equally true that its necessity is of another, much deeper kind: the nation-state has become one of the core imaginary significations of the modern Westernized world. Of course that signification/institution is perfectly adequate for the new local bureaucracies and oligarchies (be they African or other), but it takes only a moment's reflection to discover that the *nation*-state form is neither a necessary nor a sufficient requisite for their development. It is only on the imaginary ("ideological") level that, in the context of the Westernization/"modernization" of the planet, the inhabitants of eastern New Guinea, for example, or of Mali, "had to" be a "nation," barring which they would feel "inferior" to other people. And it was as promoters, protagonists, or leaders of a "national struggle" or "national independence" that those oligarchs/bureaucrats ("democrats" or "socialists") managed to rise to power, with the support of the Western world or the Russians. The problem facing us is that of *going beyond* that imaginary signification of the nation-state, toward another form of collective identification, and the difficulties encountered in embarking on that road.

Now I come to the second aspect of the question: the role of the psyche. Let me sum up my conception, briefly. Human beings start life as a monad, a self-enclosed psyche knowing nothing about reality and wanting to know nothing. That monad has to be broken, partially, so that the singular human being can survive. The requisite for that survival is its socialization, its transformation into a social individual. That socialization process begins when the mother turns her head away from her baby for the first time: that in itself is an act of violence inflicted on the psyche. The evolution of the individual, leaning on a process of neuro-physiological maturation, of course, is the accretion of a series of layers of socialization ultimately producing someone who is a man, woman, president of the Republic, worker, professor, football player, cheer-leader, or other. That process always occurs *ambivalently*: the loved object is necessarily simultaneously the hated object; the breast is always both good (present) and bad (absent), and those attributes are transferred to the person to whom it is presently linked. As demonstrated by the survival of the human race, the "positive" affect prevails over the "negative" one in the immense majority of cases,, which absolutely doesn't mean that the negative side isn't always there. This is visible in parent-child relations, where ambivalence is always present, as well as in the ambivalent relations between the sexes. In passing, and in opposition to one brand of demagogy in contemporary feminism, I would note that no ambivalence is as great as between mother and daughter. No hatred between father and son reaches the intensity and destructiveness, none is as morbid and cruel, as the hatred between mother and daughter so often revealed by clinical work. That finding makes one somewhat skeptical of the idea that men have always been the ones to inject hatred, violence and evil in the history of humanity, with women always on the side of love, guileless sweetness, and so forth.

Hatred is therefore always there, if only deep down, the most pervasive form being hatred of the other. In this respect, the organization of every society up to now may be viewed as an immense machine geared and built to deflect outward—toward the "others"—the hatred and aggressiveness existing within that society. That deflection, working in extremely varied and highly complex ways, is never totally successful. Let's take two more or less familiar cases, the ancient Greeks and modern Western societies. The Greek *poleis* spent their time, so to speak, fighting each other on entirely futile pretexts. At the same time, the main characteristic of Greek men was what Jacob Burckhardt called the agonistic element. *Agôn* meaning struggle, combat. We now talk about the Olympic "games." But in Olympia they were *agônes*, not "games": they weren't death-dealing, but the Greeks viewed them as struggles, combats. The Athenian tragedy "contest" was the *tragikos agôn*. Within the *polis*, then, the agonistic element was deflected toward "rivalries," "competitions," activities both valued and useful for the functioning of the city. Who will be the most valiant fighter during the war, the best orator speaking to the people, the best tragic poet, the most convincing arguer? And so on. The agonistic element is integrated in and used by public life. Notice that things went wrong, in Athens at least, with the Peloponnesian war, when the pursuit of primacy in the political field was separated from, and freed of, any other element: with some demagogues, such as Alcibiades. Something similar does of course exist in modern capitalist societies, in the form of economic competition, struggles between groups within hierarchical-bureaucratic structures—along with serious deflection outward. Note that in both cases, and

in spite of Montesquieu's "sweet commerce," internally deflected aggressiveness is absolutely unable to absorb it all, and there are always sufficient
residual amounts turned outward.

Because there is also a more difficult, darker side to this business: that
is, self-hatred. In every individual, profound self-hatred is always smolder-
ing. That hatred is turned toward, and against, the social individual the
psyche has been obliged to become. In the last analysis, we never accept
the being into which we have been turned by society, and the core psyche
always detests all those layers of socialization gradually deposited around
it and which frontally contradict its mightiest aspirations, its omnipotence,
egocentricity and limitless narcissism. Rarely is that hatred expressed as
such. But when we look at the most extreme manifestations of hatred of
the other, such as racism, it is impossible to comprehend them otherwise
than as a massive transferal of self-hatred to someone else (to a category
of others), which is to say as a transferal, within that complex, of the desire
and the affect, maintained as such by changing the object. I'm not the
villain; it's the Jew, the Black, the Arab. I'm not the one who should be
destroyed; it's the other. Naturally, it's all infinitely more elaborate in reality, and above all, cloaked in various rationalizations, and so on. Some
negative feature will be assigned to the other: Jews are usurers who bleed
the people dry; the Arabs smell bad and are invading the country; and so
on. Only that self-hatred can account for the dreadful extremities of racism. Were that not the case, racism in its most virulent form wouldn't
exist; there would only be attempts at forced conversion, as there have
indeed been so many throughout history. But Hitler's goal wasn't to turn
the Jews into good Nazis, and no-one was saved by his World War I med-
als or love of the German homeland. The very definition of the extreme
form of racism, a definition that no one seems to have seen so far, is that
the other is *inconvertible*. It's the exact opposite of what transpired with the
Arab conquests, for example, or with European-Christian expansion,
which aimed at converting (or exploiting) others, and were more or less
successful.

{Let me summarize, and please excuse me if you find this presentation
somewhat dry. Hatred of oneself, as the manifest self (the mental and
physical self) is always there, then, but is contained, on the whole (it works
silently). Combined with the negative component of the ambivalent investment of the other, or with monadic egocentricity—ineradicable self-
centeredness—which amounts to the same thing, it turns into hatred of
the other. This conversion enables the affect and the desire to be preserved by means of a change of object. Conversion—in the religious sense
this time—of the other corresponds to secondary narcissism: the other

must become like me; the Ego expands. The inconvertibility of the other corresponds to her elimination, irrespective of any real or reasonable consideration. The killing of King Duncan or of Banquo is "rational with respect to a goal." Auschwitz is not. It is that inconvertibility we encounter whenever we are faced with elimination for its own sake.[1]}

In conclusion, I have no ready-made answer to the enormous questions raised by all of this. A large part of the answer depends on a change of society: the socialization of individuals can be modified to tend toward their autonomy, to a better understanding of one's self and to a greater control of subconscious drives. That aspect is fundamental. And such an education will also have to give a different answer to the question, Who are we? But we are faced with a paradox here. I used to suggest, and still do, the following answer to the question "Who are we?" as the motto for an autonomous society: "We are people who give ourselves our own laws, and who can change them when we feel the need or the desire to do so." Is what we are, is this sort of society, valuable? We cannot raise human beings in such a society without having them internalize the idea that it is the only way of living in society that is truly worthy of human beings. That is what I would say, at any rate. But then, what should we say about others? About people who are prepared to kill those who think differently, for instance? Ready to kill Salman Rushdie? Are they "inferior"? Nowadays they will be said to be different. But we cannot uphold what we take to be freedom, justice, autonomy, and equality by merely speaking about "differences." Yet that is what today's repulsive pseudo-leftist or pseudo-democratic hodgepodge does, by confining itself, precisely, to small talk about that "difference." There are people who believe in freedom and democracy, and then there are people who believe thieves should have their hands cut off. The Aztecs sacrificed human beings. Is that a mere difference? Suppose a new faith arises, leading to the development of leagues of headhunters in Brussels or Paris; would we be faced with a "difference" we would have to respect?

We want to set up an autonomous society, and if we want that it is obviously because we judge it preferable to any other present or conceivable form of society, and therefore superior (since I think no one would dare contend that political regimes are like tastes for food). But knowing what autonomy is and what it postulates, it would be inconceivable for us to want to impose it on others by force: that would be a contradiction in terms. There is a fine line here, which we must walk both in the present

---

1. {This passage appears in Castoriadis' transcription but is not to be found in the recording.}

and in a future less appalling than this present. We must assert the value of autonomy, freedom, justice, equality, freedom of thought, free discussion, respect for other people's opinions, but nonetheless without considering people subhuman if they don't share that conception. All we can do is try to convince them, reasonably. Which of course seems to be an *almost* impossible task, since as soon as the other refers to a sacred Book containing a divine revelation, to convince him reasonably is *almost* meaningless, since for him the ultimate criterion is not the reasonable character of what is said, but its conformity with the divine message. But what is at stake here, too, is the identity of that community whose self-definition is its reference to autonomy, since that autonomy will only exist in itself and as a value if we are capable of giving our lives to defend it, if necessary. {In any case, the reference point of such a collective identity, without which human beings cannot be socialized, should not be a "territory" or a pseudo-historical "imaginary" past, but the project of individual and collective autonomy itself, rooted in history and tradition, certainly, but which would be the history and tradition of that struggle for autonomy and freedom.[2]}

## Discussion

*Isn't there a mystery of peace, as well? You don't talk about those peoples—the Nuer, the Trobrianders, the Muria—who never knew war.*

To say there is no comprehensive theory of war is tantamount to saying there is no comprehensive theory of peace, either. War and peace are two sides of the same coin, in that respect. We can throw some light on certain aspects of the problem, but we cannot elucidate it completely. I'm willing to admit that out of the several thousand known societies, three or four of them never experienced that atrocious phenomenon we are trying to understand. Which means that all societies, barring one-thousandth of them, experience or have experienced war. But you're right; it is the periods of peace that challenge any overall theory. You can have a theory of war of the "Newtonian-Marxist" type, with "causes" accumulating, an explosion, a phase of *détente*, then the cycle begins again. But there should be a pretty much explainable periodicity involved then. Any overall theory of war should simultaneously provide an explanation of periods of peace. I

---

2. {This passage appears in Castoriadis' transcription but is not to be found in the recording.}

have already talked about Freud's death instinct: What was it up to during peacetime? True, the region Freud lived in didn't experience any war between the 1866 conflict between Austria and Prussia (he was ten at the time) and the 1914 thunderbolt. There were of course many wars during that "peaceful" period, but they were waged far away, *in der Türkei*, in Turkey, or elsewhere, as the bourgeois say in *Faust*. People were massacring each other all over the world in Freud's day, but he only became truly aware of it in 1914, when he was affected personally, and that was when he wrote his "Thoughts for the Times on War and Death." But what was the death instinct doing, at the collective level, during that "period of peace"? Had it migrated to Plevna, Khartoum, or Port Arthur? The existence of periods of peace is definitely the most difficult problem for any comprehensive theory of war. The same thing may in fact be said of explosions of racism, since there are long phases when nothing happens—in some parts of the world, at any rate.

*About ten years ago you talked about the threat to world peace represented by the Soviet military-industrial complex. What is the situation today?*

A fundamental change has definitely occurred in that respect in recent years. I still believe that my description, in *Devant la guerre*,[3] of the Russian regime as meta-totalitarian turned into a stratocratic regime was correct for the period—not in the sense that the "colonels" had taken power, but because the entire society was oriented toward a kind of expansion that could no longer be anything but military; it could not be ideological, since the ideology was dead. That society was unreformable. There is one point on which I was mistaken: I claimed it was unthinkable that a reformist stratum emerge from within that bureaucracy. I was half wrong, if I may say so. What came out of it was Gorbachev and his group, at first. They had reformist illusions but were unable to achieve that reform, because the system was really and truly unreformable; so it was they who destroyed the system. The Russian bureaucracy is perhaps the only historical instance of a class destroying itself. The bureaucracy was not done in by an uprising or a popular movement, as in Poland, Czechoslovakia or Germany; actually, the people in the streets of Moscow in 1991 weren't shouting "Democracy, democracy!" but "Russia, Russia!" or "Yeltsin, Yeltsin!"

---

3. [*Devant la guerre*: vol. 1: *Les Réalités*, 1st ed. (Paris: Librairie Arthème Fayard, 1982; 2nd ed., 1983). An article on the same subject, originally published as "Devant la guerre (I)" in *Libre* 8 (1980): 217–50, was published in English as "Facing the War," *Telos* 46 (Winter 1980–81): 43–61.—Trans.]

*I have a problem with your definition of peace. There was the Algerian War, the war in Indochina, etc. I consider there have been wars in Europe over the last twenty years.*

Let's talk in good faith, now. I was talking about wars on the European continent after 1945. I am well aware that there have been dozens of wars during that period, maybe more than previously. Unquestionably, the European powers were involved in warfare elsewhere in the world during that period. I'm not saying that is less important, nor that the lives of the Algerians or Indochinese are worth less than the lives of Frenchmen, Belgians, Germans, and so forth. But for a number of reasons, I was talking about that continent, where, in fact, the two worldwide cataclysms that affected the lives of all other peoples originated.

*In May 1968, one of our main motivations was the Vietnam War. We were convinced that our anti-war action and militancy could be effective, as it had been, earlier, against the Algerian War. The present situation in Yugoslavia is much more disturbing; it leaves us perplexed and paralyzed. What position, what kind of action can we take in that war?*

Unfortunately, my only response to your perplexity can be the expression of my own. We are asked to sign petitions, to participate in round-tables, in short, to do what is usually done by intellectuals, who don't know how to do anything else, at a time when people are getting killed over there. But we could have said a lot more on the subject this evening, because the Balkans are extraordinarily enlightening as to the complexity of the problem and the difficulty of giving "simple" answers. First of all, there is the weight of history. There is also the mixture of population groups (in addition to the fact that a considerable proportion of the population has a Serbian father and a Croatian mother, or vice versa). In a reasonable, peaceful world, there would be nothing insoluble there. You can say: we'll set up autonomous communes, to federate as they like, and so on. But we are not in that world. There are, precisely, those impassioned identities, those reciprocal mythologies (all Croatians are pro-Nazi, the Serbs are all Chetniks, or "communists," or other). Above all, because of that admixture of populations, you can't suggest having referendums (as in some parts of Europe after World War I), since 55 percent majorities would yield regions dominated by one ethnic group, and that would be tantamount to organizing civil wars in the long run.

*In view of what goes on at present, what enables us to say that an autonomous society will exist some day?*

Nothing. But nothing enables us to claim the opposite. There is no impossibility, and there certainly is no necessity, no fatality. It all depends on the activity, the creativity of human beings. Even if an autonomous society does exist some day, nothing enables us to say that it will not fall back into heteronomy. There is no guarantee; no one can prevent a democracy from committing suicide or from sinking into who knows what madness. But I don't think we can claim it's all over, saying: that project of autonomy that already arose in Athens—even if in a very limited form—and was kindled again in Western Europe starting in the 11th century—right here, in Flanders, in Italy, and elsewhere—that movement couldn't have yielded anything greater than Bush, Mitterrand, Kohl, and the society we are now living in. I think we would be taking, what shall I say—a definitive stance—on a subject that remains open, even if the signs are indeed very sinister these days.

*What are the conditions that enabled the present rise of the extreme right in Europe? Why now and not ten or twenty years ago?*

I've already said what I think about that, in an interview published in the Paris daily newspaper, *Le Monde*, on December 10, 1991. I am not very convinced by what I hear about anti-immigrant feelings, and so on, even if such feelings do exist, of course. The phenomenon can be understood only within the broader framework of people's attitude toward the system. That system apparently doesn't even keep its promises on the "material" level; there is no longer an indefinite horizon of "progress." Faced with that situation, people have different reactions. Some are politically apathetic. I don't think I'm prey to some optimism that distorts my judgment, but I think I see signs of renewed activity among some younger people, who are more apt than ten years ago to question things, to criticize, and maybe even to do something. Also, there is, indeed, another part of the population, probably more prone to that, which expresses extreme right leanings. Here, we see a mixture of "traditional" racism, disarray, resentment toward society, and so forth, although we shouldn't underestimate the role of some political, electoral maneuvers by President Mitterrand, to take some votes away from the traditional right. Thanks to which I think the socialists will end up, one of these days, with fewer constituents than [the extreme right-wing leader Jean-Marie] Le Pen.

# PART II

# Interventions

# On the Possibility of Creating a
# New Form of Society

*Over the last thirty years, you have developed analyses of Russia and Stalinism, and extended them to China. Could you give us some of the main points, without giving a complete presentation of these? For example, you refute the expression "State socialism" and you speak of bureaucratic capitalism. More generally, what can be said about bureaucracy as a crucial phenomenon?*

The expression "State socialism" (or the more recent, involuntarily humoristic brainstorm, "dictatorial socialism") is the same as a square circle, a one-dimensional solid, and so on. Its function is purely ideological, to make people forget that the Russian regime and other similar ones have nothing to do with socialism. The existence of the State is inseparable from the existence of slavery, as Marx rightly said. Socialism has always meant the eradication of exploitation and oppression, the elimination of domination by any social group, the destruction of the economic, political and cultural institutions instrumental in achieving those relations of domination. Now, in Russia—and in China—all of the institutions, ranging from the machines and the organization of work in factories to the press and official literature, and including the army, the State, and so forth, are there to transmit, consolidate, and reproduce the domination over society of one particular stratum, the bureaucracy and its Party.

But beyond that fact, the bureaucratization process is taking place everywhere; it affects contemporary society as a whole. Bureaucratic capitalism is the social regime in every country: it is fragmented in the West and total in the Eastern countries. The first striking fact is that bureaucracy as an exploitative, exclusively dominant class initially developed in

{A talk with Edmond El Maleh, published under the title "A Talk with Cornelius Castoriadis," in *Le Monde*, December 13 and 14, 1977. This is Castoriadis' own typewritten version, including various handwritten corrections and additions.}

Russia after 1917, and, paradoxically, as the product of what has been called the degeneration of a socialist revolution. Local, accidental factors have been advanced to account for the development of bureaucracy in Russia: the country's backwardness, the civil war, the isolation of the revolution. That was Trotsky's thesis, a rehashed, watered-down version of which is now being served to us—another of history's jokes—by French Communist Party historians, and there is nothing incidental about that. In both instances the point is to evacuate the political issues raised by the fate of the Russian Revolution: the question of the meaning of socialism, the question of the role of the Bolshevik Party, of Lenin's party, and of its apparatus as the core, agent, instrument, and beneficiary of the establishment of new relations of domination and exploitation.

*You mean that those explanations are worthless?*

They beg the question; they don't explain what needs explaining. Backwardness, isolation, and so on might just as well have led to the return of private capitalism. But *why bureaucracy?* We have been told: the midwife was clumsy; the stable was poorly lit; the mare already had congenital malformations. My question is: But what, really, is the nature of the animal that was born and has been living for sixty years now? Degeneration as an explanation is used to avoid the crucial issue. Be that as it may, the discussion in those terms is totally anachronistic. Russia has been industrialized. It is no longer "isolated." Bureaucratic regimes are now subjugating one billion three hundred million individuals. All that has in no way led the bureaucracy to disappear, or lessened its power. Also, it has succeeded in dominating East Germany and Czechoslovakia, by no means "backward" countries.

*What may be made, then, of the degeneration of the 1917 revolution?*

Ultimately, the very term, degeneration, is improper. Between February and October 1917, there was "dual power" in Russia, with the interim government on the one hand, the soviets on the other. After October, another, mitigated "dual power" was established for a while, between the Bolshevik Party and what remained of the autonomous activity of the masses and the organs of that autonomy (essentially the factory committees). Mitigated because a great many workers believed the Bolshevik Party was "their" party. But that Party, and Lenin and Trotsky first and foremost, did just one thing, irrespective of its claims. It reestablished a

State apparatus separate from society and controlled by itself; it domesticated the soviets, the trade unions, every single collective organization, and worked at subordinating all social activities to its own norms and to its own viewpoint. And it succeeded. That period came to a definitive end when Lenin and Trotsky crushed the Kronstadt Commune (in 1921). From then on, the Bolshevik Party constituted a dominant social group in Russia, and only a social revolution, a revolution by the people as a whole, could have chased it from power—as it will no doubt do some day. The term degeneration can only be applied, at most, to the Bolshevik Party itself. There is definitely a considerable difference between Lenin and Stalin, between the Party in the 1903–1921 period and the 1927–1977 version of the Party. But that "degeneration" is in fact an advent, a birth, the unfolding, revelation and accomplishment of the totalitarian bureaucratic nature of the type of organization created by Lenin. Once it came into power, that Party reestablished or established hierarchy—the defining property of its own organization—everywhere, conglomerating around itself the bureaucratic, managerial strata of production, the economy, the State, and culture. That's how a dominant, exploitative, bureaucratic class came into being, fully disposing of the means and output of production, of people's time, and even of their life, behind the legal form of "nationalization."

## What about China?

On the issue of bureaucracy the case of China is even more enlightening. It illustrates the country's relative historical independence, since we can't talk about the "degenerating" of a socialist, working-class revolution there. The Chinese CP developed in the 1920s as a political-military organization modeled after the Bolshevik Party. It took advantage of the collapse of traditional Chinese society and the immense revolt of the peasant masses. When it came into power it established relations of domination, making Chinese society much the same as Russian society on the main points we are concerned with here, in spite of some obvious, unquestionably specific features. Even more clearly than in the case of Russia, this case shows us that the constitution of a totalitarian bureaucracy is not necessarily the product of an organic evolution, so to speak, of society. There is no development of the productive forces producing new relations in production which in turn generate a new class, which class finally also seizes political power. A political group is formed and takes power, after which new relations develop within production, with the corresponding infrastructure. The industrialization of China is the outcome of the access of the bureaucracy to domination, not the contrary. Here is another reason to reject Marx's view according to which classes are formed within production and defined by the position of individuals with respect to relations of production. That view is nothing but the arbitrary extrapolation to all of history of some aspects of the advent of the bourgeoisie.

*What can be said about the bureaucracy in other countries?*

In the classical capitalist countries the development of the bureaucracy may be interpreted, to some extent, using Marx's frame of reference. Because of the concentration of capital, the growing size of firms, the tendency to subject the work process to increasingly close control and to manage it from outside, production can no longer be managed by a boss with the help of an engineer and an accountant. It requires a large bureaucratic apparatus, with the power actually in the hands of the top, irrespective of any formal title of property. An individual capitalist cannot really take action within his firm unless he is at the very summit of the bureaucratic pyramid that runs it. Otherwise he is reduced to earning dividends (the amount of which is not even set by him). Ownership gives access to the top of that pyramid. But it is no longer the only entitlement, or even the main one, as shown by the groups of self–co-opted executives who increasingly dominate today's major firms.

But that Marxian interpretation is insufficient and incomplete. In the Western capitalist countries, another source of bureaucratization is to be found in the tremendous extension of the role and functions of the State, irrespective of any state control of the means of production (as shown by the case of the United States), which go far beyond the mere regulation of the economy. The State tends increasingly to manage, regulate, and control every aspect and sector of social activity, at the same time as the state and political bureaucracy proliferates. Last, the labor movement itself has been a powerful source of bureaucratization over the last eighty years. A bureaucracy has developed within the working-class trade union and political organizations, dominating them and dispossessing participants of any control over them. Which is to say that the working-class movement has adopted an organizational model that is the capitalist model, along with the capitalist significations: hierarchy, specialization, the split between order-givers and order-takers.

*How do you account for the fact that this bureaucratization, a universal process according to you, produces totalitarian regimes in the Eastern countries, whereas it enables the existence of democratic regimes in the Western countries?*

Your question leads us to the heart of some of the most profound problems facing the philosophy of history. There is unquestionably a degree of unity or uniformity in the modern world, which is why I talk about bureaucratic capitalism. At the same time, the fragmented bureaucratic capitalism of the Western countries and the total bureaucratic capitalism of the Eastern countries differ in several important ways. I view an "explanation" of that difference as impossible, if what is meant by explanation is the usual theoretical reasoning by which what happens is reduced to causes that were already there. We definitely can elucidate many aspects of the birth of totalitarianism, and identify many of the factors that have played a major role in it. But it is impossible not to see the advent of totalitarianism as a historical break, a creation. Its monstrosity doesn't prevent it from being a creation. Modern totalitarianism is an original historical figure exceeding every "explanation" one may apply to it. It is neither Asian despotism, nor tyranny, nor the inevitable outcome of the mere existence of the State, as recent, superficial claims would have it. The State has existed for at least six millennia now: totalitarianism only developed in the 20th century. It is clearly rooted, in many ways, in the evolution of capitalism. But just as clearly, that evolution doesn't "explain," doesn't "determine" it; otherwise it would have produced it always, everywhere.

*According to you, that failure of determinist explanatory models also applies to Marx's conception, which you have criticized repeatedly, in many texts, over the years. What are the main points of that criticism?*

Any criticism, and in fact any discussion of Marxism, must necessarily start with the historical fate of Marxism—barring which it is nothing but an exam paper, and a bad one at that—which essentially boils down to one massive fact: Marxism has become the ideology, the official secular religion of states that dominate, exploit, and oppress one third of the global population. An abrupt, immense question then arises: How could a theory claiming to be revolutionary and socialist become the ideological cover for those regimes? However superficial and ridiculous today's fashionable claim that the Gulag is contained in Marx, it is just as superficial and ridiculous to set a social and political theory and the effective historical practice inspired by it and accomplished in its name completely apart from each other. There is in fact a strong connection between the central elements of Marx's thinking and what Marxism has become.

*That is what you demonstrated in your 1964 paper, "Marxism and Revolutionary Theory,"*[1] *which forms the first part of The Imaginary Institution of Society, and marks your break with Marxism. That break had started with your questioning of Marx's economic theory.*

Yes, that economic theory is a central element, one which is also indicative of the belief pattern of Marxist disciples. It is no accident that the man spent forty years of his life working on his economic treatise without succeeding in finishing it. Nor that his disciples thrive on the belief that Marx had discovered the "laws" of the economy certifying that capitalism will collapse. The two aspects are closely intertwined: you had to discover "laws," and you have to believe that those laws exist. If you don't know them personally, there are the Party specialists who "read Marx's *Capital.*"

So, what about those "laws"? Let's take an example, a central one, actually. Marx believed he had discovered a law of the rising rate of exploitation under capitalism (in short: that the mass of profits/mass of wages ratio rises over time). Now you have to deliberately blind yourself not to see that this "law" is contradicted by the facts. Over the two centuries of the history of capitalism, real wages have risen, in the long term, at least as much as the productivity of labor. In other words, the rate of exploitation has remained constant, at the worst. Why? Essentially because the workers fought to obtain raises in their real wages, and they obtained them.

If we return to the theory, in search of the reason for that mistake, we note an astonishing fact: class struggle is absent from *Capital*—or more accurately, it only exists on the capitalist's side, and the capitalist always wins. That's no omission, easily righted and made good. That "absence" of class struggle is the strict equivalent of Marx's explicit thesis, the central axiom of his analysis of capitalism: labor power (or those aspects with which we are concerned here) is a commodity like any other one. As such, it has a given, constant "production cost," in material terms, whereas the productivity of a working day is continually increasing, as technology advances. (Or in terms of "value": the value produced by a day's work is constant, by definition, whereas the unit value of the goods composing the

---

1. [Excerpts of which are to be found in *The Imaginary Institution of Society* (Cambridge, Mass.: MIT Press; Cambridge, England: Polity Press, 1987).—Trans.]

supposedly constant consumption of the working class decreases over time.) Therefore, the difference between the two, what Marx calls the surplus value, increases over time, along with the rate of exploitation of the working class. That's Marx's reasoning, one that is radically wrong, irrespective of any empirical falsification. Wrong because it ignores, and must ignore, the resistance of workers, their struggles—in other words, because he postulates that labor power is a commodity.

*That is a view you have been stressing since 1953, in those texts on the dynamics of capitalism to which you often return.*

It is indeed all-important and has infinite ramifications. The "exchange value" of labor power is not a commodity. No commodity bargains over its value, or fights to increase it. Coal has never gone on strike to get its price to rise. Nor is the "usage value" of labor power in production a commodity. When a capitalist buys a ton of coal, he knows how many calories he can extract from it, at a given state of technology. When he buys a day's labor, he doesn't know how many productive, efficient motions he will be able to extract from it. That will depend on what goes on in the factory, on the workers' resistance and struggles. Neither the "exchange value" nor the "usage value" of labor power are or can be determined "objectively," independently of the activity of workers and their struggles. But Marx—like all economists—is obliged to ignore that aspect, to posit the exchange value and the usage value of labor power as *predetermined*, independent of people's activity. Now, how can you construct a system of economic "laws" if the main variable in the system is undetermined? He is therefore obliged to adopt the practical aim of capitalism—the transformation of the worker into a pure, passive object—assumed to be entirely achieved, as a theoretical axiom.

Everything said in *Capital* postulates that capitalism has eliminated every resistance within the working class. But that capitalism is a pure, completely uninteresting fiction. It is capital alone in the world, what I call the solipsistic fiction of capital. And that obviously affects all the consequences. For example: the rate of accumulation depends on the rate of exploitation (investment depends on profits). Likewise, the stability of the capitalist economy depends on its internal markets, the evolution of which will differ totally depending on whether real wages remain eternally constant or rise along with the productivity of labor. The observation that the aim of capitalism, the transformation of workers into passive objects, is unfeasible reveals a much deeper conceptual problem than that of the "economy." It enables us to understand what I have called the fundamental contradiction of capitalism.

*What do you mean by that?*

Capitalist technology, and with it the whole corresponding, supposedly "rational" organization of production, aims at transforming workers into passive objects, into pure executants of tasks circumscribed, controlled and determined from outside by an Apparatus for managing production. But at the same time, that production can only function inasmuch as that transformation of workers into passive objects doesn't succeed. The system is constantly obliged to solicit, and to use, the initiative and activity of those very people it attempts to turn into robots. A single hour of really "working to rule" everywhere, and the whole global production would break down. The system only functions inasmuch as people everywhere make it function against its own rules. The fundamental contradiction of the system is that it is simultaneously obliged to exclude workers from any essential participation in managing their activity and to constantly solicit, and use, that participation. This antinomy is incorporated in the present-day technology and organization of production—which are not, as Marx (and Lenin, and Trotsky) believed, neutral instruments, pure means of productive and economic "rationality," but rather, are consubstantial with the nature and goals of the system of domination, in the West as in the East. To surmount it therefore requires drastic changes in that technology as well as in that organization of production. Which cannot be done unless workers and their collectives take full charge of running their activities— what I call the collective management of production by the producers. And since the same antinomy is present in all spheres of social activity—as the exact other side of the growing bureaucratization of those spheres— the solution requires the collective management of social activities by the autonomous, federated organs of the participants—producers, students, and others—what later came to be called, with a more or less watered-down content, self-management. The true content of socialism—the content aimed at by workers during the Paris Commune, in Russia in 1917, in Catalonia in 1936–37, in Hungary in 1956, etc.—is the self-organization of society. But for that self-organization not to be confined to trivial matters, there must be no predefined, socially instituted limits. Self-organization meaning, therefore, the explicit self-institution of society.

*We should certainly get back to that idea. But doesn't the claim that Marx transforms the practical goal of capitalism into a theoretical axiom mean that Marx's thinking was contaminated by the bourgeois ideology from the start?*

Yes, of course. There's the Marx who writes that the point is no longer to merely interpret the world, but to transform it, and that communism is not an ideal state, but the effective movement that abolishes the existing state of affairs. That Marx begins to break with the capitalist universe, and beyond that, with the whole Greek and Western heritage. But there is also—and simultaneously, this is no chronological evolution—the other Marx, in whom the theoretical, rationalist element, aimed at establishing a system of set, potentially complete truths, constantly prevails over the former.

When Marx began to write, English and French workers had been advancing revolutionary ideas and practices that broke with the instituted world for forty years. What makes Marx great is that he understood the importance of those working-class creations and was inspired by them. But at the same time, he could only view them within the inherited framework (even if he enlarged it enormously). He was unable to challenge the traditional conception of "theory" or the corresponding postulate, the ontological bias behind it since Parmenides: to be is to be predetermined. He thought that theoretical reasoning, by inspecting and analyzing history, can discover the predeterminations, the laws explaining the future. In so doing, he partook of that immense enterprise begun by the Greeks and pursued by the Western world: the constitution of The Theory, the vision of what is as it is truly—and therefore, according to that conception, timelessly. Which enterprise cannot fully develop without eclipsing the distinctive fact of social-historical life: *doing/making* as bringing-into-being [*faire-être*], as creation, the self-institution of society. For to acknowledge that is tantamount to acknowledging indetermination as an essential, primordial dimension of social-historical being (and ultimately, of being itself), and to abandoning the inherited conception of Theory, realizing that it was never anything but a *project for a theory*, the sense of which is the ongoing activity of elucidating the world and ourselves. The Theory as something complete is a phantasm. Like any phantasm, the idea of abandoning it seems unbearable only as long as you are prisoner of it. That abandonment, far from leaving us deaf and blind, does just the opposite: it frees us to elucidate.

*And you think Marx remained a prisoner of that phantasm?*

For some key points, yes; and especially in that part of his thinking with social and historical resonances. It's very comprehensible. Marx addressed a world that was waiting—it still is—to be given *The* great, rational Theory. He owes his enormous historical impact to that "wrong reason." It is not for its revolutionary element, or for its depth and subtlety, that Marx's thinking was propagated and, simultaneously, efficient. It was because, boiled down to the few basic schemes to which *it can be* effectively, and in a sense accurately, reduced, it provides an apparently clear, simple, complete vision of the world and of what to do and not to do, usable by the obtuse disciple in Tiflis, the low-ranking cadre in Yenan, or the secretary of the Pas-de-Calais party cell.

*The time has come to talk about creation, self-institution, the imaginary, those ideas that pervade your work and your writings at least since 1964. Is this a jump into the irrational? Does the imaginary mean fiction, a fantasizing vision? Or is it the resurgence of a utopia?*

In everyday parlance, the imaginary has meant fiction as opposed to non-fiction, to the real and rational. That opposition is clear for everyday life within a given social world. But it becomes obscure and mysterious if we begin to question it. What is real? If you look at history, you see that each society institutes *its own* reality. What is and is not, what exists or does not, varies from one society to the next. Marx himself says somewhere that for the Greeks, the Apollo of Delphi was as real a force as any other. The same is true of spirits in some archaic society, of God in a monotheistic society, and so on. Likewise, what is "logical" or not, or again, the idea of what *verification* is, varies from one society to another. In each instance, the particular society *institutes* reality and rationality. The most immediate illustration is language, both the vehicle and the essential tool for structuring the world—both the "natural" and the social world, the rational lineaments of every reality, in general. Language is historically instituted, and in each instance the language instituted is different. There is no such thing as language in general, no pure, basic language of which historical languages would be isomorphic exemplars. What languages have in common is either trivial or unfathomably mysterious: that is, the ability to *signify*, to bring into being [*faire-être*] a world of significations. The most important of these significations have no assignable referent, no real or rational correspondent. It is those significations, the social imaginary significations, that hold all the others, and that particular society, together. Today, for instance, pseudo-"rationality" is one such signification. Each society institutes a universe: what is and what is not, what is valid and what is not, needs, individuals, their roles and identities, and so forth. That institution is creation. It cannot be reduced to what was there before, nor to "real" or "rational" factors external to that society. It is the work of the radical social-historical imaginary, just as an original work of art is the work of the radical imagination of an individual.

*Is that creation arbitrary, then?*

I say it is not reducible, not that is absolutely arbitrary. For example, no society can ignore the need for food or the difference between the sexes. But people eat historically instituted food, not calories; and social gender and biological sex are two very different things. Society leans on nature; it is not determined by nature. "Nature" itself is posited, represented, and enacted differently in each instance. The ancient Greeks saw it as sustained by the gods, the dryads, and the nereids. For modern society it is an inert material for humans to master. Each society posits and creates its relations with nature.

*Ultimately, both terms of the relationship too.*

Definitely, and all at once and immediately. To postulate his relation to nature as one of domination (Descartes says, as master and possessor of nature), modern man must postulate nature as a series of inert objects and society as the subject of rational mastery. The imaginary, non-real, non-rational character of that position is self-evident. Actually, that's an insane position, but an insane position that is *the* reality of today's world.

*So there is a whole critical evaluation of the powers of theoretical reason, and therefore of science itself. That partakes of what you call elucidation. But it is also, certainly, part of a political effort, since knowledge and power are increasingly viewed as one and the same.*

Let me make one thing clear. What I call the project of theory is neither empty nor vain, once voided of theoretical absolutism, of the delusion of the perfect Theory. We must rid ourselves of those twin, complementary naiveties: the idea that science knows, or will know everything, or that science knows nothing. In both cases there would be no problem. Whereas there is effective knowledge, and at the same time the object, nature, coherence and history of that knowledge are endlessly mysterious.

As for the assimilation of knowledge and power, that is a mystification propagated, comprehensibly, by those in power, but also by some people who claim to combat them but who only substantiate that mystification. In the last analysis, the belief that instituted States are all-powerful and omniscient is the only true foundation for the system. But half of the time, power is both blind and mindless, and is essentially, necessarily so. And those in power are not competent technicians and specialists (how could a specialist's specialization make her universally competent?), but people who are skilled in one particular specialty: in climbing the bureaucratic ladder. The man who became general secretary of the Russian CP was not the best Marxist, but the one who was most skilled in cutting the others down. It isn't the best engineers who run firms, but those who are best at turning the infighting between cliques and clans to their own advantage.

Seeing power and knowledge as one and the same is an essential element of the dominant ideology. No society can live without giving itself a self-representation. That representation partakes of the social imaginary significations correlative to its institution. Now, as opposed to previous societies, capitalist society does not give itself a mythical or religious self-representation; it wants that self-given representation to be rationalist, serving simultaneously as its "justification." Capitalist ideology is rationalist: it alleges knowledge, competence, its scientific character, and so on. Pseudo-"rationality" is the keystone of the imaginary of this society. That is true for Marxist ideology as well, now a secular State religion. I say rationalist, not rational. It claims an empty rationality, hanging in midair, one totally contradicted by its reality. Here again, we have something historically new. In no other society do we find such an antinomy between the society's own self-given system of representations and its effective reality. The reality of an archaic, slavery-based or feudal society corresponds to its system of self-representation. But modern society lives on a system of representations postulating rationality both as the end and as the universal means of social life—and which is denied by its each and every act. It claims to be rational, and massively produces what is irrationality even from its own viewpoint.

*After all that critical, elucidation work, is a socialist, revolutionary project still conceivable?*

Only through this sort of work can we understand that project, its origins and its content, and situate ourselves with respect to it. Socialism is not a necessary phase of history, no more than there is a science of society guaranteeing its advent and susceptible, through its "specialists," of guiding its construction. The socialist project is the project of the creation of a new form of society. And it actually was born as a historical creation, in and through the activity of a category of people. Since the turn of the 19th century, workers have been challenging the established institution of society, not only of capitalist society, but of all those societies we call "historical." It was not only economic exploitation they were combating, but domination as such: they wanted to set up a new order based on equality, freedom, and cooperation. In and through the activity of those men and women, new significations emerged, embodying themselves in new forms of organization opposed to the ages-old instituted world: the world of the State, of hierarchy, inequality, and the domination of some people over others.

That movement did repeatedly fall short of its goal in the course of its evolution. It became bureaucratic, adopted capitalist modes of organization, and the corresponding significations. Its encounter with Marxism—which, in many countries, turned into its confiscation by Marxism—is a crucial point in that evolution. At the deepest level, Marxism actually became the transmission belt by which capitalist models and significations (rationalism, hierarchy, productivity as a value, the primacy of pseudo-"theory," and so forth) were transferred to the working-class movement. But the movement went on, and still does. It still takes the elementary form of workers' day-to-day resistance to the exploitation and alienation to which the system subjects them. It stands up in broad daylight, constantly asserting the same aim, in Europe between 1917 and 1923, in Spain in 1936–37, in Hungary in 1956. Other movements with the same aim have joined in: the youth movement, which yielded May '68 in France, the women's movement, the ecology movement.

That aim may be summed up in a single word: autonomy. Autonomy means the elimination of dominant groups and of the institutions embodying and orchestrating that domination—the State, first and foremost—and the true self-government of collectives, the self-organization of society. In its fullest sense, that self-organization entails the explicit self-institution of society. Why explicit? Because society is always self-instituted, but is unaware of the fact. It is a feature of the institution of all previously existing societies, and of their self-given system of representations, to ascribe that institution to some other, outside agent: to a mythical hero, God, the laws of nature or the demands of Reason. Now, we must understand that we cannot flee our responsibility as to the institution of the society we want, not even by hiding behind "Reason." We want equality, freedom, justice: that is neither "rational" nor "irrational"; it is beyond both. It is absurd to think that the laws of history guarantee the advent of a just society (or of a society in which the question of justice could be eliminated). It is meaningless to think that we could define, once and for all, what a just society is, and demonstrate that a just society is more "rational" than an unjust one (at best, the reasoning would be circular). And it is infantile to think that any such "demonstration" would be of any help whatsoever. You don't refute Auschwitz or the Gulag; you combat them.

A *historical war* is on. It began with the Greek *dèmos* and the first Ionian philosophers, has gone through long eclipses, is periodically revived, and in our historical period takes the form of the Parisian sections in 1792 and 1793, the English workers founding their first trade unions, the communards, the workers and intellectuals of Budapest. It is a war against subservience to a dominant group, against myths, simply against any received idea, against the established institution of society qua institution of *heteronomy*. As long as society remains asymmetrically, antagonistically divided, that war will not cease. It's up to us all to choose our side.

*But what are the chances of that project of autonomy, confronted with the omnipotence of instituted States?*

There is no omnipotence of instituted States. Their power is nothing but the reverse side of people's belief in that power. For the rest, the answer is not in my hands. Everything depends on the desire and ability of women and men to change their social existence, to acknowledge their responsibility for their fate, and to fully shoulder that responsibility. If everything we have said is politically meaningful, it may be summarized quite simply. The point is to remind people of an elementary truth, of which they are well aware, but which they generally forget when it comes to public affairs: neither the expansion of the capitalist economy, nor the government, nor the laws of history, nor the Party, ever work *in their favor*. Their fate will be what they want to and are able to make of it.

# What Political Parties Cannot Do

*What, in your opinion, is the reality behind the expression "social experiments"? Do you think it aptly characterizes the new social movements?*

I think the term is ambiguous, and actually anything but innocent. It seems to be depicting as new something that is not new but whose importance has constantly been minimized or ignored by official "left" organizations. In our culture—and this is massive and obvious at least since the late 18th century—people have repeatedly made attempts and taken action aimed at concretely modifying their living conditions, including of course their working conditions. That began at the start of the labor movement, which has never been, and never could have been, just a pure protest movement against the established order. It was, at the same time, a self-organized, or to use the term I prefer, a self-instituting movement—positively self-instituting, of course. That was expressed in what can only be called forms of social *creation* (and not "experiments"), such as the setting up of the first trade unions, of mutual aid associations, cooperatives, and so on; in short, all those self-organizing activities of the working class through which it constituted itself as a class in the full sense of the term. Because capitalist machines alone do not make for a working class: those machines only bring into existence a category of people as passive objects of exploitation, a "class in itself." The working class becomes a class "for itself"; it constitutes itself as a historical class, inasmuch as it organizes itself, *doing, making,* and *making itself.* That movement of self-constitution of the working class, pervading the 19th century in the "advanced" countries of the time, was later masked by the bureaucratization of the working-class organizations. Which doesn't mean it has come to an end.

---

{A talk with Joël Roman on April 20, 1979, on "social experiments," published in *Critique socialiste*, no. 35 (June 1979). The present text is based on the transcription as reread and corrected by Castoriadis in May 1979. *Critique socialiste* is the theoretical journal of the Parti Socialiste Unifié; see note 2 below.}

Then came the women's movement. Here again, isn't it a bit strange to talk about "social experiments"? For about a century, women have been gradually modifying their situation—and men's situation as well, by the same token—through their everyday, anonymous, largely subterranean activity. They have destroyed ageless taboos, shaken attitudes and customs in ways that have incalculable, and surely still unforeseeable, consequences. That is due neither to "political" organizations nor to specific organizations (the MLF[1] and other groups have developed in the last ten or fifteen years), but to the immense number of women whose attitudes had changed and who more or less imposed that change on men too, and who therefore positively *created* something, who modified the established institution of relations between men and women. What sense is there to call that an "experiment"?

The same is true of the youth movement, over the last twenty-five years or so. And also, more recently, of other movements that are not definable as a social "category" (as the working class, women, or youths may be). People in some place, or who have shared interests or concerns, get together and try to do something on their own. Why call that a "social experiment"? To cover up the ideological and political nudity of today's "left." In those instances, the people who act are not doing so to "experiment"; they act to *do* something, to *create* something. Is it called "experimenting" because it doesn't square with the program and ideology of the official political movements? That was also true of the women's and youth movements, which were underhandedly fought, looked down on, and ignored by those organizations, until they attempted to co-opt them.

Why do people embark on those activities? Because they realize that neither state institutions nor parties respond to their aspirations and needs, that both are incapable of responding to them (otherwise people would try to use them for those activities). For example, ecology movements developed not only because the existing parties didn't concern themselves with the problem, but also because people realized that if and when parties address the ecology issue, it is out of demagogy, and that with *those* parties, it will never be otherwise.

At the same time, people are beginning to understand, more or less clearly, that it is absurd to subordinate all activity to "the Revolution" or "seizing power," following which, supposedly, all problems will be solved. That's a tremendous mystification, which guarantees, precisely, that *nothing* will be solved after "the Revolution." For one thing, self-organized

---

1. [The Mouvement de Libération des Femmes, the main women's liberation group at the time.—Trans.]

movements, partial self-management, are expressions of the conflict tearing present society apart, of people's fight against the established order, and also, secondly, they prepare something different. However embryonic, they translate and embody people's determination to take their fate into their own hands and under their own control.

*What about the idea, advanced by some people, that these movements help to replace failing institutions, or else that they are part of a new class compromise with the upper middle class, instead of leading to a political transformation of society?*

To say that as long as the regime persists it co-opts everything is tautological. But should we combat, say, freedom of the press, or even lose interest in it because the system co-opts it or integrates it? Or again, why not reason that way about trade unions, where it would be infinitely more justified, since the unions are now cogs in the functioning of the system, and have been for quite a while, and there can be no modern, "free-market" or even totalitarian capitalist country without unions to channel the working class? That's a short-sighted reasoning, as shown by the history and evolution of capitalist production and its organization. The system organizes production and exploitation in a given way; workers invent ways of defending themselves and combating that organization. Sooner or later, the system integrates or co-opts those means, and the battleground shifts; the workers invent new means, and so on. That's what history is.

Moreover, behind the argument you mention there is visibly a conception of "politics" that reduces it to fighting between parties that want to run the State. Not only is that a restrictive conception; it's a *bureaucratic* conception of politics.

*So political parties are more a hindrance than a means of developing socially creative movements?*

Definitely. That conception of political activity is necessarily embedded in what parties really are: bureaucratic organizations claiming (on the basis of a more or less lopsided ideology) to have found the Archimedean lever for the transformation of society; that is, you have to seize the State apparatus and the rest will follow. That explains why parties are unable to see what's going on in the new movements and why those "vanguard" organizations have turned out to be rearguards dragging miserably along, far behind events. With a lag of five, ten, sometimes even twenty years, brilliant political leaders and famous theoreticians have discovered self-management—we had been talking about it since 1955—women and youths—we had been talking about them since 1960—and so forth. A few days ago, I read in the papers that Mr. Séguy very seriously stated at I forget what meeting of his [Communist-led] union, the CGT [Confédération Générale du Travail], that the problem of working conditions is new and important, but difficult, and that the union should study it further before committing itself on it. No kidding! In 1979, that working-class "leader" and his union have discovered the "new" problem of working conditions—a problem over which workers have been fighting since capitalist factories have existed, that is, for practically two centuries.

"Left-wing" parties have taken two actually not mutually exclusive attitudes toward those movements. The first, corresponding to the reality of those parties, is to say: we need to govern, we need nationalizations, etc., and the rest will follow. The second turns the new demands into decorative feathers, mere cosmetics, through a series of demagogic, verbal concessions. Women are making demands? OK, no problem, they decide to give women 30 percent of party leadership positions, as if that would solve anything. Likewise: people engage in activities to change their living conditions? Well, we'll call that "social experiments" and say it's "interesting." "Experiments" as compared to what? As compared to the "certified" truths written into the party "platforms." In their existing form, "left" parties—irrespective of the intentions and ideas of the individuals of which they are composed—are organizations designed to direct and manage from outside and from above.

*According to you, then, the solution doesn't reside in present political parties at all. But would you go as far as totally refusing the notion of political organization as such?*

The solution is certainly not political parties such as they now exist. More accurately, those parties are for another solution—the bureaucratic solution, either reformist or totalitarian. But that of course doesn't solve our problem, except in the negative. There will be no transformation of society without explicit, enlightened political activity. Political activity is necessarily collective. So we need a political collectivity fighting and acting for the transformation of society, for the establishment of an autonomous society. That collective organization will have a series of all-important tasks. It will have to spread news of and publicize the true content of struggles and movements under way, discuss their meaning and possible weaknesses, the reasons for their success or failure, show what is exemplary about them. It will be universal, not because it possesses a "true theory," defined once and for all, but in its endeavor to make explicit the immanent universality already implicitly present in people's activity, and the meaning of that activity, exceeding the specific shape it took under the circumstances.

That collectivity will of course be organized in such a way as to embody and evidence the goals it pursues: it will therefore be self-managed, self-governed. That certainly is not easy. How can, say, several thousand people scattered all over France establish a non-bureaucratic (and not completely chaotic) collective, one that is effectively self-managed, self-governed (and in self-government there is not just the self part, there is also government, which many people forget)—that, to my eyes, is one of the most important problems today. Infinitely more so, in any case, than the discussions over a "United Left," and so on.

*But isn't that sort of political organization—corresponding pretty much to what we're trying to do in the PSU²—doomed to be marginalized by the ordinary interplay of present-day political institutions?*

Here too, we must rid ourselves of received ideas, and particularly of the idea that the only kind of political activity is that done by parties, meaning having city council members, deputies, and so forth. What was the most important political event in France in the last twenty years, at the least? May '68. Now who made May '68? What party made May '68? None of them. And yet, ten years later, France is marked more by May '68 than the France of 1881 was by the Commune.

*But in one sense May '68 failed, inasmuch as it didn't produce an effective political transformation; it remained only an immense social movement.*

True, and in one sense, and in part, we can say that May '68 was a "failure." I myself circulated a text during the events (published immediately afterward, in late June '68, in *La Brèche*,³ a book by Edgar Morin, Claude

---

2. [The PSU (Parti Socialiste Unifié, 1960–89), a small party to the left of the Socialist Party, was an admixture of various currents ranging from reformist to revolutionary. Although claiming to advocate "self-management," it was viewed by people such as Castoriadis as advancing a watered-down version of that notion.—Trans.]

3. [For an English-language version of Castoriadis' contribution, see *Political and Social Writings*, vol. 3: *1961–1979: Recommencing the Revolution: From Socialism to the Autonomous Society* (Minneapolis: University of Minnesota Press, 1993). —Trans.]

Lefort and myself) in which I tried to demonstrate the need to organize, to set up permanent forms of collective action and existence. Nothing of the sort was done, for reasons it would take too long to discuss here. But that in no way diminishes the immensely positive importance of May '68, which revealed and made everyone see one fundamental thing: that the true locus of politics is not where it was believed to be. The locus of politics is everywhere. The locus of politics is society.

*But isn't there a contradiction between the observation that May '68 failed because of the inability to institute, and on the other hand the criticism of existing institutional forms, be they State institutions or instituted political parties?*

There is a contradiction only if you confuse those existing institutions with any possible institution. The failure—or more accurately, the *limit*—of May '68 was the inability to set up new, different institutions: different not only in name, of course, but in their essence. The claim that we cannot enter a new phase in social life without destroying the State apparatus and without disbanding the dominating groups and the institutions consubstantial to their domination does not mean that an autonomous society is a society without institutions. There is no such thing as a society without institutions. The reign of pure desire is just as essentially the desire to murder other people, for example.

What, then, can be said right now about the institutions of a new society, an autonomous society? At any rate, we can say that they will be the embodiment of autonomy, meaning collective self-management, self-organization, self-government in every sphere of public life. This also means that those institutions won't be set up once and for all, they won't be removed from the instituting activity of society. Which is why I believe the main political problem—the only one, perhaps, ultimately—is that of the *explicit, conscious* self-institution of society. To be solved it requires both *new* institutions and a *new kind of relationship* between society and its institutions.

It is from this vantage point that we can take our bearings as to the movements we are discussing: Do they represent new, autonomous forms of collective organization? Does *another kind* of relationship develop there between people and their collective organization, enabling them to *effectively* control it? That's the essential criterion. We don't condemn the Communist Party, or any other bureaucratic organization, because it is an institution, but because it is a *bureaucratic* institution, because that institution, in its form, structure, organization, and ideology, is necessarily heteronomous, alienated and alienating, making its members and other people subservient.

Over and beyond this, there are further distinctions to be made. As long as overall society remains what it is, it is clearly impossible for fully autonomous organizations to exist in a given sector or location, since no organization can be disconnected and isolated from society as a whole. All are immersed in and influenced by it, and suffer the consequences. But that doesn't mean that they will inevitably be co-opted by the regime, all the time and 100 percent. Here too, we must denounce that absolutely pseudo-revolutionary prejudiced opinion that either you make a total, radical break or you are 100 percent co-opted by the system. That's not true.

*There is still a problem, precisely, with partial self-management or limited socially creative movements: If they can't transform society radically without destroying a number of central institutions, how can we give them the ability to converge so as to do so? What is the unifying logic of those movements?*

To determine whether any such unifying logic exists, and what it is, we must determine the true problem of the transformation of society. What is the root of social conflict in the present regime, over and beyond mere conflicts of interest? The fundamental contradiction in capitalist society—be it fragmented bureaucratic capitalism, as in the West, or total, totalitarian bureaucratic capitalism, as in the East, in what are abusively called the socialist countries—is immanent in the very organization of that society, to the division between order-givers and order-takers, between those who direct, or manage, and those who execute. This division means that people are excluded from their own lives, both individual and collective. I'm talking about the split between managers/directors and executants, not the old political philosophy opposition between those who direct and those who are directed. It is possible to be directed, whereas it isn't possible to be *purely* an executant. Now, the regime tries to reduce people to pure executants—that is an internal necessity—to exclude them from managing their own activities. At the same time, it couldn't survive if it really, fully succeeded in doing so, in making people totally passive. (That's clear if you take the organization of work in present-day enterprises.)

Now, all the movements we are discussing aim, in one way or another, to some extent, at overcoming and abolishing that division between directors and executants—between directing and executing. Inasmuch as they aren't mere explosions and don't simply let people express themselves, but are creative, socially instituting movements as well, they express and embody people's desire for autonomy. In that way they herald and prepare the only radical transformation of society: the advent of an autonomous society, taking charge, for the first time, of its own self-government, and setting its own laws. The unifying logic of those movements, and their tie with the project of radically transforming society resides in the fact that they already embody, however partially, fragmentarily, and embryonically, those all-important political significations: self-management, self-organization, self-government, and self-institution.

# Present Issues for Democracy

Modern constitutions begin with declarations of rights, the first phrase of which is either a theological creed, or something similar: "Nature commands that . . . ," or "God commands that . . . ," or "We believe that all men were created equal." That last claim is false, in fact: equality is a creation of people, acting politically. In comparison, the Athenian laws were as deep as can be: they always began with: "*Edoxe tè boulè kai tô dèmô*," "It seemed right to, it was the well-thought-out opinion of the council and of the people that . . . ," followed by the text of the law. That *edoxe* is fantastic; it is truly the cornerstone of democracy. We have no science of what is good for humanity, and we never will have one. If there were one, it wouldn't be democracy we would want to seek, but the tyranny of the person possessing that science. We would try to find him, and tell him: "OK, you are going to govern since you possess the science of politics." That indeed is what Plato and many others said, explicitly, and also what the people who flattered Stalin said, "Since you know history, economics, music, linguistics. . . . Long live the Secretary General!" Whereas the Athenians said, "According to their well-thought-out opinion, the council and the people order that. . . ." That means democracy is the regime of the *doxa*, which is well-thought-out opinion, that faculty we have of forming an opinion on questions escaping any geometrical formulation.

Take the question of the age at which citizens should be given the vote, for instance. Is there any scientific answer? Is any such science even conceivable? Of course not. From the very moment when a society raises that question, the answer implies a choice. And that's true irrespective of the political regime, even under the "dictatorship of the proletariat": Who is a

---

{Excerpts from a lecture given at the University of Montreal on April 9, 1986, partially published under its French title, "Les enjeux actuels de la démocratie," in *Possibles* (Montreal) 10, no. 3–4 (1986).}

proletarian? And at what age? Is being exploited a necessary and sufficient condition for voicing one's opinion? The main point is that in a democracy we don't have a science of political affairs and the common weal, we have people's opinions. Those opinions clash, are discussed and argued, and finally, the people—the community—comes to a decision and settles the matter by its vote. This, then, is the process of interrogation, the questioning introduced by democracy. It isn't vain questioning: We know that the people decide, or rather, we want the people to decide. And we know, or should know, that what the people decides isn't the ultimate truth; it can be wrong, but there is no other solution. We will never be able to save the people against its will; all we can do is give it the institutional means to correct itself if it made a mistake, and possibly to revise a wrong decision or a bad law, and modify it.

To begin with, there is the self-constitution of the political body, without the help of any science. We ourselves must draw and set the limits, and there can be no scientific or mathematical demonstration that we are right. We will then say—at least I hope we will—that everyone who usually lives in the territory and is concerned by what occurs there partakes of the political collectivity. That may seem obvious, but it is not at all the case in the existing legislatures, where only the "nationals" of the given State can vote (naturalization is relatively easy in America, but not in Europe). We would have to decide, then, "who participates in the life of the collectivity." The criteria for doing so will necessarily be a bit arbitrary, even for the latter definition. I don't suppose we'll say that a Japanese or French person with a stop-over in Montreal on election day can vote. Not if she stays for three hours. But what if she stays three weeks or if she rents an apartment? What I want to point up by these apparently trivial examples is the necessity for the political collectivity to define itself and to constitute itself, which necessity has been overlooked in all the theological-philosophical rhetoric of the last two centuries. What philosophy will ever be able to tell us at what age, starting with what length of residence, all human rights become automatically applicable?

But we can also delve deeper into the self-definition of a collectivity in terms of the definition of the people, of governing, and of everyone's equal participation in governing. A democratic society, whatever its size, is always composed of a multitude of individuals who all participate in governing inasmuch as each and all are equally, effectively able to affect what goes on. That is absolutely not the case, in practice, in today's democratic societies, which are what I prefer to call elective, liberal oligarchies,[1] with each social stratum defending its power, well-barricaded within its positions. No doubt, those strata are not completely impermeable. That's the free-market apologists' famous argument: "Mr. So-and-so began as a newspaper vendor and thanks to his abilities he ended up president of General Motors." Which simply proves that the dominant strata know enough to bring in new blood by recruiting individuals from the lower strata, those who are most active in the social game as organized by them. The same is true for politics, which is dominated by party bureaucracies. No matter whether they are in government or in the opposition, socialists or conservatives, in one sense they are all accomplices for the permanent power-related stakes. Leaders aren't changed according to popular will; it's the rules of the bureaucratic game of their party apparatus that produce new ones. Whatever little democracy subsists in present-day society is only the residue of centuries and centuries of successful struggles. That does not put the power effectively in the hands of the people in our so-called democratic liberal oligarchic societies. At most, the people can only express a vague electoral veto every five or ten years—and as you know, that veto is more fictitious than real, for the very simple reason that the game is rigged, not in the sense that the elections are rigged, but because the choices open to voters are always predetermined.

But that doesn't mean that the dominant oligarchies, be they capitalist or political, are constantly, systematically violating a guileless, unwilling people. Citizens let themselves be led by the nose; they are deceived by cunning or corrupt politicians and manipulated by the scoop-crazed media, but don't they have any means of controlling them? Why have they lost their memory to such an extent? Why do they forget so easily that the same Reagan, the same Mitterrand, was talking very differently a year ago, or four years ago? Has some evil spirit turned them into zombies? And if

---

1. [The term "*libéral*" is used here to designate the defense of individual liberties, as shown in Castoriadis' definition of present societies as "liberal oligarchies": "Any political philosopher in the classical ages would have recognized them as liberal oligarchies: . . . liberal because that stratum consents a number of negative or defensive liberties to citizens" (*Figures of the Thinkable* [Stanford, Calif.: Stanford University Press, 2007], 126). The broad sense, usually used by Castoriadis, of opponents of state intervention and champions of "individual freedom," is occasionally extended by him to the usual modern French use of the term, applied to right-wing, generally "neoliberal," ideological apologists of the free-market economy, to the exclusion of the American sense of the left-wing progressive.—Trans.]

so, what can be done? But I don't think they have turned into zombies; I simply believe we are going through an extremely critical phase of history, in which there is effectively a problem of political participation. It is as if people took in everything they are told with enormous cynicism— "They're all corrupt! Politicians are all part of the same mafia!"—but that doesn't necessarily prevent them from voting. . . .

On everyone's equal participation in power, in governing, I would like, first, to eliminate the confusion between equality and sameness. Giving everyone the same effective possibility of participating in governing in no way means making everyone alike; that's obviously absurd. To begin with: society involves power—and according to the democratic postulate, which you may challenge, both in the absolute and relatively, that power must be everyone's power, the power of all those who wish to partake of it. So you will say: "But maybe citizens will not all participate; there will always be inequality between active and passive people." I didn't claim that democracy achieves that equality; the regime doesn't have that ability, though it may acquire it in the long term, by educating people so that they understand that the community belongs to them. . . . I said: giving everyone the same effective possibility. If people don't want it, there's nothing to be done. Don't worry, we then fall back on your liberal government, and what happens is what often has in the past, in trade unions in particular. We cannot save humanity against its will. And no-one can preserve it from either folly or suicide. I contend that democracy requires active citizens, truly desiring to participate. But we can't take them as some absolute given, independent of the regime in which they live, and of what that regime makes of them and of what they can make of the regime.

I also contend that the effective possibility for everyone to participate in governing excludes ownership, by one individual or a group of individuals, of factories that feed two hundred thousand workers. I view that as incompatible. It's up to the collectivity to decide. I myself am opposed both to the prohibition of individual ownership and to forced collectivization, but in modern society where you have large enterprises, they are a locus of political as well as economic power.

What about the minority? Of course it must be free to express itself, to organize, and so on. Actually, whenever the majority has truly been able to express itself, it has never oppressed minorities. Minorities have been oppressed, and the majority with them, whenever one particular minority took power to wield it in the name . . . of the proletariat, the German race, or whatever. That isn't the oppression of minorities by the majority, even if 43 percent of Germans voted for Hitler in 1933. There is no historical illustration of the idea that the majority tends to eliminate the minority. Those who eliminate minorities are always minorities who have monopolized power. In the last analysis, I obviously agree with you completely: in a democratic regime, people must be free to express their opinions without being prevented or persecuted. That's not negotiable. But it is simply a consequence of a democratic regime. Because democracy can function only through discussion, open-mindedness, conflicts of opinion, and there can be no discussion if people know their heads will fall if the vote turns against them. That's obvious. But having said this, if you have any sense of reality, you realize that what protects minorities right now is not any constitutional ruling. Constitutions are made; they can be undone: fifteen sovereign Western European nations have had one hundred and fifty constitutions over the last two centuries! What, in the Constitution of the United States, prohibits a qualified majority from deciding, I don't know, that all redheads will automatically be the state's slaves? What truly protects minorities in present-day society—and the events of the 1960s have proved this fully, for African-Americans—is not so much, and not only, the rules written into the constitution, but the construction of a democratic type of individual, who has internalized the democratic components of the institutions. And who, although he himself is white, finds it intolerable that blacks in southern states are prevented from registering to vote, and who stands up to obtain their right to vote. An individual who, while respecting the law of the community, nonetheless does not revere authority, dares to intervene when a policeman abuses that authority, and takes note of his number. . . . Now, that kind of individual doesn't necessarily exist elsewhere. Not in present-day Iran, at any rate, perhaps not in Russia either, and no doubt less and less in our own contemporary societies.

# These Are Bad Times

*You didn't speak out after 1981* [when the Socialist Party came into power], *that period of "silence of the intellectuals." Now that the right is governing again, do you feel we are at an urgent* kairos, *that critical point where something must be said or done?*

Several papers in *Domaines de l'homme*[1] show that I have expressed myself whenever I deemed it useful. But it was out of the question for me to participate in that carnival, with its trivially transparent stakes, actors and motivations. In France and elsewhere, it has been a long time since the distinction between left and right either addressed the great issues of our time or corresponded to any radically opposite political options. Where is the opposition between Mitterrand and Chirac on military matters, nuclear energy, Africa, the structure and management of government, education or even the economy? For five years the so-called socialists had absolute power; they used it to run the system and—as they did during the Algerian War—to do what the right wanted and didn't dare to do. The policies of [Socialist] ministers Bérégovoy and Chevènement are the most striking examples. The "reforms" introduced since 1981 boil down to three kinds of measures: those involving areas where France was behind the times (decentralization, the death penalty); those that usefully exploit a paleo-socialist dogma for the benefit of the party bureaucracy (nationalization, replacing existing managers by "ours"); and last, those designed to facilitate the utmost penetration of the state apparatus by the socialist apparatus. On the other side, we have a "right" claiming to be "liberal"

---

{Interview by Michel Contat, published as "Castoriadis, un déçu du gauche-droite [Castoriadis, Disappointed by the Left-Right]." *Le Monde*, July 12, 1986.}

1. *Domaines de l'homme: Les carrefours du labyrinthe II* (Paris: Seuil, 1986). [A few papers contained in this book have been translated into English, mostly those appearing in periodicals.—Trans.]

and adding fifteen interventionist, authoritarian clauses to each of its measures, and which, naturally, attacks the least privileged strata, the immigrant populations and other foreigners, and which suffers irremediably from the same total lack of ideas and of political imagination.

There's a total misunderstanding; these are absurd times.

*The cretinism you denounce so bluntly isn't specific to* [right-wing] *liberals,*[2] then?

There are, notoriously, some deep, original thinkers among liberals, including the American founding fathers, Benjamin Constant, Tocqueville, and John Stuart Mill. They have nothing to do with the rehash served up by today's "liberals" without a single new idea, not a single effort to deal with present-day issues. The question raised by this wretched scene is: What has made that pseudo-liberalism so strong in recent years? I think much of that strength comes from the fact that "liberal" demagogy has succeeded in cashing in on the profoundly anti-bureaucratic and anti-state movement and mentality that have been causing social unrest since the early '60s (and which escaped the penetrating gaze of "socialist" leaders).

To view May '68 and the other movements of the '60s as the beginning of contemporary "individualism" is a terrible misunderstanding. That individualism stems from the failure of May '68, and that failure *was internal*. The movement—and others like it in other countries—carried many absurdities with it, and was unable to go beyond the stage of the subversive demonstration. It did not succeed in positively addressing the question of its own self-government. But its underlying inspiration was the aspiration to *autonomy*, in its social as well as individual dimension. Today, as always, the political task at hand is to return to the great emancipatory tradition of the Western world, and take it further: to build a democratic, self-governed society, one in which individual and collective autonomy are mutually supportive and nourish each other. But that cannot be achieved without a vast democratic movement of the population, which is precisely lacking. The failure of the movements of the '60s converged with the underlying trends of modern bureaucratic capitalism, pushing people toward apathy and privatization.

For the time being, then, the *kairos*, as political *kairos*, is lacking. There is nothing we can do about it, and it is not a complete loss. It leaves time

2. [See note 1 in the preceding chapter, "Present Issues for Democracy."]

for us to take our thinking further, to question more deeply, as I try to do in the philosophical texts in *Domaines de l'homme*.

*How do you explain that apathy?*

That's a huge question. It forms one of the nuclei of the second volume of *Devant la guerre*:[3] Why and how does a culture die? That is just as difficult as the other one: Why and how does a culture come into being? A culture comes into being by creating new imaginary significations and embodying them in institutions. The world is peopled with gods and nymphs. Or else, the world and human beings were created by an omniscient, all-powerful god. Or still again, the world is nothing but inert matter through which we can achieve what gives meaning to human life, that is, the unlimited expansion of productive forces, or of mastery, or of might. Those are the core imaginary significations of a few known societies, and it's easy to see what institutions have actively embodied them. Those institutions often go through crises, but societies also have a tremendous capacity for self-repair, which depends mainly on the ongoing vitality of those imaginary significations, meaning too, above all, on their ability to shape, vivify, inspire and motivate individuals. Do Western societies still believe in a future indefinitely filled with more and more "well-being," wealth and technical "might"? Do they really believe that future is worthwhile? Is that an idea for which people would be willing to die, for instance? Do they produce individuals capable of anything but *living off* the system?

*What you are saying, in general, isn't very encouraging or very stirring.*

Before agreeing with other people, I want to be in agreement with myself. I'm staggered, at times shattered, by the ravages of pseudo-Hegelian "realism," which is actually opportunism, very short-sighted in fact, even among intelligent, sympathetic young people. They advance, in a commiserating tone, what is meant as an argument, "But that's what was being said ten years ago; you can't say that today!" My dear friend, it's *because* something is believed today that the chances are it's idiotic. Hegel said the history of the world is the Last Judgment. For our times, this evening's

3. {The second volume of *Devant la guerre* was never finished by Castoriadis, but "The Crisis of Western Societies" *Telos* 53 (Fall 1982) gives some idea of the intended content. We hope someday to publish the chapters Castoriadis had already completed.}

TV program is the Last Judgment. Since that program is structurally and rightfully forgotten the following morning, we have a Last Judgment every evening—meaning there is no longer any judgment, last or first, no memory and no thought. In the good-mannered Parisian intellectual microcosm it has become offensive to remind people (and even to remember) what so-and-so was saying last year.

*How long can one put up with being in the minority?*

I'm not in the minority. I'm alone, which doesn't mean I'm isolated. I was alone, we were alone too, during the whole period of the Socialisme ou Barbarie group. Subsequent events showed we weren't isolated. Possibly, everything I say and write is worthless. But there is also another, less optimistic hypothesis: that people today have no wish to hear, and to make the effort required by a discourse calling for critical thinking, responsibility and refusal of sloth.

*Are you very pessimistic?*

Ours is the period when the supremely pathetic expression of "postmodernism" was invented to conceal eclectic sterility, the reign of the facile, the inability to create, the evacuation of thinking for the benefit of commentary, at best, but usually of wordplay and eructation. A period of parasitism and all-around plagiarizing. What goes as the last word in "thought" and "political philosophy" today will be viewed pityingly, I'm sure, one, two or three decades from now. Because what is being said, fundamentally? That history has stopped, or better yet, it is over. Since Ancient Greece, Europe has also defined itself by philosophy, and we are being told: Philosophy is finished; all we have to do is "deconstruct." For twenty-eight centuries, Europe has defined itself by its struggles to modify the institution of society, by its social and political struggles, its creation of the political sphere, and we are being told: Politics (true, great politics) are over. The republic, be it parliamentary or presidential (also called "democracy," respect for words having been lost long ago), that's the form for human society, discovered at long last. Of course some reforms remain to be made: the family allowances of some almost-obsolete rural policemen require updating, for example. But on the whole, the political task, the task of instituting society is over: We'll have Reagan, Thatcher, Kohl, Mitterrand/Chirac for centuries to come.

Speaking of that nightmarish vision inevitably makes one irresistibly optimistic. Because there is almost an internal contradiction in that prospect. Those people are the by-products and the parasites of contemporary regimes; in no case could they have *created* them (just as today's "deconstructionists" can only subsist because there have been philosophers). They couldn't even preserve them, in the long run. Those regimes were produced by the struggles of peoples for infinitely more radical goals: goals of true *autonomy*. Philosophy, true thought, has not ended. We might almost say it is just beginning. And great politics must be recommenced. Autonomy is not merely a project; it is an effective possibility for human beings. It is not for us to foresee or decree its advent or its disappearance; it is for us to work toward it. We're living in bad times, that's all.

# Do Vanguards Exist?

*The term "vanguard" is associated with artistic and political movements. In an-other sense, one may talk about "advanced scientific research" or "avant-garde techniques." What ties these different senses together? What is a vanguard?*

First, one historical remark: I don't think that Sophocles, Shakespeare or Bach represented a vanguard in their times. Not that their works were unanimously acclaimed: there were certainly quarrels over opinions, tastes, schools of thinking. But there was no question of a "vanguard." That idea, that military metaphor of a detachment in the forefront of soci-ety, exploring the terrain and in charge of the first contacts with the enemy, is a relatively recent invention. It implies that history is and must be a "forward march," "advancing." At best, the idea leans on tremendous assumptions as to the philosophy of history. At worst, it is frankly absurd, implying that the most recent is the best, most beautiful, and so on. That latter idea actually does prevail at present.

*Where and when was the vanguard born?*

The phenomenon probably first occurred in France, at the end of the Restoration and especially under the Second Empire. There was Baude-laire, and the condemnation of the *Flowers of Evil*, supposedly for reasons of public morality, actually even more for esthetic reasons, the scandal raised by Manet's *Olympia*, Rimbaud, and so forth. Almost immediately that spread to the other European countries (Wagner proclaimed that he

---

{Interview by Michel de Pracontal, published under the title "Cette course absurde vers le nouveau pour le nouveau [That Absurd Race toward Novelty for the Sake of Novelty]," *L'Événement du jeudi*, August 20–26, 1987. We have used Castoriadis' type-written version.} [The names of politicians of the period are anecdotal; no detailed explication is needed to understand the meaning.—Trans.]

was writing "the music of the future"). Pre-revolutionary Russia, from 1900 on, had a fantastically lively painting, sculpture, and poetry scene. Between 1860 and 1930, the great creators took their distance from and were opposed to society. What they did was judged subversive and/or incomprehensible, and they themselves were mostly enemies of the established order. It was then, too, that the misunderstood genius and the accursed artist appeared, not as individuals, but as a *type*. Van Gogh died in dire poverty, and eighty years later one of his paintings sold at the highest price ever for a painting.

*How do you explain that marginalization of creators?*

In the mature phase of bourgeois society a cultural split occurred, for the first time in history to my knowledge. The capitalist bourgeoisie lost its historical creativity; its culture became repetitive. Its great artists, then, were the *"pompiers,"* the academics, now rediscovered by the Orsay museum. Official society, the affluent, or the state as commissioner, only accepted extremely conventional works of art. Almost necessarily, authentic creators were marginal then, to enjoy only late or posthumous recognition. After 1930, and even more, 1945, that history repeated itself, but as comedy, with a race for novelty for novelty's sake, but applauded (and paid for) this time by an "informed" public, adhering to that stupid judgment: it's new, so it must be good, and what comes later has to be better than what came before. "Revolutions" and "subversions," bringing in high, fast profits, follow in rapid-fire succession.

Ultimately, that absurd race for novelty for novelty's sake lost its content and petered out, and we ended up—in architecture, first—with our famous "postmodernism," the ostentatious claim that there is nothing more to say, except by recombining what has already been said. As one of the spokesmen of postmodernism in the United States proudly stated, "We are at last delivered of the tyranny of style." An acknowledgment of sterility—repetition of what has already been done, as a program—but also statement of a profound truth: "modernity" was great and open (look at the "influence" of Japanese, African, and American Indian art on the impressionists, on Picasso, and so on). "Postmodernism" is trite and spineless. Its main merit is to make us understand, by contrast, how sublime the "modern" period was.

In short: the development and value of a "vanguard" in art and literature is a phenomenon tied to the specific, momentary features of one historical period.

*If the artistic vanguard leads down a blind alley, isn't the opposite true of the sciences, where the race for novelty seems to be concomitant with the advancement of knowledge?*

Ever since the beginning of scientific development, first with the Greeks, then, and above all, with the Renaissance, we rightly think that there is always more to be discovered, that what we have seen so far is only temporarily correct, is only correct within a given framework, and so on. Science can always go further. Whereas the idea of going further is meaningless in the field of art. No-one will ever go beyond Aeschylus, Beethoven, or Rimbaud. No-one will ever go beyond Kafka's *The Castle*. One may go elsewhere, and otherwise, but no-one will go further. In that sense, scientific development exists, whereas you can't speak of development in the field of literature or the arts. But we must be careful here: that development is not the mere accumulation of knowledge, with each piece adding to the others. It is reworked by major revolutions. The relation between the discovery of something new and what was previously accepted is strange, to say the least. The philosophical signification of the transition from Newton's physics to Einstein's physics raises some immense questions.

*Couldn't we say that the former "fits into" the latter?*

No. Those serious questions arise precisely from the non-fitting. The average scientist believes that Newton gave a first approximation, and Einstein a second, better approximation. But that's not true; there is a problem of theoretical (and not simply numerical) compatibility between the two conceptions. In a sense, Newton is purely and simply wrong. In another sense he isn't; he covers 99 percent of phenomena with his first approximation. So scientific revolutions do exist. At some points, great new imaginary schemata emerge that account for reality better than the previous ones. That's true of relativity and quantum physics. How is innovation greeted? Newton's theory was not accepted immediately; in France, for example, the Cartesians opposed it for decades. Einstein's theory, or the special theory of relativity to be more accurate, didn't raise any great uproar; there were claims that it was in the classical spirit—and yet, that isn't the theory for which Einstein was given the Nobel Prize. The general theory of relativity did totally destroy the classical framework, but for quite a while physicists viewed it as a theoretical curiosity without much real importance. To this day, one has the impression they don't realize its deep philosophical implications, and the aporias it uncovers. Quantum theory on the other hand destroyed something immediately essential for classical physics, an idea that physicists as well as ordinary people had absorbed at their mother's breast: the idea of determinism, the category of causality. That's why Einstein himself, Louis de Broglie, and Shrö-dinger never accepted it. Nowadays quantum theory is almost universally accepted. It is as if we had become accustomed to experiencing major changes. In spite of the huge theoretical difficulties experienced by con-temporary physics—the situation is truly chaotic—scientists advance and discuss the "maddest" theories. There is the understanding that reality is less "logical," in the sense of our familiar logic, where two and two make four, than was previously thought. A famous physicist, talking about a new theory, could say, "It isn't crazy enough to be true."

*But isn't that tolerance of novelty tied to a narrowly pragmatic attitude? Don't physicists use quantum physics without really trying to understand what it means?*

That is very true, as a rule. Physicists have given up trying to make sense of what they say, and connecting it with the mundane world or with the great philosophical questions from which science originated. They no longer even care about making coherent use of their own categories. Some even more fundamental categories than that of causality, the categories of *locality* and *separability*, are challenged by quantum theory. We can no longer say, in every case, that a thing is "distinct" from another, or that it is located in a given place and is not simultaneously almost everywhere and almost nowhere. Well, physicists go on working, tranquilly. They agree that at the deepest level—the deepest reached so far!—things aren't necessarily localizable or separable. What does that mean? Who knows. That lack of interest in meaning and signification, extremely serious in my opinion, is typical of contemporary physics, as it is of the period in general. In the long term, it may have decisive effects.

　　Can we speak of a scientific vanguard? I don't think the expression is meaningful here. Some scientists produce more original work than others, but they don't represent a vanguard. Rather, the distinction is between those who work at the frontiers of problems and those who continue to cultivate a well-plotted-out scientific field.

*What about political vanguards?*

At the outset, we mostly find the Leninist ideology of the Party as "van-guard" of the working class. It's always that common conception that po-litical truth exists, in this case an idea or theory of future society and of the way to get there, and that truth is already in the hands of a specific category—the Party and its leaders—by virtue of their ties with revolutionary theory. Those people therefore have the duty to guide the working class, to lead it to the Promised Land. Lenin said that the Party must always be ahead of the masses, but just one step ahead. It's important to understand what that means. If it were at the same level as the masses it would no longer be a vanguard, and if it were three miles ahead it would be completely isolated and would fail dismally. The Party mustn't isolate itself from the masses, so it must present its program as immediately feasible. The masses must be shown that it espouses their immediate demands and doesn't want to carry them too far—whereas in reality those demands are a lure to make them swallow the whole Party line.

*For someone who rejects the concept of a party, a minority group possessing the truth, what, conceivably, can the political role of a vanguard be?*

I for one rejected the idea of a vanguard long ago. But I am still, more than ever, deeply convinced that present-day society will not overcome its crisis if it doesn't radically transform itself. In that sense I am still a revolutionary. And I believe that that transformation can only be the work of the immense majority of the men and women who live in this society. The question then arises: What kind of relationship can we see between a population—be it French, English, or American—and those individuals who think (or believe they think) a little more, and above all continuously, about the great political issues, and who want to act on the basis of their thinking? That relationship inevitably involves two completely opposite phases. For instance, in the present phase the population is totally politically apathetic and completely privatized (that's what is glorified under the heading of "individualism"). Very exceptionally this situation is disturbed by some little surface ripples (such as the November–December 1986 student movement). If we believed that everything real is rational, that what happens is what has to happen—a truly monstrous idea—we would say that the game is up. Everyone minds his own business, writes poems, buys a video camera, goes on vacation, and so on. During a period like the present one, I think the role of people who think politically and have a passion for politics (a passion for the *res publica*) is to say what they think, loud and clear, even if few people hear them. To criticize what is, and also to remind people that there have been phases in their history when the people itself was different and acted historically creatively, acted as an *instituting* force.

Let's suppose, now, that all of a sudden, when it is thought that nothing can happen any more, a minor incident causes a flare-up; part of the population begins to make new claims, new demands, inventing forms of action and of organization. That's exactly what happened in May '68. . . . In that kind of phase, true historical creation is in the making, and we must understand that we probably have much more important things to learn from the movement under way than what we could teach it, assuming we could teach it anything at all. Consequently, that tiny minority of people who formerly attempted to speak out or act—the "vanguard"—can no longer view itself as anything more than one component of that whole movement.

So, rather than saying that an individual or a group forms a "vanguard," we can say that they may eventually represent a positive leavening agent, given the state of the mass of society during certain periods. But that is never final. When history really goes to work, when society becomes an instituting force again, those groups return to the rank and file, or at best, they become spokespeople, or loudspeakers for the collective movement. That's the role Dany Cohn-Bendit played, to some extent, during the first days of May. But there are other historical instances of people who played that valuable role of spokesperson for a collective movement on a more lasting basis.

*The concept of leadership isn't objectionable, then?*

It's fashionable in the leftist or left-wing tradition to condemn (in words only) the concept of leadership, seemingly a "right-wing" idea. That position is hypocritical and mistaken. Some individuals are occasionally, sometimes lastingly, more capable than others of expressing what everyone feels, and sometimes even of inventing things with which other people identify. They are leaders.

*What role do you see for leaders in present-day society?*

As long as apathy, privatization and pseudo-individualism prevail, a creative movement of the whole community is unthinkable, nor can we imagine some politically creative individual who, by playing that role, would cause other people to raise issues. It's a truism, but at the same time a profound truth, like most truisms, that a society has the leaders it deserves. What do we see right now? A fellow I don't know from Adam, whose existence I discover one morning in my daily paper, is in third or fourth position in opinion polls on French people's positive opinions of so-called politicians. That fellow's name is François Léotard. Who is Monsieur Léotard? I don't know. What has he done? I have no idea. Did he discover America, invent a mathematical theorem, win the *Tour de France*, invent some gadget, found a successful business, climb the Himalayas? No. Did he ever have the most minute personal idea? If so, he hides it carefully in his diary; he makes sure never to say anything but the most innocuous platitudes. But as I understand it, he was able to set up a little operation, an *apparat*, as they say in the Eastern countries. He's an apparatchik with a good understanding of our media-dominated period and who managed to persuade the TV people to make him telegenic. Thanks to which Mr. Léotard is a political leader, and a most appropriate one for France in 1987, precisely because he hasn't a single idea in his head—a new idea, one of his own. Mr. Léotard is the adequate expression of what France is right now. From a Hegelian standpoint, he should be elected president of the Republic in 1988. He won't be, which proves, once again, and fortunately, that history isn't completely rational. Fortunately the French people is not merely what it is, like all of us, in fact. It's in man's nature not to be what he is and to be what he is not (that's Hegel again). There is more, and something else. Only for the time being that more, that something else, is dormant.

*Doesn't that political apathy go along with exaggerated trust in the power of science and technology?*

It's a fact that the passivity of contemporary people rests on that imaginary signification: techno-science as capable of solving problems in their stead. Between 1950 and 1980, the main mystification was that politicians were technicians: they are the ones who know; it's too complicated; how can we understand that nuclear business, how many bombs the Russians have, and so on. A randomly selected individual, we are told, couldn't understand what it means that the Russians have two thousand bombs and the Americans have one thousand five hundred; it's too much for them; you have to be a specialist—not a nuclear specialist, a specialist in "politics"!—to understand. That same individual couldn't understand why the French government has to throw out eight hundred million dollars to get planes[1]

---

1. {In 1976, on the basis of unreliable reports, the firm Elf signed a several-hundred-million-franc contract for the purchase of a patent on a device supposed to enable planes, known as "sniffer planes," to detect oilfields from afar.}

that can smell oil from an altitude of five miles. To understand the need for that you have to come from the right schools, and be ex-president Giscard d'Estaing. That farcical idea that politicians are technicians prevailed for quite a while.

At present, two dimensions coexist. [Socialist] Laurent Fabius, for instance, still embodies the mystification of technical skill: he is the "expert." Even if Léotard didn't play in westerns, he embodies the other pole, the one Reagan created, and . . .

*. . . he's a marathon runner.*

There you have it. This is a country of classical culture; the marathon is Léotard's western. People find him charming, a pleasant sight on TV, reassuring. . . . Actually, people's attitude toward political leaders can be summed up in three points: (1) there's nothing we can do, anyway; (2) problems are increasingly being solved by techno-science, anyway; (3) in the meanwhile, we'll take a cocktail of techno-politicians and video-politicians, the former supposedly to manage things and the latter to tell us stories so we can go on sleeping. That may seem a bit premature as a description of the French situation: I don't think it is. But at any rate, it's obvious with Reagan in the United States. Video-politics. Stories that let you sleep. "I'm going to make America great again." "I'm going to eliminate the budget deficit, waste, etc." "I will restore morality in public affairs." Now, everything Reagan has done so far in foreign policy has been a failure, or at best, has ended in a draw. The budget deficit is huge, reaching a point no Keynesian could ever have imagined. The foreign deficit has become almost incredible, and thanks to Reagan the United States has been turned into one of the world's main debtors. One person out of two in Reagan's immediate entourage is involved in one way or another in scandals involving corruption. And Reagan remains very likable; most people have a good opinion of him. It took Irangate to change that somewhat. And at the same time, the now autonomous march of techno-science continues to destroy the terrestrial environment and to create huge risks for an increasingly less distant future.

*But what would have to be done to change that? Stop everything?*

In the present context, there isn't much to be done. If your goal in life is to have more and more objects, you should continue doing the same. If your goal is to forget we're all mortal, you can always go on sleeping, while awaiting the next medical miracles that will bring the life expectancy at birth up from 72.1 to 72.3 years. A different context is needed—resulting from a radical transformation of society. And in that context, we would have to become deeply aware, first of all, of the fact that there can be no guarantee that any techno-scientific activity is innocent: the moment when a mathematician discovers a theorem is innocent, but there's no knowing whether that theorem won't be crucial, some day, for producing a bomb. A great, and very respectable English mathematician, Hardy, a pacifist during both world wars, said he had chosen mathematics because it could never be used to kill human beings. That's nonsense. One of the first equations you learn to solve in differential calculus is called the gunner's equation, because it is used to calculate parabolas for shooting.

There is no scientific innocence, not even in paradise: that is already clearly stated in Genesis. First, everyone must be deeply penetrated with that conclusion. Moreover, in those sectors where research is seen to involve risks, temporary bans should be decided effectively, not just on paper. But that would only be a weak stopgap. What must be changed is the attitudes of contemporary men and women, of contemporary society, the conception of the goals of life, of what is important, of what we are and what we should be for each other. That's what true politics is—and in that sense the real question of our times is the political question, and the more the opposite is vociferously proclaimed, the more that is true.

# What Revolution Is

*What is irreversibly new in a revolutionary event/break? What makes it more than a mere continuation of an old legacy, as some people contend nowadays?*

First of all, it's worthwhile to dispel the confusion around the very word "revolution." Revolution doesn't mean civil war or a bloodletting. A revolution is a change in some of society's central institutions by the activity of that society itself: the explicit self-transformation of society, condensed in a short span of time. Had the king of England been better advised, the American Revolution would not have had any military or violent side; it would have been no less of a revolution. Cleisthenes' "revolution" in Athens—of which we are all still the heirs, in some sense—was not violent. The February 1917 revolution in Russia was hardly a violent one: on the second or third day, the tsar's regiments refused to fire on the crowd, and the old regime collapsed.

Revolution means that most of the community enters a phase of *political*—meaning *instituting*—activity. The social instituting imaginary goes to work and explicitly tackles the transformation of the existing institutions. Inasmuch as it encounters resistance from the previous institutions, and therefore from the established government, it understandably tackles the governmental institutions, that is, the political institutions in the narrow sense. But this awakening of the social instituting imaginary naturally calls into question all sorts of other dimensions of social life, formally instituted or not. That is in fact a requisite, since everything in society hangs together. Of course there is a risk that things will get out of hand, but that is true of *every* human action. We know what monstrosities may be committed by so-called revolutionaries driven by the illusion of the tabula rasa

---

{An interview conducted by François Dosse, on November 24, 1987, published in the periodical *EspacesTemps. Réfléchir les sciences sociales*, (1988): nos. 38–39 under the title "L'auto-constituante [The Self-Constituting Body]." Transcription by F. Dosse, reread by Castoriadis.}

and the will to control, literally, absolutely every manifestation of social life. You don't transform people's family, language, or religion by laws and decrees, even less by terror. Changes in those institutions, if they are to come about, derive from another sort of labor performed by society on itself, a process with its own rhythms, its own time frame. Revolution is a hub in this process—both the outcome and a mediation enabling the self-transformation of society to proceed.

As for the "mere continuation of an old legacy," there really is not much to discuss. No revolution is the outcome of a tabula rasa, nor can it produce a tabula rasa, even if it wants to. It is socially/historically prepared; it occurs under specific conditions, often continues already existing trends—or falls back on them. None of that allows us to do away with the moment—the moments—of social-historical creation embodied by the brief, dense figure of the revolution. You can go on repeating that the French Revolution, for instance, "only" extended and completed the centralization process already begun long ago by the Ancien Régime. Why, then, do people avoid asking what that process would have yielded, what the outcome would have been, *without* the Revolution? Can the sovereign will of the people, democracy, human rights, religious freedom, popular education, and so forth, as ideas—social imaginary significations—along with the institutions in which they were more or less successfully embodied, be reduced to a centralization process? Clearly, the idea of universality was absolutized, mechanically, so to speak, especially during the Jacobin excesses, so that the centralization process too came into its own through the Revolution. But the Revolution cannot by any means be reduced to that.

*So you don't think that 1789 was the beginning of a history of abuse leading to unavoidable terror, negating the initial ideas?*

If I had the time, I would really like to work on a few lines of thought that have apparently been overlooked, unless I'm seriously misinformed. First of all, how 1789 was prepared, in the depths of society. What part of the intellectual agitation, the ideas of "philosophers," filtered out and spread, and how that was adopted and re-elaborated by the various strata of the people, in the provinces, and so on. It's not enough to know that Robespierre had read Rousseau. We would have to reexamine the registers of grievances from that angle, with their successive formulations, look at their content in connection with what we now know about the subsequent movement, and so on. Another approach would be to study the immense institutional creation process that began in 1789 and did not stop, in fact, even under the Jacobin dictatorship. As we know, the Napoleonic Code is the outcome of all the legislative work prepared by the members of the Convention, but the same is true for the transformations in the administration, in education, in the military organization, and so on. All that was set in motion during the 1789–92 period; it was a fantastic labor of explicit self-institution of society, unequaled anywhere, to my knowledge. I think the Federation played a decisive role in that process. The country showed its will to re-institute itself, by re-composing itself on the basis of its "natural" or apparently natural constituents—that is, local communities. The Federation is a magnificent symbol of the outburst of instituting activity and of its self-symbolization. That all represents the fertile period of the Revolution. Then, as we know, a number of factors, and some internal fatality dooming all revolutions, caused the people to gradually withdraw from the scene, even the people of Paris. Long before the 9th Thermidor, the Jacobins were no longer able to muster the sections. From that point on, and because the people withdrew, an absolutist power was established, whose efforts further accentuated that withdrawal, of course.

*But can't we say that the process of mobilization of the masses is necessarily followed, here and elsewhere, by a withdrawal, a loss of impetus, a demobilization of the forces active in the revolutionary process?*

It's a fact that aside from the American and English Revolutions, and even there, the revolutions of modern times have all been beaten, or went wrong—sometimes with an even worse outcome. (Which by no means takes care of the question of their signification and effects, as already said.) And it's true, there was that withdrawal of the population, every time; to say it isn't inevitable doesn't mean it isn't meaningful, or that it doesn't raise an enormous question. That question—of the "degeneration" of the revolution or, better still, of its confiscation by groups that develop during the revolutionary process and aim at establishing their own power—has been a concern for me for forty years, and for forty years I have been writing that there is no a priori theoretical answer to it. All we can say is what should be done, generally speaking: that is, fight for institutions that enhance the possibilities of collective self-government, combat all those leanings, those tendencies going in the opposite direction. At one point in the French Revolution a split developed between the Paris assemblies (which were, moreover, soon affected by manipulations) and the rest of the country, whose participation in the process dwindled. Those are the conditions behind the Jacobin dictatorship and the Reign of Terror.

As we know, Hegel, in *The Phenomenology of Spirit*, views this as a necessary course of events: the vertigo of freedom aspiring to be absolute leads to Terror as the supreme form in which freedom is reversed, becoming its opposite. A nice philosophical demonstration—unrelated to historical effectivity or to the underlying issues of democracy as individual and collective freedom. The idea of *absolute* freedom is clearly a phantasm. But it is true that freedom knows no externally imposed limits; it cannot rest on a norm given in advance once and for all. Meaning that on the collective and political levels, as on the individual level, freedom is inseparable from risk—which risk cannot be averted by setting up a constitutional monarchy; it can be averted only by *self-limitation*. Democracy can only exist by and with self-limitation. Moreover, democracy is a tragic regime: it never guarantees a "happy end," and is always threatened by its own hubris: look at the Athenians in 413 and 406 BCE (in Sicily, and with the Arginusae).[1] But I myself am threatened by hubris, and nonetheless, I don't take refuge in slavery.

*Talking about 1789, what do you thing of the idea that "the revolution is over"?*

Let's avoid misunderstandings. I think that when François Furet wrote, "[T]he French Revolution is over," the accent is on "French." What he meant, or what I think he meant, was that the historical cycle begun in 1789 is over, and that the French people should stop playing their political combats in the disguises of 1789. But we have to look at the contemporary situation, and we must do so on a global scale. Can we imagine that all those enormous issues facing humankind right now can be solved by the existing institutions? To make that claim—and the idea that the age of revolutions, of major institutional changes, is over is tantamount to that—would actually be to claim that the political history of humanity is over. There are indeed some people who, laying the blame on metaphysics as allegedly leading to totalitarianism, and rejecting any philosophy of history, implicitly profess a metaphysics and a philosophy of history postulating that with present-day "democracy" the suitable form of political community has been found at last. Now, that "democracy" (actually, the

---

1. {On those two examples of the hubris (excess constituting a transgression) of Athenian imperialism, see Thucydides, *The Peloponnesian War*, book VI, and Xenophon, *Hellenics*, book I, chaps. VI and VII.}

liberal oligarchic regime) is far from representing any last stage of history: it is presently dying from privatization (magnificently called "individualism"), people's apathy, and the incredible deterioration in the political personnel. Moreover, those "democratic" countries represent only 12 percent of the global population—and will be down to 6 percent in twenty-five years. Whereas the same "liberal" model is visibly unable to spread everywhere, spontaneously. The great European issue, the issue of emancipation and of self-governing political communities, is still present. Some rights and freedoms have been gained, of course—gained by long battles—but those gains are qualitatively insufficient. Greece and Europe are the historical birthplaces of a project of autonomy, both social and individual. That project is far from being achieved, and its requisites are threatened again, today, by new forms of bureaucratic, manipulative domination, producing the atomization of society and feeding on it. Left to themselves, they may even gradually do away with the advances won by earlier struggles, in the long run.

*For society to be unblocked, and that creative autonomy achieved, the path is inevitably political, then?*

Not exclusively, but politics is definitely part of it. An idea has been going around, I know, for the last decade or so, according to which we should, more or less, leave the State alone and try to create "spaces of freedom" "alongside" of the State and ignoring it (and which the State would no doubt ignore, irrespective of what goes on there?). That, once again, is backing down from *the* problem of politics, which is deeply rooted in the heart of Western political philosophy: the problem of power as something collective. There is one crucial postulate: that power necessarily takes the form of a State, and there's nothing we can do about the State. That way of thinking is abysmally far from the political philosophy of the Greeks. That philosophy is not to be found in Plato and Aristotle, where, by a huge, truly laughable misunderstanding, it is usually sought: it is what is expressed in the practices and institutions of the democratic *poleis*, and in particular in those of the Athenians. Those practices make no distinction between citizens, the citizens' collective, and the "State." There is no "State." There is the *dèmos* or the *koinon* of Athenians. "Athens" for the Greeks, for Thucydides for instance, is a geographic expression, not a political one. The political entity is always designated as the Athenians, the Lacedaemonians, the Great King. But for the moderns, at least since the

17th century, the central postulate of political philosophy is the unchallengeable existence of an untouchable monster, the Leviathan, what Tocqueville calls the tutelary power. It is out of the question for society to
govern itself; it is fated to be governed by a State separate from itself. At
best, we can limit the movements of that State, that Minotaur, fencing it
in (with paper fences), periodically providing it with young boys and girls
so as to sate it for a while—that's all. None of that is changed when, once
every four, five, or seven years, that mysterious alchemy takes place by
which, on some Sunday, the government "dissolves" and is reincarnated
in the evening (is this Holy Communion?), once again becoming the "hy-
postasis" of the people, personified by its "representatives." Politics does
not and cannot yield an answer to everything—but there can be no fundamental change in society that does not encompass the dimension of power.
The present structure of power is alienating and atomizing; it relegates
everyone to private life and childishness.

*Since a complete break it is still conceivable, where can it come from? Is any
moving force perceivable?*

It is no longer meaningful to talk in terms of a moving force. For a long
time now, I have been thinking and writing that there is no privileged
bearer of the project of autonomy, no "class" destined to be hegemonic.
The problems facing our society affect 90 to 95 percent of the population.
Will that population become politically active again? I don't know, of
course, and there is no doubt that we are going through a very bleak
phase. . . .

*What do you think of the idea that the true crux of the May '68 movement lies
in the onset of individualism and hedonism?*

What is now called "individualism" is mostly what I have been calling
privatization, since 1959. It existed long before May '68. No, the May '68
movement was a reaction against that trend. Following the May interlude,
privatization flourished again, more than ever. The ideologies of the death
of the subject, and the death of meaning, which had been circulating between the rue de Lille and the rue d'Ulm[2] until then, swamped the popular
idea market then: they were forms of theorization of the failure of the
movement.

---

2. [Two meccas of Parisian intellectualism—Trans.]

*What do you think of the 1986 movement of youths in schools? Was it in continu-
ity with the 1968 movement?*

The 1986 movement was completely consonant with the spirit of present-
day society; whereas the May '68 movement called into question the contents of what was taught, the teacher-student relationship, the relations
between what is taught and life in society . . . ; nothing of the sort occurred
in 1986. Quite the opposite, students had nothing to say about the curric-
ula, never mentioned their own privileged situation, and tried to ignore
general and political problems. There was, of course, a political awareness
afterwards, of which we are glad, of course—but what remains of it? What
remains of the whole movement, all in all? Nothing—whereas the society
we live in is deeply influenced by May '68, in spite of its failure. [Writers]
Luc Ferry and Alain Renaut got the order of the figures wrong in their
book: their "'68 way of thinking"[3] is in fact the "'86 way of thinking."
The attempt, in '68, to raise the question of education, is absent in '86;
the calling into question of every social issue in '68, absent in '86; support
from the rest of society in '68, absent in '86, when the movement remained
confined to a minority. May '68 is one of the last movements to date to
partake of the great tradition of emancipatory movements in the Western
world—the question does not even arise for '86.

*What do you think of the present self-commemoration trend?*

Every society is self-commemorative—but today, the commemoration of
'89 is like [architect] Bofill's fake neo-classical buildings behind the Mon-
tparnasse railroad station. A postmodern commemoration—which is to
say, phony. The thing to do would be to use it to remind people of the
spirit and the contribution of the Great Revolution. To try to use it to
shake things up. But who will do that?

---

3. [L. Ferry and A. Renaut, *French Philosophy of the Sixties: An Essay on Antihumanism*
(Amherst: University of Massachusetts Press, 1990).—Trans.]

# Neither a Historical Necessity nor Simply an "Ethical" Exigency: A Political and Human Exigency

*In a recent interview, you say, "We see no will, in this society, as to what it wants to be tomorrow—no will other than the panicky, nagging desire to maintain what already exists today." Isn't that the ordinary state of every society?*

It almost always has been, almost everywhere, in traditional societies. It was not the case in societies in *our* tradition, in which the project of freedom, self-government, and autonomy emerged—in the democratic *poleis* of Greece and in modern Western Europe. Those societies, sparked by a project of individual and social autonomy, called their own order, their own institution into question. It is that kind of calling into question that is waning today. Of course, one may contend, as reactionary thinkers always have, that this state of apathy is desirable. Which also amounts to saying that the present state of affairs is perfect—or the least imperfect humanly attainable. It's amusing, actually, to hear that being said today by neo-liberals—including some former revolutionaries—who maintain that the search for a better society leads to totalitarianism, and that this society is in fact the best possible. Naturally, those of us who identify with their history cannot cease to struggle for another society, a free, autonomous one in which people govern themselves collectively, and where such self-government is articulated with individual autonomy. *Self-government* obviously means self-management of production and work.

Now, the broad movements of the '60s and '70s, have been followed by two mutually reinforcing trends: one toward depoliticization, with more

---

{An interview conducted by Philippe Frémeaux and Pierre Volovitch, published in *Alternatives Économiques* (January 1988), under the title "Une exigence politique et humaine [A Political and Human Exigency]."}

and deeper privatization, and the other a strong comeback of the dominant strata that have succeeded in imposing what they couldn't even dream of twenty or thirty years ago. They managed to get the population to accept an unemployment rate of 10 to 12 percent or more; in the United States, the trade unions have signed contracts in which they accept wage cuts. That's partly due to the "crisis" (thoroughly exploited to that effect), but also that "crisis" itself reflects a regression within the dominant strata, incapable of managing the system. Over and beyond the circumstantial fluctuations, these are times of decadence for Western societies, for all classes, in which everything that held them together is rapidly falling apart.

However, the present state of privatization and apathy isn't tenable for this society, in the long run. The "liberal republic," which is to say the liberal oligarchic regime, can't function permanently on cynicism and "individualism." Those people who have to make it function can't all be totally cynical, or the regime will collapse. Now, nothing in "liberal" discourse or in the "values" of our times accounts for why—barring the threat written into the Criminal Code—a judge would not put his judgment up for bids, or a president use his position to get rich. But for the Criminal Code itself to function, *honest* judges are needed. Moreover, the dominant strata no longer have any "policy." They have ongoing demagogy (in the classical sense), admirably illustrated by the television interviews with simultaneous, continuous polling, which some imbecile whose name I forget has the nerve to call the fulfillment of direct democracy.

*At its start, syndicalism wanted to abolish wage labor. Haven't present-day trade unions come to the point of demanding that wage labor be maintained? What role can today's trade unions play in advancing toward a society composed of autonomous, responsible individuals?*

It's true they called for the abolition of wage labor at first, but they soon set that aside. For a long time now, trade unions have contributed to integrating the labor force in the system. For decades now, when workers are really determined to struggle, be it in the United States, in England, or even in France and Italy, they have had to set union structures aside and invent autonomous forms of organization. There's another factor at work in the role played by the unions: it's the fantastic quantitative decline of the "conventional" proletariat within the population at large, and even, more broadly, of what used to be the combative categories of wage earners. The new jobs, when there are any, are found only in the service industries. Everywhere else we see accelerating destruction, de-industrialization, with the great traditional industrial regions wiped off the map, in entire countries. Even the United States is actually being de-industrialized. But the crisis in trade-unionism had begun long before that happened: workers had had the real-life experience of the bureaucratic, conservative transformation of the unions.

*What social forces hold the promise of an alternative at present? Or is it the very idea of a link between an alternative and some definite social forces that is mistaken?*

That idea is in effect mistaken, at least for modern societies. It is out of the question today to claim that the "proletariat" is historically destined to transform society, now that the proletariat is becoming a small minority, or that the "wage earners" have that role, since almost everyone is a wage earner nowadays. At present, if we are to transform society, the whole population must participate, and the entire population may be sensitized to that exigency—except perhaps some 3 to 5 percent of diehards. Another mistaken idea must be stressed, one that is deeply anchored in the "left": the idea that the poor are politically/historically on the right side. That's part of our Christian heritage. Logic and historical experience show that the very idea is absurd, and that the true "poor people" are rather inclined to kowtow to the dominant classes.

*So there is no longer any group capable of constituting itself nowadays. . . .*

It's true that the issue may be put in universal terms today. The example of May '68 is very striking in that respect. The most active students were immersed in an archaic ideology, according to which they were nobodies; they had to galvanize the working class, parade around the factories, and so on, whereas most of the working class was still shackled to the CP and Communist-dominated CGT [Confédération Générale du Travail] union. At the same time, by their very movement, the students were showing that the most radical, most important demands were no longer supported by the working class but by themselves and by the other strata that took action at the time.

*But if there isn't any historical necessity any more, what defines the left, aside from an ethical exigency?*

It isn't only an "ethical" exigency, it's a political and human exigency: I want to be free; I want to be responsible, to participate in the decisions that affect me; I don't want my fate to be decided by others.

*The market economy ideology, and business, may also be positive values, values of self-assertiveness, and individuality, and correspond to the demand for autonomy. Maybe your pessimism isn't justified.*

I am not pessimistic; I try to understand what is going on, and I discover that the social fabric and the values that held it together are falling apart. The "individualistic values" you're talking about are illusory. Bernard Tapie[1] has "succeeded," but only one out of fifty thousand people can be a Tapie, by definition, since we are living and will continue to live in an economy based on large productive units. Take the idea, "I'll get myself a little shop and I don't give a damn about society." But society gives a damn about you; it imposes all sorts of things on you: pollution, noise, taxes, war, maybe. "Individualism" is infantilism. In no other society I know of are people as immersed in society as they are today. People in fifteen million homes are pressing the same buttons at the same time to see the same thing. What a laugh!

*Isn't that one of the things that makes the present consumer society so strong?*

That's absolutely obvious. I'm not pessimistic, as you said earlier, but the situation really is serious. What's going on isn't going on behind society's back: people want this kind of consumerism, this kind of life; they want to spend so many hours a day in front of their TV set and to play with their home computers. There's more involved than mere "manipulation" by the system and by the firms it benefits. There's a huge, very coherent, very gradual trend: people become depoliticized, privatized, they turn inward toward their little "private" sphere, and the system provides them with the means of doing so. And what they find in that "private" sphere diverts them even more from being responsible and politically active.

---

1. [Bernard Tapie is an unorthodox, self-made businessman (one-time owner of Adidas and president of a prestigious football club, among others), media darling, and member of the Socialist Party at the time. His claim to fame was a televised pre-electoral encounter with the excellent debater and extreme right-winger Jean-Marie Le Pen, in which he was perceived as having won. He was the only prominent Socialist to agree to debate with Le Pen.—Trans.]

*The strength of liberalism lies in the fact that in this society, consumption is one way of expressing freedom through the possibility of choice; in comparison with that, the project of a different society seems totalitarian. How can consumerism be criticized today in a way that effectively rejects the terrifying side of present-day consumerism without being a throwback to authoritarian regulation of consumption?*

An autonomous society is a society in which the consumer is truly *sovereign*. The kind of mere "freedom" of consumers they talk about today is the possibility of choosing between the goods proposed (but even that isn't true, actually). Whereas when consumers are sovereign, they can say (and nowadays this can only be true collectively, essentially): what I want is such-and-such goods. The same is true politically. There too, there is no true freedom without sovereignty. Sovereignty would mean, for instance, that consumers could say, "I don't want a city that is constantly jammed with traffic, constantly defaced by cars; I want public transportation, or another kind of car, or the collective management of cars."

*Behind what you are saying, isn't there the idea that the market in itself isn't a bad thing, but what is bad is a number of social conditions, inequalities, and so on?*

Of course. Free-market economics depicts the market as a consumer "voting" place. That vote is rigged, obviously: the "vote" of some magnate who wants his own jet weighs a million times more than the vote of someone who is out of work, or of a starving immigrant. On the other hand, there is the absurd Marxist idea that the market as such—commodities as such—"personifies" alienation. That's absurd because interpersonal relations in an extended society can't be "personal" the way they are in a family. They are always, and always will be, socially mediated. In any even slightly developed economy that mediation is called the *market* (exchange, in other words). Provided a number of givens are established, as I have shown in *On the Content of Socialism*[2] the market can become a sort of ongoing referendum, ratifying or canceling decisions on what to produce. Neo-liberal discourse contends the market does that right now—and it doesn't, in reality.

---

2. In *Political and Social Writings*, vol. 1: *1946–1955: From the Critique of Bureaucracy to the Positive Content of Socialism* (Minneapolis: University of Minnesota Press, 1988).

# When the East Swings to the West

*For a long time you contended that there is no going back on a communist regime once it has been established. Gorbachev seems to be proving you wrong.*

I was very surprised by Gorbachev's coming into power, by his ability to stay there and to make a number of changes. My vision of what bureaucracy is made me exclude that. But the extremely improbable does happen sometimes. Second, the event must be interpreted. I think a fraction of the ruling strata clearly realized that they could no longer resist Western pressure, the relative rearmament, or massive armament of the United States, with such a decrepit economy. The military people must have increasingly felt the need for a civilian industry functioning as efficiently as the military-industrial apparatus. Everything we learn these days actually corroborates, and more than corroborates, what I was saying in *Devant la guerre*.[1] In an interview with the newspaper *Le Monde*, Sakharov says the working-class population receives less than 30 percent of the national product. Where does the rest go? It can't go entirely to dachas and caviar for the bureaucracy. Also, military spending is still rising by 3 percent annually, whereas American military spending has leveled off or declined since 1985. In this respect Gorbachev's very astute foreign policy not only gives him enormous publicity but it also enables him to placate his military-industrial establishment by beginning to prepare the redeployment of military spending, and by shifting from quantity to quality.

---

{An interview conducted by Jean-François Duval, published under the title "Quand l'Est bascule vers l'Ouest" in *Construire* 44 (November 1, 1989). *Construire* is published by the Swiss cooperative Migros.}

1. [*Devant la guerre:* vol. 1: *Les Réalités*, 1st ed. (Paris: Librairie Arthème Fayard, 1982; 2nd ed., 1983). An article on the same subject, originally published as "Devant la guerre (I)" in *Libre* 8 (1980): 217–50, was published in English as "Facing the War," *Telos* 46 (Winter 1980–81): 43–61.]

But that's not all. As happens periodically in Russia, those ruling strata also want to become more civilized, more Westernized. They are well aware of the tremendous gap between life in Russia and life here. In that sense, Gorbachev is a sort of tsar with a civilizing mission. But is there any chance that the road he has chosen will go somewhere? There is talk about *self*-reform, but look at what's happening in Hungary. What will happen there in the coming years if no outside pressure is exerted (aside from its membership in the Warsaw pact)? It will become a capitalist, parliamentary republic. Things are slightly less clear in Poland. Nonetheless, the system isn't being reformed in either case; it's collapsing. What we have in the USSR is not reform but continuous backing down from the system without the features of a new system in sight, in spite of some huge changes such as *glasnost*, elections, the new Supreme Soviet, parliamentary debates on TV, and so on. For the time being, the regime—which ceased to be truly totalitarian after Stalin's death—is clearly moving toward a sort of very moderate absolutism, with an autocrat, Gorbachev, who does what he likes while allowing a lot of things to be decided by the Supreme Soviet.

But what does the future have in store? There's no need to enumerate all the enormous existing problems—the different nationalities, Eastern Europe, the political regime, and so forth. The great unknown is the economy, of course. And from that standpoint the situation is growing worse by the hour, with no solution in sight. When they say there will be two, three or four hard years, those are empty words. I don't see what will change in two or four years if they continue on the present course.

*There is talk about the end of communism. But replaced by what? Do you think they are unable to imagine the future, and to establish truly new institutions for themselves?*

That's the crucial point. I've always thought that a revolution, in the true, full sense of the term, is not only not excluded in Russia, but it is one probable prospect. I can't see a lasting relapse to a Brezhnev-type regime, at any rate. But in what sense could Gorbachev's reforms succeed, since in the most difficult area, the economy, we don't even see what he wants and what the content is? When a society is faced with urgent, seemingly insoluble problems, we have the definition of a pre-revolutionary situation. No-one sees any solution; everyone knows there has to be one; and an explosion occurs. There are no signs of that for the time being, except for the miners' strike, where they showed remarkable organizational capacities and abnegation.

If society does resuscitate in that way, the question is whether its political imagination will be awakened. What I find striking and saddening in the evolution of the Eastern countries, however much I rejoice at the collapse of communism of course, is the total lack of political creations—however much we admire people's tactical genius in Poland and Hungary, and their success against regimes which are military dictatorships. But when they go on to reconstruct society, what do we see? They revert to the allegedly well-tried recipes of free-market capitalism: the market, parliament, and so on. There are no new ideas. They are as short of ideas as in the West. Now, institutions are the work of human creativity, the work of the radical imaginary that founds every society. If the Hebrews lived to worship God and we live to increase the gross national product, it's not because of nature, the economy, sexuality, or other. Those are primary imaginary positions, fundamental ones that make life meaningful.

*That's one of your main ideas.*

Absolutely. Political discourse is terrifyingly empty in our society. Neoliberal discourse is empty: it's a second-rate, hackneyed version of what the great liberals of the past were saying. The socialists have nothing to say. There's a political regime they call democracy, but which is not democracy. Any classical political philosopher would have said that those regimes are oligarchies. It's the same people, not even 1 percent of the population, who govern and are co-opted in almost hereditary fashion. The hereditary transmission of money, positions and relations is still enormously important. Our political system is what I call a liberal oligarchy. The requisite for and effect of which is apathy toward public life, and the vanishing of any true conflict, be it social or political. Social conflicts have become purely corporatist. The population votes every five years, and rights things a bit if some leaders go too far. It can dismiss them and replace them by others, but those others are just the same. We're seeing that in France, and it should soon be seen in England, now that Thatcher is gone, and replaced by the Labour Party.

*As we know, people have deserted the institutions, the systems, the political parties. . . .*

What has been called individualism, hedonism, narcissism, and so on, all misnomers, is attended by an essentially cynical attitude. But it's ridiculous

to talk about individualism when people in twenty million homes are turning the same switch at eight o'clock every evening, to watch the same
program. No! What we have is historically unprecedented *privatization*, as
I have been calling it for the last thirty years. Which is to say, the pursuit
of trivial pleasures in a world devoid of projects and prospects other than
people's petty individual well-being—what I call consumerist, televisual
onanism. That's all it is.

Given this state of affairs, people's attitude toward institutions is unclear: they are both tolerant and constantly making demands. We are
not the State, but as soon as a problem arises we turn to it, and that goes
hand in hand with the corporatism I mentioned. Ours is a *lobby* and *hobby*
society. It's as if society were a soup, or a mayonnaise gone bad: what
holds it all together no longer depends on people's being active in a
comprehensive whole with which they are concerned. Make as much
money as you can and try to be seen on TV, that's the philosophy and
morality of the system. What kind of individual, of human being, can
that produce? The fact is, it does work like that, with a pseudo-market
dominated by monopolistic firms and fantastic state intervention, since
in every country the State controls 50 percent of the national product,
directly or indirectly. It works, but for how long? We mustn't forget that
capitalism's huge success rests, among other things, on the irreversible
destruction of the biological resources accumulated on earth over a period of three billion years. That's a sort of wall against which we are
being hurled at top speed.

*What you want, fundamentally, is a social body capable of doing self-analytic,
elucidating work similar to that of the patient on the psychoanalyst's couch . . .*

That's quite correct, although I don't really like that sort of comparison.
The two are deeply akin, however. True democracy was born in the Western world precisely as an attempt at self-government, that is, as people
making their own law. But to do so, society must incorporate an enormous
dose of reflexive thinking, of reflection on itself. True democracy is the
regime of reflexive thinking. That doesn't mean it's a regime of absolute
knowledge or of transparency. It may make mistakes, as we all can, however much we reflect on things. But we don't act randomly; we try to be
careful. We deliberate with ourselves. True democracy is a reflexive regime
because it's a deliberative regime. It implies the liberation of collective
activity, and passion for public affairs. Also, for any truly democratic regime to be established, that activity and that passion would have to be

sweepingly deployed. Now, we don't see any signs of that (except during the '60s and '70s). The fact is particularly terrifying since we're running up against a block of granite, the ecological impasse. If humankind doesn't react, and get a grip on itself, there's a serious risk that it will then end up with a totalitarian regime.

*What about Europe?*

Any attempt to go beyond the nation-state is a good thing. But we can't approve the capitalist, bureaucratic form it is taking right now.

# The Market, Capitalism, and Democracy

*One increasingly hears people on the left say, "If the plan doesn't work, then we'll have to go back to the market. A complex modern society requires impersonal forms of mediation, impersonal forms of collective regulation"—in short, in Habermas's terms, there is a distinction between system and lifeworld. Habermas argues that, although systems should ultimately be controlled by the lifeworld, we can't abolish the system as such. There will always be a market and some forms of administrative-bureaucratic regulation of society. That's the basis of his critique of Marx: that Marx has some notion of collapsing all social relations back into the immediacy of the lifeworld. Much of your inspiration seems to come, albeit indirectly, from the early Marx. Where does your concept of autonomy place you in this debate?*

Marx was certainly wrong in thinking that all impersonal mediations should be abolished. Yet that is what is behind his critique of the commodity, and also of money. I broke with that position as early as 1957 in a text for the review *Socialisme ou Barbarie* called "The Content of Socialism," which is in my *Political and Social Writings*.[1] It's quite obvious: you can't have a complex society without, for instance, impersonal means of exchange. Money has that function and is very important in that respect. It's another thing to deprive money of one of its functions in capitalist and pre-capitalist economies: that of an instrument for the personal accumulation of wealth and for the acquisition of means of production. As a unit of value and as a means of exchange, money is a great invention, one of humanity's great creations. We are living in a society; there is an anonymous

---

{Excerpts from an interview with Peter Dews and Peter Osborne at the University of Essex in February 1990, published in *Radical Philosophy* 56 (Autumn 1990): 35–43.} [The present text is a revised version taking the French translation into consideration.—Trans.]

1. *Political and Social Writings*, vol. 1: *1946–1955: From the Critique of Bureaucracy to the Positive Content of Socialism* (Minneapolis: University of Minnesota Press, 1988).

collectivity; we express our needs and preferences by being willing to spend so much on one particular item, and not on some other one. I don't see that as a problem. But you have to be very careful when talking about the "market," you know. To return to that text from 1957, I said that the socialist society will be the first society to have a genuine market, because a capitalist market is not a market. A capitalist market isn't a market, not only if you compare it with the manuals of political economy, where the market is transparent and where capital is a sort of fluid moving from one area of production to another instantaneously because profits are bigger there—that's all nonsense—but also because prices there have practically nothing to do with costs. In an autonomous society you will have a genuine market in the sense both of the abolition of all monopolistic and oligopolistic positions, and of a correspondence between the prices of goods and the actual social costs.

*But will you have a market in labor-power?*

That is, indeed, problematic. My position is that you can't have a market in labor-power in the sense that you can't have an autonomous society if you maintain a hierarchy of salaries, wages and incomes. If you do maintain that hierarchy, then you retain all the motivations of capitalism, of *homo economicus*, and all the old hodgepodge starts again.

*Won't that undermine the market?*

I don't see why. There are no economic and rational grounds on which I can say, "One hour of this man's work is worth three times that of some other man's work." Here lies the whole problem of the critique of value theory, and the critique of what underlies value theory, which is the idea that the result of production can be imputed to this and that other factor, in a definite way. But actually, no such imputation is possible. The product is always a social product and a historical product. You always have to consider that whatever imputation of costs you do, it's a relative imputation, geared to social needs and geared to the future—although it must of course have some relation to historical costs and reality. But there can be no rational or even simply reasonable justification for any differential labor costs. That's apparently a very hard point to swallow.

*So you don't think that there is any rationality to the capitalistic distribution of social labor through the wage relation, in terms of productivity? It's purely political?*

Exactly. The present distribution of income, both between groups and between individuals, is the sheer outcome of a struggle of forces. Nothing else. Naturally, this creates problems in relation to workplace discipline, for example. If the workers' collective is not capable of establishing enough solidarity and discipline to have everybody working according to some accepted collective rules, we reach the political hard core of the problem. There is nothing to do, in that case: no more than there is in the field of political democracy, if people are not willing to be responsible for the decisions of the collectivity, to participate actively and so on. Which doesn't mean you have to maintain bureaucratic and hierarchical structures in production—on the contrary. The division of tasks and the division of power are two different things.

I spent a lot of my time trying to analyze the functioning of capitalist factories, and I came to the conclusion that capitalist planning of production in the factory is absurd, half of the time. Factories work because the workers transgress the capitalist organization of production. They work against the rules, or at a distance from the rules, so production can go on. If they were to apply the rules, production would stop immediately. The proof is that "working to rule" is one of the most efficient ways of bringing it to a standstill. So much for the capitalist organization of production. As soon as you have hierarchy, you have this fundamental opacity in the production sphere, because you have the division between those who manage and those who execute, the order-givers and the order-takers. By virtue of their position, the workers have to hide what is going on from the eyes of the directors. This reaches delirious proportions in a fully bureaucratic society, but it's the case practically everywhere. It's up to the collective to make the basic decisions. It can delegate, but it elects its delegates and can revoke them if it likes.

*This will entail very high levels of political culture and activism.*

Yes, people have to feel fully responsible, there's no doubt about that. You cannot have a truly democratic collectivity, involving not only self-management of production, but also the purely political level, unless people are really active. But we shouldn't fetishize this: one can think of institutions that facilitate this participation. Today, to be responsible, to attempt to participate, you would have to be heroic twenty-four hours a day. We have to create a situation whereby you can participate without being heroic twenty-four hours a day.

*This would mean a reduction of working time.*

Certainly. But that would occur for other reasons, too. What is working time spent on? In the United States, production doubled between 1939 and 1942. And actually, workers were probably spending only about four hours doing their job. The rest of the time they were playing the numbers, or playing cards, or "working for the government," as they say—"Leave me alone; I'm working for the government." That meant he was doing something to be taken home. In France they call it *"la perruque."* And in Russia, you know the tremendous extent of it. I would argue that under different conditions of participation of the workers, present output could be reached in four or six hours instead of eight.

*Would it be true to say that you are in favor of what is sometimes called indicative planning, via some general democratic framework at a social level?*

More than indicative. I don't think there is a contradiction between market and planning in this respect. In an autonomous society one must have a true market, not just with consumer freedom, but with consumer sovereignty. Consumers, in the day-to-day vote represented by their purchases, are the ones who must decide which specific items are produced for consumption, *with everyone having an equal vote.* Today, Mr. Trump's vote is worth one million votes of the average American. That's not what I mean by a true market. But you have to have general decisions about at least two things: the apportionment of the national product, or national income, between consumption in general and investment in general, and the respective shares of private consumption and public consumption within the mass of consumption. How much society decides to devote to education, to roads, to erecting monuments, to all public endeavors, and how much it decides that individuals are free to spend as they like. You need a collective decision about this. You have to have proposals and discussions, and the implications of decisions must be made clear to everyone.

In this sense, you must have planning, because the implications of the decisions about investment and consumption have to be foreseen. If you decide that you will have a given amount of investment, that defines, more or less, the levels of consumption you can count on for the coming years. If you want more investment, then you will have to consume less. But maybe you will be able to consume more in five years' time. If you want more education, you can't have it for nothing. You will have to devote resources to education, and you have to decide where you take these resources from. Do you take them from private consumption? Or do you take them from investment, which is to say from the future growth of productive facilities? Do you care about any future growth of productive ability, or do you just want to renew the existing capital? All this has to be brought to the forefront, and cannot reasonably be decided by market forces.

*This sounds like the kind of debate currently taking place in the Soviet Union.*

In a sense, yes. But I don't accept that idea of Habermas's that because you have to have the system you must accept a degree of alienation or heteronomy. I don't say that you can be master of everything. You can't control everything. That's not the problem. The point is that you can always look back, always change things, and establish mechanisms whereby the functioning of society is made controllable by people, though certainly not fully transparent. . . .

# "Democracy" without Citizens' Participation

*Whenever the question of present-day democracy is broached, what is meant is always parliamentary democracy, be it praised or criticized. That doesn't take us very far. Can you help us take that interrogation further, toward the participatory democracy form, for example?*

I personally prefer to speak of *direct democracy*. Nothing is possible if citizens don't participate in public life; that's self-evident. But it doesn't suffice to repeat: participation, participation. The question is, Why on earth would citizens participate? If they aren't participating now, there must be reasons.

*It's because nobody asks them to in a parliamentary democracy. Plus the fact that most people don't think they are free to do so.*

As Rousseau said, speaking about the English, they are only free on election day. But are they even free on that day? The dice are loaded, the pseudo-options have been predetermined by the political parties—and they are empty, to boot. What "programs" do political parties have today, in France, England or elsewhere?

*Perhaps, indeed, the differences aren't very clear. So, speaking about contemporary democracy . . .*

It is organized, construed to make it *impossible in fact* for citizens to participate. After which politicians come wailing about their crisis in representativeness. Look, Mr. Fabius, the Socialist, is now lamenting over a bunch of unknown continents he has discovered: people are privatized; citizens have lost interest; his party's "program" is empty. Or take those socialist

---

{An interview conducted by Anne-Brigitte Kern, published in *Transversales Sciences/ Culture* 7 (February 1991) under the title "Où en sommes-nous de la démocratie? [Democracy: Where Are We At?]."}

parliamentary representatives who describe the void in contemporary "politics," including in their own party, only to conclude by inciting us to firmly uphold "the [socialist] President's political line."[1] Ridicule hasn't killed anyone for a long time in this country.

*Citizens think there's nothing they can do about that state of affairs.*

Within the present regime it's true; there's nothing they can do. For people to participate, they must have the conviction, constantly corroborated, that their participation or their abstention will make a difference. And that is possible only if they are participating in making effective decisions that affect their lives.

*But that can't be done by isolated individuals. Only collectivities are in a position to support action that leads to decisions.*

Definitely. Participation must be rooted, first of all, in places where people are led to join together, whether they like it or not. Those places exist, formally at least. They are workplaces, public services, municipalities, and large city neighborhoods, for instance.

*You say "formally." Which suggests that doesn't go without saying.*

That's right. Bureaucratic capitalism, which governs the business world and all of social life, as well as the overall evolution of our culture—what I call the instituted social imaginary—tends either to destroy the places where people traditionally socialize and join together or else to turn them into empty shells. Bureaucratic-hierarchical structures destroy any kind of solidarity. Our culture is frantically driving individuals into privatization, leading them not only to lose interest in the affairs of the community but also to view others as objects or potential enemies preventing them from moving forward in the overall traffic jam. Nonetheless, it must be said that the establishment of a true democracy makes tremendous demands on everyone.

*Because it brings individual autonomy into play. . . .*

It postulates that individuals are autonomous, which is to say lucid, reflexively thinking and responsible. It also postulates that individuals realize, contrary to the mystifications circulated by liberalism,[2] that their fate is

---

1. In the French daily newspaper *Le Monde*, December 11, 1990 (a "Manifesto" written by twelve socialist parliamentary representatives).
2. [See note 1 (page 127) in the chapter "Present Issues for Democracy."]

radically tied to everyone else's, that they are part of the same planet as their fellow creatures, and that they and their fellow creatures are presently destroying it.

*But so many of the issues facing the community seem abstract. Since people don't understand them, they think it's unavoidable that they be excluded from decision-making.*

That's the illusion of technicality, the *illusion of the expert appraisal*. But countless absurd decisions have been made by experts, or on their recommendation, over the last thirty years, including the Villette slaughterhouse project and the national electricity company's over-equipment in nuclear plants. We have, or soon will have, specialists capable of modifying the human genome. Should we let them decide about that? Specialists almost always disagree among themselves; they aren't the ones who decide. When people in charge want an "expert opinion" with a given orientation, they can always find specialists to produce the report they need. I don't think the French people would have voted for the construction of "sniffer planes,"[3] had there been a referendum. You had to have studied at the best engineering school and be a great specialist in economics, like President Giscard d'Estaing, to swallow that.

Technological progress would make it possible to have expert appraisal serve democracy. Wide-ranging public debates could be organized, in which democratically controlled specialists would lay out the feasible options, for example, with the main arguments for each one, and their respective implications and consequences. That way people could decide knowledgeably, instead of suffering from the effects of decisions taken in their absence and perfectly opaquely, as happens today. But all that assumes a radical change in a great many of this society's structures.

*Starting with the educational system in which you still only learn to obey. . . .*

Obedience *and* anarchy, *one or the other, one and the other*, which brings us back to some essential features of the crisis in Western culture. Successive ministers of education each produce a "reform" of the educational system, programs are endlessly—and very superficially—being reworked, and it all

---

3. {In on the basis of unreliable reports, the firm Elf signed a several-hundred-million-franc contract for the purchase of a patent on a device supposed to enable planes, known as "sniffer planes," to detect oilfields from afar.}

amounts to zero. Why is the educational system falling apart? There are three basic factors, which are never mentioned. First, there can be no education if pupils aren't interested in learning and in what there is to learn. Right now, no-one is capable of addressing that question. The only real answer is a ridiculous one: with that piece of paper you will be able to find work—which isn't even true. So schools become factories producing certificates of vocational aptitude. Second, there's the question of teachers. Teaching isn't just any old job, a job to "make a living." To teach is to succeed in getting children to learn to love the fact of learning, and to do so you have to love to teach and to love children. You can't transmit anything if you are not possessed by those two loves, and if you are not able to inspire love.

*The fashioning of a human being, of a citizen, begins at school. That's where you learn to understand, to make choices . . .*

Definitely. Which brings me to the third point. To make choices requires the ability to get one's bearings and to have a hierarchy of values. *Where are those values in today's society?* Where are they, in a society for which the only actual, affirmed value is money, and which is incoherent, even with respect to that, since it pays the computer scientists it needs thirty or forty thousand francs a month as soon as they get their diploma, whereas it pays their professors only fifteen thousand? Who will become a professor of mathematics in the future? And what will make a judge, who may have to decide cases involving hundreds of millions, stay honest?

*If we follow the American model in every respect . . .*

But we do. As Marx said about England in his day, it's the mirror in which we can see our future. The American elementary and secondary school system is in a pitiful state, as we know. It used to be very partially made up for by the university system. And now, statistics show that those universities, with their wonderful libraries, the best laboratories one could dream of, and so forth, have to recruit almost a majority of foreign professors, along with foreign postgraduate students. The United States is not even capable of producing its own cultural elite.

    This is all to say that the issue of democracy goes beyond politics. It's a comprehensive question. Society is dominated by a mad race, defined by three terms: *technoscience, bureaucracy, and money.* If nothing stops it, democracy will increasingly be out of the question. Privatization, indifference, and egoism will be all-pervasive, with a few savage explosions of those who are in the excluded minority and are unable to express themselves politically.

*But the capitalists' and bureaucrats' dream of controlling things, of complete mastery of the system, doesn't come true!*

That's obvious. The more we extend partial skills and partial achievements, the more we have overall *non-power*. No-one dominates or controls the situation.

*Maybe that's humankind's fortune, our chance to achieve greater wisdom. . . .*

We do need wisdom, and we need the will.

# The Gulf War: Setting Things Straight

We must refuse to ask whether or not the war should have been waged as long as we have no clear vision of the nature of the conflict, the real motives on both sides and the potential effects of the foreseeable outcomes.

Saddam Hussein doesn't give a damn about the Palestinians or about the Koran. Both came to his mind when he had to find allies fast, after the violent reactions aroused by his annexation of Kuwait. He conquered Kuwait for strictly territorial, financial and power-related goals. Kuwait's borders are artificial, but so are Iraq's and those of every other country in the region (and many others as well). Saddam didn't attack Iran in 1980 to free the Palestinians, but to aggrandize his territory and his resources, and to get the Western world and the Soviet Union to arm him to the teeth. He doesn't represent the poor against the rich, or the South against the North. He rules over a naturally rich country that he has ruined to arm himself and to maintain a regime of terror. He cuts his opponents to pieces, and gasses the Kurd minority. Only "progressives" are prepared to forget all that because Saddam beautifully completes the collection of oppressors (Stalin, Mao, Castro, Pol Pot, and so on) they have always upheld so fervently.

The Western countries talk about "law." What a strange thing it is to uphold law, and human rights, in the company of Assad and King Fahd. They also talk about "international law." That infinitely elastic law was and still is left in abeyance where the West Bank, Lebanon, Cyprus, Grenada, or Panama is concerned. No-one is opposed to the self-determination of the Kuwaiti. But one should also demand the self-determination of the Palestinians, then, and of the Kurds (massacred simultaneously by Saddam, the Iranians, and our allies, the Turks), the people from Timor, and from some vague Baltic countries, Armenia, Georgia, and so forth.

---

{Published in the newspaper *Libération*, February 5, 1991, under the title "La guerre du Golfe mise à plat."}

The West also says that they could not allow Saddam to become uncontrollably powerful, or he would have ended up directly or indirectly (by dictating prices) controlling much of the world's oil resources, dominating the Middle East, and attacking Saudi Arabia and/or Israel. But if Iraq actually is crushed, that will set up an even more formidable regional superpower, Iran, and make Syria, with its sights on Lebanon and its score to settle with Israel, even more threatening.

The true goals of the United States have very little to do with oil, contrary to claims: when the price exceeds twenty-five dollars a barrel, other sources of energy become profitable in the middle term. Those goals mostly express their (very shortsighted) determination to impose their "order." That means crushing Iraq. Suppose they succeed. The result will be even greater chaos in the region and in all Muslim countries (Turkey aside, for the time being). The idea that an "International Conference" could solve anything whatsoever is a fairy tale. Hatred and resentment not only of Arabs but also of Muslims (look at Pakistan, right now) are at fever pitch as of now. Whatever comes next, Saddam will be—he already is—turned into a hero. That's what makes religious fanaticism akin to paranoid systems: if you win, you owe your triumph to God; if you lose, he offers you the crown of martyrdom. The effects would have been very much equivalent if they had allowed Saddam to swallow up Kuwait. The West was and still is trapped in a trap it set up by arming Saddam, letting the Palestinian conflict degenerate, and so on. It is now creating a situation the abominable effects of which will be felt for decades.

Fanaticism has reached a point where even someone such as the Algerian Aït Ahmed,[1] who probably thinks otherwise in private, feels obliged, when speaking on the Europe 1 radio station, to give every possible proof of his "Arabism." Characteristically, the few Arab intellectuals who seemed to earnestly value criticism and reflection until now are presently actively contributing to a mythologized version of Arab history in which the Arabs have been doves, white as snow, over the last thirteen centuries, and all their ills have been inflicted on them by Western colonization. (It's surely Wall Street that caused them to be enslaved by their brothers in religion, the Turks, for four centuries? It's Western imperialism that explains why they now maintain, in one case the Kurds, in another the Berbers, and in the case of Mauritanian Arabs the Black people in their country, in slavery?)

---

1. [Aït Ahmed, a key figure in Algeria's revolutionary fight against France for the country's freedom, and still very active on the Algerian political scene, is not only not an Arab nationalist, by any means, but is a Kabyle, which is to say, not an "Arab," from Algeria, considered an "Arab" country.—Trans.]

The Palestinians are still the losers. Arab solidarity is a joke, at the State level. Not only do all of the Arab governments care nothing about the Palestinians, but it's in all of their interest that the Palestinian problem not be solved. For only a few dollars in some cases, or empty words in others, those corrupt regimes get themselves, for cheap, a diabolical foreign enemy on which to deflect the passion and hatred of their people. Israel doesn't want to give the territories back, and will never do so voluntarily. Had it wanted to, that would be done by now. The quibbling over whether or not the PLO [Palestine Liberation Organization] is representative is all right for the Middle Eastern bazaars. Internationally monitored elections in the territories would have shown who is representative and who isn't. What the Israeli "right" wants, and the "left" doesn't dare to refuse, really, is the definitive annexation of the right bank of the Jordan, the stepping-stone to a greater "great Israel." The absolutely exorbitant nature of that goal makes no difference. The Western world is unable to understand what nationalism backed by religion (in both the Israeli and the Arabs) can be, although they themselves were deep into it only three decades or three centuries ago.

Then there's the techno-military illusion, electronic warfare and an instant, fake, "Nescafé" victory: twenty days after the onslaught, the Iraqis are still able to shoot down a few of the coalition's planes, and an Iraqi army column penetrates, unseen for dozens of hours, thirty kilometers into Saudi Arabia. Maybe a bunch of Iraqi colonels will put lead into Saddam one of these days, or his foot soldiers in Kuwait will disband. But maybe (and much more probably), the Iraqis will resist for a long time. Strategists were in a hurry to proclaim that Iraq isn't Vietnam, and that the bombs would bring the Iraqis to their knees for want of a jungle in which to hide. Once again, the strategists have committed their favorite imbecility: they have forgotten about people. The jungle and the desert aren't the same, but barring proof to the contrary, Iraq and Vietnam have one decisive thing in common: both have a great mass of men ready to die rather than surrender (whether their "reasons" are mad or not makes no difference). When they will have to extract the Iraqis from their shelters with a toothpick, and the number of victims on the coalition side begins to rise sharply, it will be sociologically interesting to study the trend in public opinion, both in the West and in North Africa.

With few exceptions, Western intellectuals haven't done much better than their Muslim colleagues so far. The vast majority say nothing. Among those who do speak out, there are those who give in to the blackmail of "Arabism," "Islam," "the West's guilt," or give vent to their stupid hatred of the United States whatever it does, or even to their shameful fascination with tyrants and brutal force. The others, obsessed by the absolute horror inspired by Saddam, his regime, and the fanaticism he galvanizes, prefer not to dwell on the motivations and aims behind the war in the Western countries, their shameful alliances, the hypocrisy of evoking "law," the way Bush pressed forward full steam toward the war, and the intolerable practices and attitudes of the Israeli government.

Whereas, as has rightly been said, one of the main victims of the war is any chance (slight to begin with) of having democracy and secularism in the Muslim world, the war also sheds harsh light on the functioning of that famous Western "democracy." As was to be expected, the "executive" has "executed" everything, and the role of citizens in defining the ends and the means has been nil. They'll say that the polls show there is popular support for government policy. What a joke! A few days before the hostilities began, the polls contended that more than three-fourths of the French people thought that "no cause, however just, justifies resorting to war." That's a monstrous position: had that lofty principle been systematically enforced, those very same French people would still be serfs, doing their master's bidding. Never mind: the government didn't give a darn about that finding. For good reason: a few days after the hostilities began, more than two-thirds of those same French people approved of the war. That about-face can't be due to some further thinking on the subject (all the information was already available early in January) or to the artificiality of polling. It's sad to say: people sided enthusiastically with the winners, in their fascination for the big American airlifted, electronic penis. This "democracy" fashions that kind of "citizens."

By now the conflict has greatly exceeded the case of Iraq and Saddam Hussein. It's on the way to turning into a confrontation between societies in which the religious imaginary is still tenacious and even being strengthened in reaction, and Western societies which have more or less successfully rid themselves of that imaginary but have turned out to be incapable of transmitting anything other than techniques for warfare and for the manipulation of public opinion to the rest of the world. Both parties have their share in that incapacity. What is important for us is that the present state of our society makes it unable to exert any influence other than material. A society that worships consumerism and zapping on TV cannot erode the anthropological hold of the Koran or of Hinduism. Peoples who are at a loss in the modern world and adhere tensely to their religious identity can't find any example worth imitating or any incitement to think for themselves in those apathetic citizens, huddled up in their petty private worlds, who leave government to the political, economic, and cultural oligarchies, to the party apparatuses and the mass media.

So what should we do? Should we get another people, as they say? Of course not. Should we get people to change? But who can do that? People themselves have to change, as a people. Everyone can contribute to that change, all of us, within ourselves and around us whenever we can speak out. Without that change, there will be only false answers to monstrously wrongly posed problems.

# Gorbachev: Neither Reform nor Backtracking

*In 1987 you wrote a paper, "The Gorbachev Interlude,"[1] in which you clearly showed how a top-down reform was a blind alley in the Soviet Union. That has turned out to be quite true.*

To be fair, I thought at the time that Gorbachev would be unable to relinquish the empire abroad. But he had to. In countries like East Germany and Hungary, the attempts to make minor reforms were dismal failures: he was ultimately forced to withdraw, and the Red Army had to consent. Why? Because the Russian ruling classes came to the realization that they had bit off more than they could chew. So they had their backs against the wall. Conversely, I was right about the impossibility of any in-depth reform of the Russian economy. Now that the totalitarian imaginary, the Marxist-Leninist ideology, has totally fallen to pieces, what do we see, coming out of the present chaos? The only thing that holds water is what the papers call the military-industrial complex, which is what I called the stratocratic elements of Soviet society: the army, the KGB, the steel-devourers.

Since the government was reshuffled last January [1991], four extremely important new positions are occupied by high-ranking members of the military industry. The KGB and the privileged stratocracy, who are just about everywhere, are obviously not about to give up their privileges or to jeopardize their social existence. So the situation is completely chaotic, and the three predictions I made at the end of that paper are coming true

---

{A talk with Philippe Thureau-Dangin, published in *Dynasteurs*, no. 7 (March 1991), under the title "En Russie, réformer l'économie est impossible. Revenir en arrière également [In Russia, It Is Impossible to Reform the Economy. Or to Backtrack]."}

1. "The Gorbachev Interlude," *New Politics*, new series 1 (Winter 1988): 60–79.

simultaneously: Gorbachev is dismissed because he is powerless; furthermore, he has watered down his reforms; and last, the population is becoming active and the army is intervening.

*One wonders why Gorbachev never tried to reform the KGB or the army, and why those forces gave him free rein for nearly four years, after all.*

We must rid ourselves of the illusion that history, real history, is the outcome of people's rational, plotted decisions. None of this was foreseen, or foreseeable. Gorbachev took power *with* the support of the KGB and the army, no doubt, and with the intention of reforming the system so it could survive. At the outset he had nothing else in mind, and didn't want anything else. As late as the spring of 1988, Gorbachev, speaking at the Czechoslovakian Communist Party Congress, explained that Marxist-Leninist ideology is the "touchstone" of the whole system. During that period the attempt at top-down reform turned out not to be feasible, and failed completely. National reactions were then sparked within the "prison of peoples" as tsarist Russia used to be called. And the pace of events sped up.

The great question mark here, if we look at things from Gorbachev's standpoint, is, Why was *glasnost* necessary? Why did they open the windows? Why did they allow all those things about the Stalinist era to be published? Why did they give newspapers some freedom? First of all, it was to discredit any reactionary tendency. Second, Gorbachev and the people around him wanted to civilize Russia, to Westernize it somewhat. But at some point an uncontrollable social dynamic developed, one which Gorbachev and his people are trying to stop. It's probably a bit late.

*Does that dynamic logically lead to a dictatorship, as many people are saying?*

The present development may go as far as a military dictatorship, but some irrevocable changes have taken place. In particular, the Marxist-Leninist ideology—the totalitarian imaginary, which actually no longer functioned by then but nonetheless continued to be a sort of corpse playing its role on stage—has been definitively smashed to pieces. There's no going back on the assertion of national identities, either.

To survive, the regime has to make the republics obey it. Can the present balance between the central government and Russia, Ukraine, and the other republics be maintained?

No, because the present government doesn't control the situation. Usually, when someone issued an order in a factory or a ministry, there were what Clausewitz called "frictions," which is to say, delays and diversions. But on the whole, it was carried out. Right now, the control levers aren't even made of rubber; they're jelly. Gorbachev can go on gesticulating in the Kremlin, signing decrees and making statements; nothing happens. Where are the only functional control levers? In the KGB and the army, but both are increasingly autonomous. If the Ukraine declared its independence and Gorbachev told the army not to intervene, would they obey him?

But what do the KGB and the army want these days? A return to the old status quo? That the USSR remain as it is?

I don't like the expression USSR very much, because there is no union, no soviets, no republics and no socialism. The present situation is chaotic, since none of the protagonists seems to have any project. What does Gorbachev want? A half-liberal system, a planned economy with little injections of liberalism? That can't work. The army can seize power; there's absolutely no doubt about that. But to do what? Can factories be made to work by shooting the workers? I don't think it's possible to return to the system as it was in 1980, from the economic standpoint. That system functioned, after a fashion, because for decades people all holed up in some niche, cheating on the production norms, but nonetheless spending half of their time productively (the other half was devoted to moonlighting— what the French call "*la perruque*"). In short, everyone got by, one way or another, and still pretended to be working. Now they don't even pretend. One wonders how come there's still any electricity in Russia, or trains that run, or planes taking off from the airports.

*If they go on privatizing, is a social movement conceivable?*

What's most amazing is that there still isn't any social movement in the USSR or in the satellite countries, although it has been five years since the lid has been raised a little. And we now discover that the lid is smashed to pieces, held together by band-aids. There was the great miners' strike in 1989 and a few small strikes, that's all. The great movements we see are national, not social. Even in Russia, we hear Boris Yeltsin explain that Russia is the most exploited of all the nations in the union. Yet we don't hear of any social movement, or of any political movement for that matter. The reformers in parliament want the government to be reformed, but they have neither a program nor any vision. It must be said that civil society, trade society, and farming society have all been wiped out, demolished by seventy years of the Leninist-Stalinist regime. Stalin physically destroyed the Russian peasantry. To this very day, there is still less livestock than in 1930. Russia lacks that anthropological foundation of habits, behavior, mentalities and petty know-how on which reforms may rely. On the other hand, the Czechs, Slovaks, or the Polish people may think, "We're going to have a hard time for two, three, or four years, but still and all we'll have obtained something. We've rid ourselves of the Russians, and our nation is independent." What can the Russian peoples say to themselves, so as to go on tightening their belt? Nothing.

*The Hungarian historian Janos Szucs sees "three Europes":[2] Western Europe, East-Central Europe, somewhat hybrid, and Eastern Europe (Russia and Romania). Won't the latter ever experience anything but the tyranny of boyars, tsars, or the party?*

I wouldn't speak of three Europes, but of two. Of course there's a difference between France, Holland, or Germany, and Poland. But Poland, Czechoslovakia, Hungary, Slovenia and the Baltic countries all participated more or less in the European movement. Those countries were more backward in some respects, but they played a role in the great European movement toward emancipation. Conversely, the second Europe, comprising Russia, Bulgaria, Romania, most of Yugoslavia, Albania, and even Greece, never took part in that European emancipation movement. If you look at the shape of that whole, you'll see that it corresponds to the zone of expansion of the Orthodox religion as it was constituted by Byzantium, and later by Russia, and to the area in which it has remained alive. Orthodox Christianity is the true Christian religion in the sense that it is theocratic, meaning there can't be any objection to what the emperor says, since the emperor is the embodiment of Christ on earth.

*In that Caesaro-papism, it isn't the pope who governs, it's Caesar who names and dethrones the patriarch of Constantinople. Later, in Russia, the tsar is afraid that the patriarch of Moscow is too powerful, so he replaces him with a puppet Holy Synod. In all those countries, what I call the dominant social imaginary has always been a national religious imaginary.*

*So you agree with the idea that there is a continuity between the tsars and the communists?*

---

2. *Les Trois Europes* (Paris: L'Harmattan, 1985).

The Stalinist ice age replaced the religious imaginary with a totalitarian imaginary. Henceforth Caesar is no longer the representative of God on earth but of the laws of history. In a sense, Gorbachev's action follows the same lines as the attempts at top-down reform made by Peter the Great, Catherine, Alexander II, Stolypin, and so forth. Those reforms never really succeeded, but they did create an academy, some universities, and above all heavy industry, mainly for military purposes. They never transformed Russian society in depth. So there remains that very deep-seated tradition, rooted in people's minds, one of obedience to the authority of the tsar or of his replacement.

*Is the Western model of emancipation as strong as it was a century ago? Is the self-image projected by Western society potent enough to incite the Russians to change?*

That's a relevant question indeed, with respect to Russia and the orthodox Christian societies, but also for Islam and Hinduism. What does the West have to offer? Gadgets, plastic goods. You can't erode the influence of the Koran by peddling Madonna! Western democracy has become a shell—I don't say an empty shell: human rights are of a defensive, negative nature, we have habeas corpus and *habeas opinionem*. People have become completely passive. Each person looks out only for her narrow personal circle, and to hell with the Earth! That's what I call privatization. According to a recent poll, 70 to 80 percent of French people stated that no cause, however just, would justify going to war. That's terrifying. Those people don't realize that they would still be serfs had that been true. It took mountains of corpses, floods of blood, people burned by the Inquisitions, others thrown into the Bastille, workers gunned down during strikes, and so on, to get the freedoms they now have in the Western world.

*In Russia as well as in the West, aren't intellectuals throwing in the towel, incapable of thinking differently and of continuing the movement toward emancipation?*

Since the 1920s, intellectuals in the West have almost all supported communism, at least for a while: take Romain Rolland, H. G. Wells, Sartre, and so forth. In the East, on the other hand, intellectuals have played an opposite, critical role: the best of them were opposed to that sinister regime. Now that that phase is over, it seems they have nothing more to say. It's not their fault. In the present period, Marxism, liberalism, and the ideology of progress are all worn out. Nonetheless, it's clear that capitalism, in its present Western form, is infinitely preferable to the Soviet "non-planning," which actually was total anarchy.

*You mention the failure of liberalism. What do you mean by that?*

Nobody really believes in progress any more. Everyone wants to have a bit more next year, but no-one thinks that happiness resides in a 3 percent annual rise in consumption. The imaginary of growth definitely still exists: it's even the only imaginary that subsists in the Western world. Western man doesn't believe in anything, except in the fact that he'll soon be able to buy a high-definition television set.

I'm not minimizing the importance of the market for regulating demand, and therefore also supply, but the way today's neo-liberals worship the market is ludicrous. They seem to have forgotten that academic economists such as Keynes, Robinson, Chamberlin, and others smashed the liberal ideology to pieces as early as the '30s. They pretend to forget that the present economy isn't based on competition; it's an oligopolistic economy. The marketplace logic would require, for example, that a rational basis be found for the price of capital, its true value. Now that's impossible; capital doesn't have any "objective value." Take the price of oil, for example: What does it represent? A balance between supply and demand? The true availability of oil? In 1991, or in 2050, when there will no longer be any oil? Does the price of oil reflect the cost, for humankind, of the exhaustion of the reserves? To believe that would be absurd. It merely reflects oligopolistic levy. Now, that price acts as an input for the formulation of the price of goods in general. So, if the price of oil is in no way rational, the same is true for the other prices. A fact which neo-liberals blithely ignore! Actually, we are now digging our own graves. . . . We need a frugal management of the planet's resources, on a global level, not individuals who are exclusively obsessed with getting more of their own so-called pleasure.

The only thing that seems to hold out in the face of the ideology of growth is the concept of the nation, in both the East and the West. Can that be seen as something other than a nostalgia for the period before the great market?

Here too, we see the failure of conventional interpretations, both Marxist and liberal. For those ideologies, the nation has no reason to exist. What's more, it was fated to be dissolved by the advances of the Enlightenment and the market. For Hobbes, Montesquieu, and Benjamin Constant, war should be replaced by "sweet commerce." The same is true of the Marxists, who believed that capitalism would unify the world and lead the proletariats of the world to fraternize. Now, it didn't happen that way. The nation has remained a lump that is hard to swallow. The imaginary of the nation resists all the more since every other belief has fallen apart. The nation is the last remaining pole of identification, and it too seems very fragile. In the early '80s, when Russia was still a threat, most French people thought the government should negotiate in case of an invasion. The "true" nationalists are more or less impotent in the face of the consequences of the global extension of capitalism. First, there is increasingly less possibility for decision-making centers to be national. Second, national cultures are being dissolved in a global soup, an atrocious one for the time being, but which could and should be something very different. National identities are increasingly being diluted, but nothing is replacing them. So they survive in the form of some tense assertion: "we are French," or "we are German," and so forth. The nation is a legally outdated form, historically speaking, but not at all so in the facts. That's the great contradiction of our times.

# On War, Religion, and Politics

*Is the Gulf War incidental or does it mark an important date in North–South relations?*

The Gulf War is certainly not incidental. It sheds glaring light on some fundamental factors of the global situation today. For one thing, there is the evolution—or rather the non-evolution—of the third world. Saddam Hussein and his regime are extreme, but also typical instances. There are dozens of petty tyrants and military regimes in Africa, Southeast Asia, and Latin America. Next, for the first time since the Vietnam War, the Western world—that is, the United States—is imposing its conception of the "global order" (the "new" one) by force. This has nothing to do with law, or with humanism; it has to do with the constellation of forces around the world. No-one cares at all about the countless other violations of either human rights or UN resolutions, and the Ethiopians can go on massacring each other and dying of hunger without any risk of having the Russians or the Americans land there to restore order. The object of the Gulf operation was not so much oil as showing who's the boss. And doing so in such a tremendously important region, on so many counts. Nevertheless, beyond the short range, American politics is blind. Iraq's crushing defeat did have a major psychological effect, but the problems of the region have been worsened (look at the Kurds, Lebanon, the Palestinians), and the politics of the Israeli government has become more unbearable than ever.

{An interview with Pierre Ysmal on May 1, 1991, published in *Humanisme. Revue des francs-maçons du Grand Orient de France* 199/200 (September 1991), under the title "Péripéties et illumination . . . [Episodes and Illumination . . .]." We have used the typewritten version, revised by Castoriadis.}

*"Colonialism was the Western world's main sin. However, I don't see any great
leap forward in the vitality and plurality of cultures since its disappearance," says
Claude Lévi-Strauss in* De près et de loin.[1] *What do you think?*

The statement is historically false. The Greeks, Romans, and Arabs all
successfully undertook huge colonizing operations. Moreover, they assimilated or converted the people they conquered, whether they liked it or
not. The Arabs now portray themselves as the eternal victims of the Western world. That's a grotesque myth. The Arabs have been conquerors ever
since Muhammad's times, extending their nation into Asia, Africa, and
Europe (look at Spain, Sicily, and Crete) by Arabizing the peoples they
conquered. How many "Arabs" were there in Egypt at the turn of the 7th
century? The present expansion of the Arabs and of Islam is the outcome
of the conquest and the more or less forced conversion to Islam of the
peoples they subdued. Then they in turn were dominated by the Turks for
over four centuries. Western semi-colonization lasted only one hundred
thirty years in the worst case (Algeria), and much less in the others. And it
was the Arabs who first introduced the trade in black slaves in Africa, three
centuries before the Europeans.

All that in no way lessens the weight of Western colonial crimes. But we
must not overlook one essential difference. In the Western world, internal
criticism of colonialism began very early (with Montaigne), and by the
19th century it had already led to the abolition of slavery (which actually
still exists in some Muslim countries), and in the 20th century, to the refusal of the population of Europe and America to fight to retain the colo-
nies (in Vietnam). Never have I heard such "self-criticism," criticism of
one's own culture, from any Arab or Muslim whatsoever. Quite the opposite: look at present-day Sudan, or Mauritania.

*What good is the UN? Does it make decisions or is it just a place for idle talk?*

The UN is a place where the super-powers make an effort, when it's con-
venient for them, to settle their disagreements peacefully. As long as the
conflict between Russia and the United States occupied the forefront, the
UN was a forum for idle talk and demagogy. Now that Russia is no longer
a great power, its role tends to be somewhat like the Holy Alliance between 1815 and 1848, or the Concert of Europe following the Congress
of Berlin in 1878.

---

1. {Claude Lévi-Strauss and Didier Eribon, *De près et de loin* (Paris: Odile Jacob,
1988; 2nd ed. "Poches Odile Jacob," 2001).}

*The military-industrial complex you have denounced so often still has a promising future, then?*

Definitely. In Russia, after a relative eclipse since 1985, it's raising its head and is beginning to weigh in on events again. In the United States, there hasn't been any significant cut in military spending, in spite of the tremendous change in the international situation in recent years. In France either—and they're preparing to put out a new fighter plane: to fight whom? The Algerians have nothing to eat, but they're asking China to help them build a plutonium processing plant to make their own nuclear bomb. Against whom? Who is threatening them?

*Can the Islamic imaginary, and the religious imaginary in general, accept the idea of progress?*

If we're talking about progress in the manufacturing of weapons or of consumer goods, they certainly can. What they cannot accept is human emancipation, individual and social autonomy. The emancipation movement and the project of autonomy, born in Greece and reasserted in much greater breadth in Western Europe, free both individual and collective creativity, making thoughtful self-change possible for both. Now, religions have always represented a formidable conservative and reactionary factor in that respect. Comprehensibly so, philosophically speaking, since they always refer to a source of law and of institutions *external* to society, one which therefore eludes, and *must* elude human action. (To my knowledge, the religion of ancient Greece is the only exception in this respect.) There is no lack of historical examples. It's easy to see how the closure of present-day Islamic societies is tied to their religion, which still aspires to run political and civil society in the name of a revealed law. But Christianity was no different. In those societies where Christian theocracy has not been called into question, they're still suffering the consequences. That's true of Byzantium and all of its offspring: Russia and the Balkans, including modern Greece. In Western Europe, it was only because the emperor, the kings, and most towns fiercely resisted the papacy's pretension to exert temporal power that things went so differently. But true Western Christianity is the Christianity of the true Middle Ages, and medieval Western society, from the 5th to the 11th century, was a closed society. It viewed history as a process of decline: novelty and innovation—*novum, novatio*— were derogatory terms. When a writer wanted to set forth a new idea, he immediately ascribed it, falsely, to an earlier writer.

To this day, as soon as the pressure lets up, the old ecclesial demons raise their heads again. The archbishop of Paris vaguely mouths something about secularity and denounces Martin Scorsese's film about Christ. In Poland religion is being taught in the schools again, and the church is demanding a ban on abortion.

*All in all, what do you think about religions?*

What an immense question! Religions have been central in the institution of all heteronomous societies, which is to say, pretty much, of *all* societies. They have provided institutions with a source outside of society, an imaginary, sacred one that made them unquestionable. They have been both the grounds for the validity of the institutions and the root of the meaning of human life, of the world, of being. But religions couldn't have been maintained so long, and above all, they couldn't have elicited and inhabited those imposing cultural creations they have nourished had they not, at the same time, played another role: that of providing humankind with a representation of the Abyss, Chaos, the Bottomless Pit, under a variety of guises and disguises. In that sense, religion is always a compromise formation, and certainly, in the last analysis, also a form of idolatry. But without that second side of religion, there would have been no Romanesque or Gothic cathedrals, no Giotto, or Greco, or Bach, or Mozart's *Requiem*.

When philosophy and politics came into being, the deceptive dimension of religion was clearly evidenced. It became obvious that society and its institution have no transcendental foundations; rather, society itself is the source of its law. The self-institution of society (which had of course always taken place) became explicit: it is we who make our laws. At that point, the central problem of democracy appeared, as well: that of its self-limitation. There is no divine law, no norm outside of society. It is therefore up to us to impose limits on ourselves, ones that are not traced anywhere beforehand. Autonomy strictly means self-limitation. In the contemporary Western world religion definitely is regressing enormously, but there is also a crisis in the project of autonomy. Capitalism has succeeded in instituting consumerism (illusory in many respects) as the sole meaning of life, and in almost totally depoliticizing and privatizing individuals.

*What is an autonomous society?*

A society whose institutions, once interiorized by individuals, facilitate to the utmost their access to their personal autonomy and their effective participation in every explicit power existing in that society.

*Does communism still exist?*

The communist ideology (Marxism-Leninism) has been shattered to smithereens. But the communist apparatuses subsist. Sometimes they are governing (as in China, North Korea, and Cuba), sometimes within communist parties, which have survived, strangely enough. Strangely, too, they still have a vague ideological influence—in Latin America, for example. Even in Europe, no more than fifteen years ago, Habermas advanced the reconstruction of historical materialism as an objective.[2]

*Was the springtime of the peoples of Eastern Europe merely an illusion?*

It was a victorious revolt against totalitarian tyranny. Spontaneous movements were able to topple regimes that were armed to the teeth, through peaceful demonstrations. Their boldness and strategic and tactical intelligence were magnificent. But they didn't go beyond overthrowing the totalitarian tyranny. They didn't develop any new organization or institutional form; we didn't see any new move toward autonomy. As soon as the tyranny was overthrown, the movement vanished, to be replaced by blind adoption of the institutions of liberal capitalism. The dream of a consumer society . . . but without consuming. Like a local sign of the global depoliticization characteristic of our times.

*Won't immigration become* the *explosive problem for France and Europe?*

It may. The problem isn't economic, of course. Immigration can't create problems in countries with a declining population, as is the case in Europe: to the contrary. The problem is profoundly political and cultural. I don't believe in today's idle talk about the coexistence of different cultures of any sort whatsoever, with their diversity. That may have been possible—hardly so, actually—in the past, in a completely different political context, essentially one in which people who didn't belong to the dominant culture had limited rights, as for the Jews and Christians in Islamic countries. But we proclaim equal rights for all (what goes on in reality is something else). That implies a shared common ground of basic beliefs within the political body; that believers and nonbelievers are on equal footing; that no Revelation and no sacred Book determines any societal norm; that the integrity

---

2. {See Jürgen Habermas, *Zur Rekonstruktion des historischen Materialismus* (Frankfurt: Suhrkamp Verlag, 1976).}

of the human body is inviolable, and so on. How can that be "reconciled" with a theocratic faith, with the penal provisions of Koranic law, and so forth? We must get away from the widespread hypocrisy characteristic of contemporary discourse. Muslims can live in France only inasmuch as they consent, concretely, to not being Muslims on a whole series of points (such as family law and criminal law). A modicum of assimilation is necessary and unavoidable, in this respect, and in actual fact, it takes place.

*Has secularity as a value been lost?*

Secularity as a value has not been lost; it's more important than ever. It is part of the philosophic foundations of democracy (the origin of the law is human, not divine), and it is one of the guarantors of individual autonomy: the political body prohibits its own intervention in private beliefs. As I have said, it is endangered by the revival of the Church's political pretensions.

*Isn't racism the modern plague?*

Racism has been in existence for an immensely long time, if not forever. But we need to understand what is now making it so virulent again. There is an overall crisis in civilization, a crisis in significations, that obviously cannot be surmounted by the void of consumer society. People are seeking meaning, confusedly. Some turn to religion, others toward racism. The meaninglessness of racism has an apparent meaning: when one is unable to define oneself positively, one does so by hating the other. That's true for public and private life.

*Voltaire, in his* Essay . . . , *says that "the only way to prevent men from being absurd and nasty is to enlighten them." Are people any more enlightened in 1991 than in the 18th century?*

They may be better informed, but not necessarily more enlightened, since enlightenment isn't a passive state. You must want to be enlightened. The Enlightenment can't be served to a passive humankind by a few beacons. The reception of the Enlightenment is just as creative as its creation. The receiver has to shake herself up enough to be able to be enlightened. Nowadays, the public mostly remains passive in the face of the excessive accumulation of information of all sorts, and there's no way of purely and simply excusing it.

*Who embodies contemporary culture? Cornelius Castoriadis? Michel Serres? Bernard-Henri Lévy?*

Sociologically speaking, contemporary culture is fittingly embodied by B.-H. Lévy, Jean-Edern Hallier, Sulitzer, Séguéla, and Madonna.[3]

*"Everything has already been said. Everything always remains to be said again. That massive fact alone could lead to despair." Does that conclusion of yours make you despair?*

Certainly not, as shown by the fact that it introduces a paper[4] calling for opposition to the unbridled advance of autonomized technoscience.

---

3. [All people who owe their popularity essentially to the mass media in one way or another, whom Castoriadis obviously views as epitomizing mediocrity and superficiality.—Trans.]

4. {"Dead End" (1987), in *Philosophy, Politics, Autonomy: Essays in Political Philosophy* (New York: Oxford University Press, 1991).}

# Communism, Fascism, and Emancipation

*Communism and fascism seem to be two ways of solving the problems of modern times and mass societies. What do you think about that? And what do you think about the common view that makes no distinction between communism and fascism?*

Communism and fascism *are precisely not* two ways, however monstrous, of solving the problems of modern times. Both destroy the societies of which they take hold and can last only as long as their combination of lies and terror succeeds in surviving. The facts show the perpetuation of such regimes to be highly improbable. They are regimes that are unable to regenerate and maintain themselves.

That common opinion which doesn't distinguish between fascism (or better, Nazism) and communism isn't entirely wrong. From the standpoint of the ordinary citizen, the two regimes produce identical results: slavery. They are also deeply similar in their totalitarian character. In both cases, the distinction between public and private is abolished; the private sphere of each citizen is absorbed by the government; and the public sphere itself becomes the secret "private property" of the dominant group. People's minds and souls must be shaped in conformity with the views of the Party, and society cannot sustain any truth other than official "truth."

There are two major differences between the two regimes, however, and they tend in opposite directions. On the one hand, Nazism is less dangerous than communism, from a global-historical viewpoint. Communism has a universalist vocation and could have taken over countries everywhere, whereas Nazism, whose proclaimed mission is the domination of one single race, was doomed to fail rapidly. Eighty million Germans couldn't have dominated five billion individuals. On the other hand, the

---

{Interview published in the Italian newspaper *l'Unità*, September 28, 1991. The text is based on Castoriadis' own typewritten French version.}

Nazi imagination, however monstrous and absurd, was not internally contradictory. Nazism says what it does and does what it says, give or take a little. Communism is condemned to say one thing and do the opposite. It speaks of democracy and installs tyranny; it proclaims equality and achieves inequality; it invokes science and truth and practices lies and absurdity. That's why it very rapidly loses its grasp on the populations it dominates. But it's also why people who believe in communism are moved by very different motivations than those of the Nazis, at least until communism comes into power. They are possessed by a "revolutionary illusion"; they generally believe that the Communist Party really aims at establishing a democratic, egalitarian society. Which is why a communist who discovers how monstrous real-life communism actually is may break down, psychologically, or become a social-democrat, or else continue to uphold a project of radical social transformation divested of Marxist-Bolshevik messianic tendencies. A fascist or a Nazi can find nothing in his previous beliefs that incites him to change them.

*Given the outcome, has communism represented a progressive or a reactionary utopia for our times? What is its legacy?*

Real-life communism represented a monstrous misappropriation of the revolutionary working-class movement. It put a new dominant class, the Party/State bureaucracy, in power, which has exploited and oppressed the population more than any historically known regime, for no other regime had comparable technological and ideological means of sowing terror, of interfering in people's everyday lives, and of manipulating them ideologically. It destroyed the working-class movement in other countries by subordinating it to Russia's imperialist policies. It has irrevocably corrupted and prostituted the ideas and vocabulary of the revolutionary movement; it has discredited the idea of social transformation; it has made entire populations view the capitalist regime as paradise on earth. Nowadays, when you criticize capitalism in an ex-communist country, people leave the room (I had that experience last June in Hungary). The only legacy it has left is the demonstration, on every point, absolutely one and all, of what should not be done, of what is the absolute opposite of a policy of emancipation.

*In an interview with our newspaper last year,[1] you said that each political regime has a corresponding anthropological type, a type of public spirit. What type was that in the Eastern European "socialist" countries?*

---

1. {April 1990.}

The communist regime tried to create a new anthropological type that corresponded to it: the individual—or Party member—as disciplined as a corpse, both enthusiastic and passive. That attempt soon failed, in the face of the reality of the system. After that, two different human types were created: the cynical, lying, manipulative bureaucrat obsessed with power and the ordinary citizen, apathetic, fearful, avoiding any responsibility and cheating as much as possible to maintain a miserable little niche for himself. In both cases, any previously existing seeds of democratic attitudes have been destroyed, and who knows when and how they may be re-created. That too is one of the most weighty legacies of the communist regimes. It's also one of the reasons why nationalism and chauvinism are emerging again so forcefully in all those countries. Because when everything else is collapsing, they seem to provide the only identification to which people can still cling.

*Do you think the democratic revolutions in Eastern Europe will change the idea of revolution, and in what way?*

The democratic revolutions in Eastern Europe have shown once again what we have always known: when a radical movement embraces the vast majority of the population, it has no need to resort to violence. The identification of revolution with violence, terror, and so on, is a mystification invented by conservative propaganda, aimed at scaring people, and which was able to find evidence in the communist putsches, beginning with the October 1917 Bolshevik putsch. But another aspect of the Eastern European revolutions should be emphasized. As much as the population proved to be determined, heroic, and capable of wonderfully efficient self-organization in overthrowing the communist tyranny, once that tyranny had crumbled it virtually abandoned any political activity. It went home, leaving the fate of society in the hands of professionals, old and new. Of course that attitude may be explained by the population's enormous disillusionment with what it had been led to view as "politics," but that's a factor that weighs very heavily on the social and political situation in those countries.

*Now that communism has ended, what's left, in terms of a theory of social change? How can we best use the great legacy of communist-and left-wing socialist-led struggles, which contributed to the establishment of the Western democracies?*

The emancipation movement doesn't need a "theory of social change." There can be no such theory: society and history aren't ruled by laws susceptible of theorization. History is the domain of human creation, which creation is subjected to some requisites. But those requisites form a framework; they don't determine creation. The notion that a "theory" of social change is possible is one of Marx's catastrophic illusions. It leads to the monstrous idea of *orthodoxy*, first introduced in the working-class movement by Marxism. But orthodoxy implies the existence of a dogma, and when you have a dogma, you have custodians of the dogma, which is to say, a church, or a party. And where you have custodians of the dogma, you have an inquisition, which is to say, the KGB.

That doesn't mean that just anything can happen or that we're blind to what goes on. We can and must elucidate what is happening and what cannot happen. But each human action creates new possibilities, and great action creates new forms of social-historic being.

We don't want social change for its own sake. We want a radical trans-formation of society because we want an autonomous society fashioned by autonomous individuals, and because contemporary capitalist society, even in its pseudo-democratic form, is a society dominated by an economic, political, state, and cultural oligarchy, condemning citizens to passivity and giving them only negative, defensive freedoms. That's what I call the project of individual and social autonomy.

That project stems from way back (to the democratic *polis* of ancient Greece) and has reemerged in a variety of forms in modern Western Europe. The elements of democracy that subsist in today's rich Western societies weren't produced by capitalism; they are what is left of the democratic struggles of peoples and especially of the working-class movement. But at one point that movement was led astray by Marxism, then by Marxism-Leninism, which introduced the idea of orthodoxy, the idea of a leading role (actually, dictatorship) for the Party, a mystifying, pseudo-religious messianism, scorn for the creative activity of the people, and a typically capitalist imaginary of the centrality of the economy and of pro-duction. If all you're interested in is increasing production and consump-tion, you may as well keep capitalism; it does that quite well. If what you're interested in is freedom, you have to get a different society.

The legacy of the working-class movement is invaluable in that respect, both positively and negatively. The working-class struggles have shown that the people possess immense capacities for self-organization. They have created forms such as the workers' councils that are still examples for us. But they have also shown what we must not do: that is, surrender one's sovereignty and initiative to a party, or believe that there can be civil servants disinterestedly serving the human race.

# Ecology against the Merchants

The idea that ecology is reactionary rests either on abysmal ignorance of what is at issue or on some leftover "progressive" ideology: get a higher standard of living, and . . . come what may! Of course no idea is inherently shielded from perversions and misappropriations. As we know, some of the themes only seemingly tied to ecology (such as the earth, the village, and so on) have been and still are used by reactionary movements, including Nazism and the Pamiat movement in Russia today. The way anti-ecologists use that fact is more reminiscent of Stalinist amalgamations, to my mind.

Ecology is subversive in that it calls into question the capitalist imaginary that prevails everywhere. It rejects the central leitmotif according to which we are fated to constantly increase production and consumption. It shows the catastrophic impact of the capitalist logic on the natural environment and on people's lives. That logic is absurd in itself and leads to a physical impossibility at the global level, since it causes the destruction of its very premises. It's not just the irreversible dilapidation of the environment and the squandering of irreplaceable resources. There's also the anthropological destruction of human beings, transformed into producing, consuming animals: into mindless zappers. There is the destruction of the milieus in which they live. Cities, for instance, that wonderful creation of the late Neolithic period, are being destroyed at the same pace as the Amazonian forest, dismantled into ghettos, residential suburbs and office areas that close down at 8 P.M. So we're not talking about some bucolic defense of "nature," but about a struggle to save human beings and their habitat. It's clear to me that saving them is incompatible with maintaining the existing system and that it requires a political reconstruction of society

{This text appeared under the title "L'écologie est-elle réactionnaire? Sauvons les zappeurs abrutis [Is Ecology Reactionary? To the Rescue of Mindless Zappers]" in a collection of papers on ecology published by *Le Nouvel Observateur*, May 7–15, 1992.}

to turn it into an effective democracy, not just a democracy in words. That, actually, is the point on which present ecology movements usually fall short, in my opinion.

But behind those obvious facts, some more difficult, deeper issues arise. What prevails nowadays is the autonomization of technoscience. One no longer asks whether there are needs requiring satisfaction but whether some scientific or technical exploit or other is feasible. If it is, it will be achieved, and the corresponding "need" will be fabricated. The side effects and negative repercussions are rarely considered. That too must be stopped, and that's where the difficult questions begin. We all want—I want, at any rate—the development of scientific knowledge. We therefore want excellent observation satellites, for instance. But their existence implies the totality of contemporary technoscience. So must we want all that, too? There can be no question of restricting freedom to do scientific research. But the limits between pure knowledge and its possibly lethal applications are extremely fuzzy, if not to say nonexistent. Hardy, the great English mathematician who was actively opposed to both world wars, said that he had chosen mathematics because it could never be used to kill a human being. Which proves that you can be a great mathematician and be unable to reason outside your own field. The atomic bomb would have been unthinkable without the help of several great "pure" mathematicians, and when differential calculus was invented it was immediately used to calculate the parabolas of cannon shots.

Where should we draw the line? For the first time, in a non-religious society, we must face up to the question of whether the expansion of knowledge itself should be controlled. And of how that can be done without producing a dictatorship over minds. I think we can set up some simple rules: (1) We don't want an unlimited, mindless expansion of production; we want an economy that is a means, not the finality of human life; (2) we want free expansion of knowledge, but we can no longer pretend to ignore the fact that such expansion contains dangers we cannot define in advance. To deal with them, we need what Aristotle called *phronèsis*, "cautiousness," or "prudence," as the bad Latin translation calls it. Experience shows that the present technobureaucracy (economic as well as scientific) is organically and structurally incapable of possessing that cautiousness, since its very existence and moving force is nothing but the delusion of unlimited expansion. So we need true democracy, establishing the broadest possible procedures for thought and debate, with the participation of the citizenry as a whole. That in turn is only feasible if those citizens have true information, true training, and opportunities to exert their judgment, in practice.

A democratic society is an autonomous society, but autonomous also, above all, means self-limited. Not only with respect to any political excesses (a majority that doesn't respect the rights of minorities, for instance), but also in the works and acts of the collectivity. Those limits, those boundaries, cannot be set in advance—that's why *phronèsis*, cautiousness, is required. The boundaries do exist, and when we will have crossed them it will be too late, by definition, just as the heroes of ancient tragedy only learn that they are inhabited by hubris, by excess, once the catastrophe has taken place. Contemporary society is fundamentally rash.

# The Revolutionary Potency of Ecology

*What does ecology mean to you?*

Understanding of the fundamental fact that social life must necessarily be primarily concerned with the environment in which it takes place. Strangely, that understanding seems to have been much more present in the archaic and traditional societies of the past than nowadays. In the 1970s, there were still villages in Greece that recycled almost everything. In France, concern with maintaining waterways, forests, and so on, has been constant for centuries. People had a "naive" but correct awareness of their vital dependence on the environment, without any "scientific knowledge" (the film *Dersu Uzala* gives another example). That has changed radically with capitalism and modern technoscience, based on the continuous, rapid growth of production and consumption, catastrophically affecting the ecosphere of this planet, as is already visible. If scientific discourse bores you, just look at the beaches, or breathe the air in large cities. So there can no longer be any conception of politics worth speaking about in which ecology is not a major concern.

*Can ecology be scientific?*

Ecology is primarily political; it isn't "scientific." Science as such is unable to set its own limits or its ends. If we ask it for the most efficient or the most economical means of exterminating the global population, it can (and actually must!) furnish a scientific answer. In its role as science it has strictly nothing to say about whether that project is "good" or "bad." We

---

{This interview, conducted by Pascale Égré on November 16 and 29, 1992, appeared under the title "La Force révolutionnaire de l'écologie" in a collection, "Planète verte—L'écologie en question [Green Planet—Questioning Ecology]," in the periodical published by the Students of the Paris Institut d'études politiques.}

can and certainly should, call upon scientific research to explore the effects of various kinds of productive activity on the environment, and occasionally to explore ways of preventing some undesirable side effect. But in the last analysis the response can only be political.

To claim, as do the people who signed the "Heidelberg Appeal" (I personally prefer to call it the Nuremberg Appeal), that science and science only can solve every problem is absolutely dismaying. On the part of so many Nobel Prize winners, it indicates a basic illiteracy, a lack of thought about their own activity, and total historical amnesia. They make those statements, whereas just a few years ago the main inventors and makers of atomic bombs were publicly doing acts of contrition, beating their breasts, proclaiming their guilt, and so forth—take Oppenheimer and Sakharov, to mention a few. It wasn't philosophers who built atomic bombs—nor was it the scientists who decided whether or not to use them.

It's precisely the development of technoscience, and the fact that scientists don't and never will have anything to say about its use, or even about its capitalist orientation, that has created the environmental problem and made it so serious today. What we realize now is the huge margin of uncertainty as to the facts and prospects for the future of the environment on Earth. That margin goes both ways, of course. My personal opinion is that the darkest prospects are the most probable ones. But the true question is elsewhere: it's the complete disappearance of cautiousness, of *phronèsis*. Since no-one can say conclusively that the greenhouse effect will or will not cause the level of the oceans to rise, or how many years it will take for the ozone hole to extend to the whole atmosphere, the only proper attitude is that of the *diligens pater familias*, the conscientious father who says to himself, since the stakes are so huge, even if the probabilities are unknown, I'll proceed extremely cautiously, and not as if the problem didn't exist.

Now, what we're seeing presently, at the Rio carnival (known as the Rio Summit), for example, is total irresponsibility. It's Bush and the neoliberals relentlessly pushing on, precisely invoking the argument of uncertainty in reverse (since it hasn't been "proved," we can continue on the same course . . .). It's the monstrous alliance between right-wing American Protestants and the Catholic Church to oppose any aid for birth control in the third world, whereas the link between the population explosion and environmental problems is obvious. At the same time, the height of hypocrisy is their so-called concern with those peoples' standard of living. But to improve their standard of living would require a further acceleration of the production and consumption that are destroying non-renewable resources. . . .

*Still and all, the Rio Summit adopted two conventions that some people view as historic: the Climate Change Convention and the one on biological diversity. Are they part of the "carnival"?*

Yes, since they don't propose a single concrete measure or include a single sanction. They are the tribute paid by vice to virtue.

Just a word about biodiversity. Really, the signatories of the Heidelberg Appeal should be reminded that no-one knows how many living species exist on Earth right now. The estimates range from ten to thirty million, but some people have even advanced the figure of one hundred million. Now, we know only a small fraction of those species. But what we do know practically surely is how many species we are causing to disappear each year, especially by destroying tropical forests. E. O. Wilson estimates that thirty years from now we will have exterminated approximately 20 percent of existing species, representing an average of seventy thousand species a year, or two hundred a day, based on the lowest estimate of the overall total! Any other consideration aside, the destruction of a single species can cause the breakdown of a balance and therefore the destruction of a whole ecotope. . . .

*When reading some of your writings, one has the impression that ecology is only the tip of an iceberg behind which it's not just science that is called into question, but the political and economic system as well. Are you a revolutionary?*

Revolution doesn't mean wanton bloodshed, taking the Winter Palace, and so forth. Revolution means a radical transformation of societal institutions. In that sense I am a revolutionary. But that sort of revolution would require profound changes in the psychosocial structure of people in the Western world, in their attitude toward life, in short, in their imaginary. The idea that the only goal in life is to produce and consume more—an absurd, humiliating idea—must be abandoned. The capitalist imaginary of pseudo-rational pseudo-mastery, and of unlimited expansion, must be abandoned. Only men and women can do that. A single individual, or an organization, can only prepare, criticize, encourage, and sketch out possible orientations, at best.

*What parallel can be drawn between the decline of Marxism and of ideologies, and the rise of political ecology?*

The relationship is a complex one, of course. First of all, you have to see that Marx is already entirely in step with the capitalist imaginary. Like the dominant ideology of his time, he thought that everything is conditioned by the increase in productive forces. When production will have reached a sufficiently high level, then we will be able to talk about a truly free, truly equal society, and so on. Nowhere in Marx can you find any criticism of capitalist technology, be it as technology for production or as to the kind and nature of goods made. He views capitalist technology and its products as an integral part of the process of human development. Nor can you find any criticism of the organization of the work process within factories. He does of course criticize some "outrageous" aspects, but he sees that very way of organizing it as a pure and simple rational achievement. Most of his criticism has to do with the way that technology and that organization are used: their use for the benefit of capital only instead of for all of humankind. He doesn't see that the technology and organization of capitalist production should be criticized as such.

That "omission" is strange, in Marx, since many other writers of his time did reflect on the subject. Think of Victor Hugo's *Les Misérables*, to take a well-known example. When Jean Valjean carries Marius through the Paris sewer system to save him, Hugo indulges in one of those digressions of which he is so fond. Basing himself, no doubt, on the calculations by the great chemists of the time, probably Liebig, he says that Paris evacuates the equivalent of five hundred million French gold coins a year to the sea through its sewers. And he contrasts that with the way Chinese peasants fertilize the earth with their own excrement. That's why, more or less in his words, China's land is as fertile today as on the first day of the Creation. He knew that traditional economies were based on recycling, whereas contemporary economy is an economy of squandering. Marx overlooked all that, or considered it marginal. And that was to be the attitude of the Marxist movement to the end.

Starting in the late 1950s, several factors combined to change that situation. First, after the 20th Congress of the Russian CP, and the Hungarian revolution that same year (1956), followed by Poland, Prague, and so on, Marxist ideology lost its attraction. The capitalist ideology then began to be criticized. Let me say, in passing, that in one of my writings dated 1957, "On the Content of Socialism,"[1] I developed a radical critique of Marx as

---

1. [In *Political and Social Writings*, vol. 2: *1955–1960: From the Workers' Struggle Against Bureaucracy to Revolution in the Age of Modern Capitalism* (Minneapolis: University of Minnesota Press, 1988). Written under the pseudonym Pierre Chaulieu, it was first published as "Sur le contenu du socialisme," *Socialisme ou Barbarie*, no. 22 (July–September 1957).—Trans.]

having totally refrained from criticizing capitalist technology, especially in production, and as having completely shared the views of his contemporaries in that respect. At the same time, people were beginning to discover the ravages wrought by capitalism on the environment. Rachel Carson's *Silent Spring*[2] was one of the first influential books on the subject, describing the way pesticides ravage the environment. Pesticides destroy plant parasites, but also other insects, and therefore the birds that eat them: a clear illustration of the circularity of an ecological balance and of how it is totally destroyed by the destruction of one single element.

An ecological awareness then began to take shape, and has developed all the more rapidly since young people in rich countries, unhappy with the social regimes there, can no longer express their criticism through the traditional Marxist channel, which has practically become pathetic. Criticism emphasizing the most sordid aspects was no longer relevant: you can no longer accuse capitalism of starving the workers when working-class families all have a car, and sometimes two. At the same time, the specifically ecological themes merged with antinuclear themes.

*So is ecology the new ideology of the late 20th century?*

No, I wouldn't say that, and at any rate we shouldn't talk of ecology as an ideology in the traditional sense of the word. But it's obvious that any true, serious politics must take the environment and the balance between humankind and global resources into account as a central issue. This is made necessary by the unbridled advance of autonomized technoscience and by the huge population explosion whose effects will continue to be felt for at least another half-century. But that taking into account must be integrated in a political project that will necessarily exceed "ecology" alone. And if there is no new movement, no revival of the project of democracy, "ecology" can very well be integrated in a neo-fascist ideology. In the case of a global ecological catastrophe, for instance, one can well imagine authoritarian regimes imposing harsh restrictions on a terrified, apathetic population. The insertion of an ecological component in a radical democratic political project is indispensable. And it is all the more imperative since any such project implies calling into question the values and orientations of present-day society, which is inseparable from the criticism of today's underlying imaginary of "development."

---

2. {*Silent Spring* (Boston: Houghton Mifflin, 1962).}

202

*Do the French ecology movements convey that project?*

I think the political component of both the "Verts" and "Génération Écologie" is inadequate and insufficient. They are not developing any thinking about the anthropological structures of contemporary society, or about political and institutional structures, the nature of true democracy, the issues that would be raised by its institution and functioning, and so forth. Those movements are exclusively concerned with environmental issues, almost not at all with social and political issues. That they want to be "neither left nor right" is understandable. But making a point of honor, so to speak, of not taking sides on crucial political issues, is highly open to criticism. It tends to turn those movements into lobbies of a sort.

When we do see an awareness of the political dimension, it seems insufficient to me. That was the case in Germany, where the Greens had established the rule of rotation/revocability for their parliamentary representatives. Rotation and revocability are central notions in my political thinking. But cut off from the rest they're meaningless. That's what happened in Germany where they no longer had any sense, integrated as they were in the parliamentary system. Because the very spirit of the parliamentary system is to elect "representatives" for five years, so as to get rid of political issues, to hand them over to "representatives" so you don't have to take care of them, which is the exact opposite of a democratic project.

*Does that specifically political component of a project for radical change include North–South relations as well?*

Of course. It's nightmarish to see well-fed people watch Somalians die of hunger on the news, and then return to their football game. But it's also, from a crudely realistic viewpoint, a terribly shortsighted attitude. You close your eyes and let them die. But they won't let themselves die off, in the long run. Clandestine immigration is increasing as the demographic pressure rises, and we haven't seen anything yet, for sure. The Mexicans crossing the Mexican–U.S. border practically meet no hurdles, and soon it won't be only the Mexicans. For present-day Europe, it's the straits of Gibraltar, among other places. And they aren't just Moroccans; there are people coming from everywhere in Africa, including Ethiopia and the Ivory Coast, who endure inconceivable hardships to get to Tangiers and pay people to smuggle them across. But soon it won't be only Gibraltar. There are something like forty thousand kilometers of Mediterranean coasts bordering what Churchill called "the soft underbelly of Europe."

Iraqi fugitives are already crossing Turkey and entering Greece illegally. Then there is the whole eastern border of the Twelve [European Union countries as of 1992]. Will they build a new Berlin wall, three or four thousand kilometers long, to prevent famished Easterners from entering Europe-the-affluent?

There is a tremendous economic and social imbalance between the affluent West and the rest of the world, as we know. That imbalance isn't declining; it's increasing. All that the "civilized" West exports to those countries by way of culture are techniques for coups d'état, arms, and television exhibiting models for consumerism that are out of those poor peoples' reach. That imbalance can't go on, unless Europe becomes a fortress run by a police state.

*What do you think of Luc Ferry's book,[3] in which he explains that the Greens are the bearers of a comprehensive vision of the world that calls into question man's relations with nature?*

Luc Ferry's book attacks the wrong enemy and finally turns into a diversionary maneuver. With the house on fire and the planet in danger, Luc Ferry takes on an easy enemy, in the form of some marginal ideologists who are neither representative nor threatening, and says nothing or next to nothing about the real problems. At the same time, he sets an extremely superficial "humanist," or "anthropocentric," ideology in opposition to a "naturalist" ideology. Human beings are anchored in something other than themselves; the fact that they are not "natural" beings doesn't mean they are hanging in thin air. There's no sense in harping on the finitude of human beings when you're talking about the philosophy of knowledge if you forget that finitude when talking about practical philosophy.

*Is any philosopher the founding father of ecology?*

I don't see any philosopher who could be called the founding father of ecology. There is of course a "love of nature" among the English, German, and French romantics. But ecology isn't "love of nature": it's the need for self-limitation (which is true freedom) of human beings with respect to the planet on which they happen to exist by chance, and which they are now destroying. Some philosophies, on the other hand, definitely

---

3. {Luc Ferry, *Le Nouvel Ordre écologique; l'arbre, l'animal et l'homme* (Paris: Grasset, 1992; 2nd ed., LGF, 1994, 2002).}

display that arrogance, that hubris, as the Greeks called it, the presumptuous excess that establishes mankind as the "master and possessor of nature," a most ridiculous claim, actually. We aren't even masters of what we will do, individually, tomorrow or a few weeks from now. But hubris always brings on nemesis, punishment, and that's what may well happen to us.

*Would we do well to rediscover the dimension of balance and harmony in ancient philosophy?*

Rediscovering philosophy in general would be a good thing, for we are experiencing one of the least philosophical, if not to say anti-philosophical periods of the history of humankind. But the ancient Greek attitude is not one of balance and harmony. It is grounded in acknowledgment of the invisible limits to our actions, of our inherent mortality, and of the need for self-limitation.

*Can growing concern with the environment be viewed as one aspect of the revival of religion, in the form of belief in nature?*

First of all, in spite of everything people are saying, I don't think there is a revival of religion in the Western world. Next, when correctly conceived (and it almost always is, from that standpoint), ecology doesn't turn nature—any more than mankind, in fact—into a deity. The only link I can see is quite indirect. It has to do with the hold religion has on almost all societies. We are living in the first society since the inception of the history of humankind in which religion is longer central to social life. Why did religion occupy such a tremendous place? Because it reminded you that you are not the master of the world, that you are living on top of the Abyss, Chaos, the Bottomless Pit, that there is something other than humankind, something that it "personified" in one way or another, and which it called taboo, totem, Amon-Ra, Olympian gods—or the Fates—or Jehovah. . . . Religion showed the Abyss, and at the same time masked it, by putting a face on it: it's God; God is Love; and so on. By the same token, it gave meaning to human life and death. It did of course project essentially anthropomorphic, anthropocentric attributes on the divine powers or the monotheistic God, and that's precisely how it "gave meaning" to everything in existence. The Abyss became familiar, something like us, so to speak. But at the same time it reminded humans of their limits, reminded them that Being is unfathomable and uncontrollable. Now ecology, as a part of a political project of autonomy, must simultaneously mark that human limitation and remind us that Being has no meaning, that it is we who create meaning at our own risk (including in the form of religions). So there is a proximity, in some sense, but also, in another sense, there is an insurmountable opposition.

*So you are for the defense of humankind, even more than the defense of nature?*

Defending humankind against itself, that's the question. Humankind is its own main threat. No natural catastrophe equals the catastrophes, massacres, and holocausts produced by people, against people. Today, human beings are still, or more than ever, their own worst enemy, not only because they continue as much as ever to slaughter their fellow creatures, but also because they are digging their own grave by destroying the environment. It's the awareness of that fact that we should try to awaken again, at a time when religion can no longer play that role, for very good reasons. People must be reminded that there are limits, not only individual, but social. It's not just that each of us is subject to the law and will die some day; it's that we all, collectively, cannot do just anything; we have to limit ourselves. Autonomy—true freedom—is that necessary self-limitation, not only with respect to the rules of social behavior but also in the rules we adopt in our behavior toward the environment.

*Are you optimistic as to that revival of that awareness of human limits?*

The creative power of human beings, their power to change what exists, is indeterminable and unforeseeable by nature and by definition. But it is neither positive nor negative in itself, and to talk about optimism or pessimism at that level is rash. Man as creative power is just as much man when he builds the Parthenon or Notre-Dame in Paris as when he organizes Auschwitz and the Gulag. Only afterwards can we discuss the value of what he has created (and that's clearly most important). At present, there is definitely the agonizing interrogation about the way contemporary society is bogged down in increasingly empty repetition; then, supposing that this repetition gives way to a new surge of historical creation, about the nature and value of that creation. We can't ignore those interrogations or be silent about them, nor can we answer them in advance. That's what history is about.

# A Society Adrift

*You denounced the growing immodesty, the lack of critical minds, and of true political thinking, as early as 1979, in connection with the "new philosophers." Those tendencies are to be found everywhere nowadays. . . .*

What is going on in the "intellectual" sphere is deeply tied to the overall evolution of Western societies. The most striking thing, when you compare the present phase with earlier phases in the history of those societies, is the almost complete disappearance of conflict, be it economic/social, political or "ideological." We are witnessing the triumph of an imaginary, the capitalist-"liberal" imaginary, and the quasi disappearance of the other major imaginary signification of modernity, which is the project of individual and collective autonomy. Superficially, that took the form, in the early '80s, of the victory of what is known as the "neoliberal" counter-offensive, epitomized by the politics of Thatcher and Reagan, which counter-offensive imposed some previously inconceivable things, such as the pure and simple cutback in real—and sometimes even nominal—wages, or again, unemployment levels that I myself thought, and wrote, in 1960, had become unthinkable because they would have caused an outburst of social revolt. But no such thing occurred. There are a number of reasons for that, some contingent—the threat, mostly bluff, of a "crisis" linked to the "oil crisis," and so on—but others, the ones we will discuss here, much deeper. In short, we are witnessing the total domination of the capitalist imaginary: the centrality of the economic sphere, the unlimited, supposedly rational expansion of production, consumption, and more or less planned and manipulated "leisure."

What that evolution expresses isn't simply the victory of the dominant strata seeking to increase their power. Almost the entire population participates in it. Conservatively withdrawn into their private sphere, people

{An interview by Marc Weitzmann, published under the title "A Society Adrift" in *L'Autre Journal*, no. 2 (March 1993).}

content themselves with bread and spectacles. The spectacles are mostly provided by television (and "sports"); bread by all the gadgets you can get, depending on your income. In one way or another, every echelon of society has access to that sort of minimum comfort; only the minorities that don't count are excluded. It's as if they had found a way to compress the overall amount of woes generated by society into the "lower" 15 to 20 percent of the population (Blacks and Hispanics in the United States, the jobless and immigrants in Europe). Most of the population seems to be content with leisure and gadgets, only occasionally making a few inconsequential corporatist objections. They don't seem to nourish any collective desire, any project aside from maintaining the status quo.

With this atmosphere, all the traditional safeguards of the capitalist republic are collapsing one after the other. There is no longer any control over political life: no sanctions, aside from the Criminal Code, which is less and less functional, as shown by all the recent "scandals." In any case, it's always the same question that arises in situations of this kind: "Why on earth should judges themselves, or their 'supervisors,' be exempt from the wholesale corruption, and for how long will they be? Who will keep the keepers?" The lack of safeguards makes for an intensification of the inherent irrationality of the system. The people in charge think they can do anything, or just about anything, provided the political poll ratings aren't too bad. The fact is, they no longer govern, really; their only concern is to get into power or to stay there. Traditional ideologies, be they "right" or "left," have become completely empty. The programs of the different parties don't differ on anything essential. In this respect, there's not even any need to "make an assessment" of the "left" (whatever happened to the series of [socialist] President Mitterrand's famous "proposals"?). But the same is true for the "right": When it claims there is a catastrophe, even if you use a microscope you can't see anything in its proposals that is commensurate with that catastrophe. There isn't even any "reactionary" or conservative program; there's nothing. Only their names and their emblems differentiate them.

*Can't the development of an ethical stance, of humanitarianism and human rights, be an objection to your observation of a state of bankruptcy?*

Those phenomena don't constitute an objection to my observation but, rather, a corroboration. Those ideas are used as so many cover-ups to hide the political void. You mustn't confuse the substance of the ideas themselves and the form in which they have been put into circulation. Who would possibly be "against" human rights? Very few people. But when did they begin to talk about them? They were mostly invoked against the totalitarian tyrannies of the Eastern countries. Fine. But then there was an attempt to turn them into the very substance of all politics, which is ludicrous. Once human rights have been ensured, there remains the question of what people do together, in society, and what they make of society. There is of course an ultraliberal answer consisting of saying, that's not a legitimate question, or even a meaningful one; everyone should just do as he likes. But that answer completely overlooks what constitutes the underlying nature of society as such. No society can survive if everyone does what she likes within the few minimal limits imposed by the Criminal Code, and even so, no criminal code can be written in complete disregard for a few substantial values that go far beyond the "rights of the individual."

Or take ethics: here again, the point of departure was mostly (there were a few others) the actions of dissidents from the Eastern countries: there were Solzhenitsyn, Sakharov, the Poles, Havel, and so forth. They took ethics as a minimal guideline, claiming that "in our situation—that of the USSR and the Eastern countries over the last thirty years—we don't know what to do on the political level, but there are some ethical safeguards that will enable people to behave decently, and at the same time will undermine the regime." "Don't lie," for instance, as Solzhenitsyn said. That's understandable, not only in their situation, but generally speaking: no politics worth speaking of can be based on lies. But it's also clear, precisely, that you can't set ethics up as the opposite of politics, as is increasingly done nowadays. I would go further, in fact, even if that will make some people scream: in the last analysis, politics in the full sense prevails over ethics; it's the more architectonic, as Aristotle would say. "Never lie" isn't tenable in every situation, for example. Solzhenitsyn couldn't tell the truth to the KGB, and in any case it would have been wrong for him to do so when they interrogated him on where his book *The Oak and the Calf* was hidden or who had helped him send *The Gulag Archipelago* to the West. Writing and publishing those texts were political acts, and everything that contributed to their achievement couldn't be measured solely with respect to "You shall not lie." Another example: "You shall not kill." Can that be raised to an absolute norm? Obviously not. If a terrorist threatens to kill dozens of hostages, should you absolutely refuse to kill him if you can? Similarly, in the present support for an armed intervention in Bosnia to stop the massacres, can that be done without possibly having to do some killing? All those decisions are political ones, in which ethics are only one element, if a very crucial one. The ethic of the Gospel is an a-cosmic ethic. If it has never truly been enforced in social life—the hypocrisy of the Church aside—it's also because it couldn't be.

*Talking about Bosnia, precisely, the partisans of an intervention want to wage an ethical war, not a political one.*

That's another absurdity. I won't discuss the issue of whether or not we should intervene militarily in Bosnia. But if you do, how do you avoid the question of the political objectives of that intervention? OK, you have to stop the bloodbath, but then what? You camp there forever? You put the country under mandate? The problem is even more flagrant in the case of Somalia. Because in Yugoslavia, it isn't completely impossible to imagine that once the bloodbath has been stopped (and alas, once much of the ethnic cleansing has been done—as it almost is, already), they might set up three or four political entities that would at least respect the minimal rule of any society, the taboo on murdering anyone you care to. But in Somalia? We absolutely do not know what to do. Humanitarian aid is all very well; we should prevent human beings from dying of hunger if we can. But what do you do if humanitarian aid is systematically plundered and taken over by armed bands? You would have to establish—impose?—a political regime, but which one, and using what means? What ethic has an answer to those questions? Without a political conception, without an answer to the question, "Why and how do we live in society, to do what, what do we view as important in life?" well, there isn't even any true answer to the ethical questions, except perhaps for some Saint Francis of Assisi.

*Paradoxically, those questions are raised twelve years after a left-wing party whose program embodied political rationality came to power.*

I have never thought that French socialists were socialist. In 1981, their program was already an archeological monument. Take "nationalizations," for instance. For decades, people of my ilk had already been demonstrating that "nationalizations" had nothing to do with socialism. Moreover, the French State had always influenced, and even actually run the economy, and it still had the means to do so, if only because it controls credit and the banking system. That point in their program, like almost all the measures they adopted, aside from the day-to-day management of things, was purely demagogic. The only exception, to date, is the creation of the RMI, the minimum income: in a society that continues to be capitalist, you have to have a social safety net. That's not philanthropic, either: someone who is hunger-stricken can't be a citizen, even in the present sense of the term—that's visible in the United States. In 1981–82, the socialists tried to "reflate" the economy, and they failed miserably. Why? Because—and the fact has a more general validity—they were ignorant of the rules governing the society they wanted to reform. You can neither reform nor preserve a social system if you don't have an overview of it. You can't budge a single part of that immensely complex mechanism without taking into account the repercussions on the other parts of the system. The socialists had more or less correctly learned how the capitalist economy works, and they applied the rules with boundless enthusiasm. So that their only claim to fame is that they introduced and enforced the neoliberal program in France. What the population might have had difficulties in accepting had the right done it, it grumpily accepted from the socialists. That's the only reason they have to go down in history, and it's extremely laughable.

*Is the very notion of a political program still meaningful?*

One can—I can—formulate a political program. But that program will be worthless if the vast majority of the population isn't prepared, not to vote for that program, but to participate actively, not only in achieving it, but in expanding and developing it and, if necessary, in changing it. At present, that program cannot be anything other than the project of a society that is self-governed at every level. And it's tautologically clear that such a project is meaningless if people don't have the desire and the will to govern themselves and don't do what it takes for that. But that isn't what we observe nowadays. Does that mean we should give up? I don't think so. History and politics don't allow for any serious predictions. Just before May '68, Pierre Viansson-Ponté wrote his famous article "*La France s'ennuie*" ["France Is Bored"]. It's true; it was so bored that it exploded a few weeks later. I certainly don't mean we're nearing a new May '68. But simply, no opinion poll and no empirical induction can foresee how a population will behave in the short run, not to speak of the middle or long term.

*But the desire to participate implies belief in the possibility of participating.*

Definitely. It's a question of belief, and it's also a question of will, and the two are inseparable in the political sphere. Human history is creation. The development of new social-historical forms isn't foreseeable since it is neither producible nor deducible on the basis of what came before. A sociologist-ethnologist-psychoanalyst from Mars who landed in Greece around

850 BCE would certainly not have been able to foresee Athenian democracy. Or predict the French Revolution in 1730. Now, to say that those forms are the outcome of undetermined creation by human beings means that their creation looks like a vicious circle, from the standpoint of conventional logic. It wasn't the peasant who venerated his lord who participated in the movements that preceded and followed the night of August 4. At the same time as a collective movement takes place, individuals are transformed, and at the same time as individuals change, a collective movement arises. There's no sense in asking which comes first: the two postulates depend on each other and are created simultaneously. It's like the chicken and the egg, or even better, like the emergence of the first live cell. The functioning of cellular DNA presupposes the existence of the products of that functioning. It's like a ring, all the parts of which are held together, and the new creation can only be posited in the wholeness of its complexity. It's true that people today don't believe in the possibility of a self-governed society, so the outcome is that such a society is impossible today. They don't believe in it because they don't want to believe in it, and they don't want to believe in it because they don't believe in it. But if they ever start wanting it, they'll believe in it and they'll be capable.

*The disappearance of the political promised lands should make for greater autonomy and a greater capacity for political creation. But what's happening is very much the opposite. Theoretically, these should be fantastic times.*

And in fact they're nil. That's true, and there is no real "explanation." You can advance several factors that make the fact somewhat comprehensible, or susceptible of elucidation, but you won't have a real explanation. The phases of societal decomposition are as inexplicable as the phases of creation. In Athens, in the sixth and fifth centuries BCE you have the creation of democracy, the great tragic poets, all sorts of other extraordinary creations. By the fourth century it's all over, and there isn't a single great Athenian poet, for example. Why? The Peloponnesian war and the defeat of Athens were certainly part of it. Thucydides wrote some immortal pages on the overall corruption generated by the war (but why not by previous wars?), including the corruption of language, with words coming to mean the opposite of their original meaning, and being used in contradictory senses by the different parties (doesn't that bring anything to mind? nowadays, the word "democracy," for instance). But defeat isn't enough of an "explanation." Why isn't the *dèmos*, the people, the same people anymore?

Why do individuals, as well as societies, lose their creative power? The fact can be partially elucidated, but it can't be explained.

The same is true for the contemporary period. There have been all those immense emancipatory movements over the centuries. There was the labor movement, which has been more or less confiscated by Marxism; Marxism itself has evolved, giving birth to two opposite currents, social democracy and Bolshevism; the former has produced we know what, and the second produced the Gulag. The outcome of which is that the passion and energy of the working class and of all those who wanted to go along with it have gone to waste.

Furthermore, those ideologies not only saw the situation as necessarily sordid and going downhill—the French CP defended the doctrine of "absolute pauperization" of the working class until a rather recent date—but they revolved around the thesis that capitalism was unable to "solve the problem of the development of the productive forces," meaning that you had to establish socialism so that the masses could have access to consumer goods. Now, obviously, developing production and consumption is exactly what capitalism does: you can't compare the "standard of living," which is to say consumption, in the capitalist sense of the term, of a worker in 1840 and in 1990, in the affluent countries. If that's really what we want, and nothing else, why bother changing the government, as the song goes.

At the same time, the outcome of that development is that the population increasingly values money and goods, power, people like Bernard Tapie,[1] and so on. In other words, there has been a sort of depolarization of values, and the negative pole, the subversive pole, has been swallowed up by the capitalist imaginary. All that doesn't "explain" anything, but enables us to elucidate some aspects of the decline, or the waning of conflict and of social and political activity, and to show some of what's behind them.

*What about the need to believe, then? Isn't it intolerable to think that our laws, our beliefs, life in society, don't rest on anything, that there is no absolute foundation for any reality?*

I don't think so, otherwise I wouldn't be here. But that really is what's at issue. Contrary to what Aristotle claimed, what people desire most isn't knowledge, it's belief. In affluent societies—which in fact represent only one seventh of the global population, at most—the end of political beliefs

---

1. [See note 1 (page 154) in "Neither a Historical Necessity nor Simply an 'Ethical' Exigency: A Political and Human Exigency."—Trans.]

and the waning capacity of society to create new, potentially meaningful values has led to the reign of what Pascal would have called amusement, or distractions, that is, oblivion. We don't want to know that we are mortal, that we will die, that there is no reward or compensation in some afterlife. We forget ourselves by watching TV . . . Tapie, or Madonna, or who knows what. . . . Which means that we are not living in a society of the spectacle, but one of oblivion: forgetting death, forgetting the fact that life only has as much meaning as we have been capable of giving it. The spectacle is there to facilitate and cover up that oblivion. We have neither the courage nor the ability to admit that the meaning of our individual and collective life can no longer be provided by a religion or an ideology, that it can no longer be given to us as a gift, and we therefore must create it ourselves.

*Doesn't that lack of courage mean the failure of your project of autonomy?*

I don't think so. The project of autonomy has been advanced in a few societies, including Athenian society and Western societies during the great modern period. In each instance it was borne by movements that unreservedly, except for a few footnotes, were deeply aware of the fact that the meaning of our life is in this world, that no transcendence can give meaning to life if we ourselves disinvest it. Transcendence, in the religious sense, is always an imaginary creation of human beings. The ancient and modern movements of emancipation all began by taking their distance, if not from transcendence itself, at least from the idea that transcendence could affect immanence, for instance by solving the question of society and its just institution. What they believed, essentially, is that there is meaning to our life that is not a mystification, which is the meaning that we ourselves can create.

*You yourself wrote that one of the causes of the present morose atmosphere is the feeling that every value, every standard, is purely contingent. Creating meaning ourselves seems to confront us with radical absurdity. If there is no absolute meaning, how can we avoid thinking that nothing is meaningful?*

First of all, there's a fact that will have to be assimilated one day or the other, which is that we are mortal. Not only us, not only civilizations, but humanity as such and all of its creations, its entire memory, are mortal. The life span of an animal species averages two million years. Even if for some mysterious reason we were to survive indefinitely beyond that point, the day when the sun reaches its terminal phase and becomes a red giant it will extend to somewhere between Earth and Mars. The Parthenon,

Notre-Dame, Rembrandt's and Picasso's paintings, the books containing the *Banquet* and the *Duino Elegies* will be reduced to the state of protons feeding energy to that star.

There are two possible responses to that. The first is the one Pascal and Kierkegaard give: I can't accept that; I cannot or will not see it: somewhere, there must be a meaning; I am incapable of formulating it, but I believe in it. The "content" may differ—it may be given by the Old Testament, the Gospel, the Koran, the Veda, it doesn't matter. The other attitude is to refuse to shut ones eyes, and at the same time to understand that if we want to live, we can't live without meaning, without signification. In that sense, socially, historically created significations are neither contingent nor necessary. They are, as I have written, metacontingent: without them there can be no human life, individual or collective. It's that same life that enables us to understand, at some point, that those significations don't have an "absolute" source, that their source is our own meaning-creating activity. The task of a free man is to be aware of his mortality and to stand up straight on the brim of this abyss, in this chaos bereft of meaning and in which we bring signification into existence. Now, we know that men of that kind and a community of that kind can exist. I'm not even talking about the great artists, thinkers, scientists, or other. Even craftspeople worthy of the name, the ones who made tables, vases, and so on, not statues of the gods, were absolutely invested in their work: the fact that the vase was beautiful, that the house was solid, was an accomplishment in itself. That investment in an activity giving shape, and therefore meaning, has existed in every civilization, without exception. There is less and less of it nowadays, because the evolution of capitalism has destroyed everything that makes work meaningful.

We can't all be Beethoven or Kant. But everyone should do some work in which she can invest and involve herself. That presupposes a radical change in the idea of work, in contemporary technology, in the organization of that work, and so forth—which change is incompatible with the continuation of the present institution of society and of the imaginary it embodies. Even ecologists don't see that tremendous side of the question: they see only the consumption and pollution side. But work is also a part of human life. So we have to make it meaningful once again to work, produce, create, and also to participate in collective projects with other people, to govern oneself individually and collectively, and to decide on social orientations.

It's difficult, of course. But that has existed in the past, to some extent. Among the Greeks, until the end of the fifth century BCE, there was no belief in immortality, or not in any "positive" immortality, at least (life after death was infinitely worse than life on earth, as the shadow of Achilles teaches Ulysses in the *Odyssey*). It's more complicated for the moderns. They have always harbored, more or less hidden, the remains of belief in transcendence of a religious sort. That didn't prevent them from going very far, all the same. But another shift came into play here as well: they postulated an earthly paradise at the "end of history" (for Marxism) or as history's asymptotic trend (for liberalism). As we have every reason to know, today, those were two forms of the same illusion; there is definitely no "immanent meaning" in history, and there will only be as much meaning (or non-meaning) as we are able to create. Now, the people who were fighting to the death on the barricades knew that: it's the fighting that is meaningful, not the prospect of a perfect society two centuries from now. In part, today's morose atmosphere probably also represents the work of mourning for the death of that illusion of an idyllic future.

*The way ethics is being elevated to something sacred at present seems to be a way of staging the lack of meaning. People haul bags of rice, denounce massacres and rapes, knowing, all in all, that if something more important isn't done, there can be no end. At the same time, the tremendous expansion of the media and advertising seems to consecrate that lack of meaning by creating a time that doesn't pass, a sort of immense present.*

That's true. More accurately, there's an imaginary time now, consisting in denying the real past and the real future; a time with no real memory and no real project. Television does indeed constitute an extremely powerful, highly symbolic image of that. Somalia was a scoop yesterday; it isn't one today. If Russia explodes, as it seems to be on the way to doing, they will talk about Russia for two days, then it will be forgotten. There is no longer any true scansion; there's what you call a perpetual present, actually more a sort of molasses, a really uniform soup in which everything is blunted and nothing is more meaningful or important than anything else. Everything is caught up in that shapeless stream of images, which is all of one piece with the loss of any historical future, the loss of any project, and the loss of tradition, with the fact that the past is either an object of scholarship for our excellent historians, or a past for tourists. You visit the Acropolis the way you visit Niagara Falls; you tour Italy the way you tour the Seychelles Islands. The past is materially part of the tourist circuit: a day in Athens, a day in Mykonos, a day in Delphi, and so on. There's no difference between the greatest triviality and the utmost depth, here. In that sense too, triviality is what epitomizes the spirit of our times.

# On Political Judgment

I agree with Vincent Descombes on most of the points he raises. But there are some issues that require a more radical view, in my opinion. I will briefly discuss four of those.

1. First of all, what do we call political judgment? It's true, as Vincent Descombes reminds us, that political judgment, like practical judgment, doesn't strive for the "true" but for the "good." It isn't of the type "I think *a* because *b*," but rather, "I want *x* because *y*." The issues pertain to the *sphere* of *x* and *y*, which is within but not co-extensive with the *prakton* {the sphere of action}, and also to the specificity of that *because*.

We need to distinguish between political judgment within a regime and the political judgment bearing on the regime itself. Suppose we are in 1788: in ordinary language, both a judgment such as "Necker should do *x* to save the monarchy" and another, such as "the monarchy must be abolished and replaced by the republic," will be called political. In the absolute, the former admittedly does not raise any philosophical issue. It states, however implicitly, an "axiom" (the monarchy must be saved), on the basis of which it can develop consequences in an instrumentally rational (*zweck-rational*) manner. That may be atrociously complicated in reality but as such has nothing to do with principles (except if other clauses are introduced: "by any means," for instance).

The (considerable) ambiguity can be eliminated if we agree to distinguish between politics in the narrow sense [*le politique*]—pertaining to the power-related dimension within society, how it is exerted and access thereto—and politics in the broadest sense [*la politique*], bearing on the institution of society as a whole, including of course the power-related

{Published under the title "Sur le jugement politique" in *La Pensée politique*, no. 3 (1995): 209–12, an issue with the theme "The Nation." This paper, along with several other contributions, was intended as a response to an essay by Vincent Descombes, "Philosophie du jugement politique," *La Pensée politique*, no. 2 (1994): 131–57.}

dimension.[1] In its narrow definition, politics does not question the ends and the principles, and it is necessarily encountered in every society, whereas politics as an activity that comprehensively raises the question of the best regime or the good society is essentially a Greek and European creation.

2. This clarification is imperative, I think, if we are to answer the question raised by Vincent Descombes: Is everything political? Of course not, if political means power-related. But certainly yes, by definition so to speak, if we take politics in the broad sense defined above. We must, however, avoid misunderstandings. We (or at least most of us) would definitely want to set limits to any explicit instituting (law-making) activity: but *that itself* is a political position and decision. The idea that everything *should not be* political (or subject to "heavenly law," or other) is a very recent social-historical creation (more or less equivalent to the creation of democracy). Moreover, those limits themselves are subject to political decision. It takes a political decision—an instituting decision—to proclaim and make sure that the *ekklèsia* has no decision-making power over what takes place in the *oikos* and the *agora*, within the limits set by that very decision.[2]

The political (instituting) character of that decision is demonstrated by the fact that the opposite decision not only can be made (as Communist or Nazi totalitarianism did) but actually was made by almost all societies throughout history. That was so, as we know, in all "religious" societies, be they primitive or historical, which always regulated an enormous portion of both "private" activities (within the *oikos*) and private/public ones (within the *agora*) on the basis of "divine" injunctions and principles, just as today's hard-line Islamic societies still want to do. If none of them was able to do so one hundred percent (or, cognizant of the impossibility, did not attempt it), it was for other reasons, essentially because it is impossible to totally control people and circumstances, although they often came close, thanks to complete internalization of the institution.

---

1. See my paper "Pouvoir, politique, autonomie," first published in the *Revue de métaphysique et de morale*, no. 1 (1988), and reissued in *Le Monde morcelé* (Paris: Seuil, 1990), 113–39) {2nd edition, "Points Essais" (2000), 137–71}. ["Power, Politics, Autonomy," in *Philosophy, Politics, Autonomy* (New York: Oxford University Press, 1991), 143–74).—Trans.]

2. my paper "Fait et à faire," first published in the *Revue européenne des sciences sociales* 86 (1989), reprinted in *Autonomie et autotransformation de la société: La philosophie militante de Cornelius Castoriadis*, ed. G. Busino (Geneva: Droz, 1989), 500–509 {and in *Fait et à faire* (Paris: Seuil, 1997), 62–72}. [The English version, "Done and to Be Done," appeared in *The Castoriadis Reader* (Malden, Mass., and Oxford, England: Basil Blackwell, 1997), 361–417.]

3. I don't think the case of the "good Nazi" is a proper example, and far from being "set up to be difficult," it contains several ad hominem elements: the prevalent horror of Nazism and, above all, its defeat. It is both "politically correct" and historically opportunistic. What if we asked, What "good is there, in any sense whatsoever (instrumental or ultimate)" that the rector of the university of Tehran is a good Islamist, or while we're at it, that the 16th-century rector of the university of Salamanca was a good Christian? "Whether, then, you eat or drink, or whatever you do, do all to the glory of God" (1 Corinthians 10:31). Now as we know, the interpretation of what God's glory demands has varied enormously over time, and it would be risky to contend that the most extreme interpretations were incompatible with the survival or even with the expansion of the societies that entertained them. After all, history has known few expansions as massive and rapid as that of Islam, starting in the 7th century.

4. What can the *because . . .* be, for political judgment? How can we justify our wanting a given kind of society, and not some other one? Let's assume that no-one will accept a statement such as "because it is written in Leviticus 20:13 that . . ." as a valid justification, any more than a reference to Bossuet's *Politics Drawn from the Very Words of the Holy Scripture.* That, to begin with, sets us apart from the immense majority of human beings throughout the ages, for whom a justification of that kind was not only legitimate but the only one conceivable. We are located in a social-historical *camp*, the camp of *logon didonai*, accounting for, giving an explanation. But how do we give an explanation?

Vincent Descombes is right in denouncing what I myself had called the confusion between universal history and a philosophy seminar in Frankfurt, and in rejecting what he dubs foundational [*fondationnaire*] philosophy. What one should want, politically, should not be the outcome of reasoning deduced discursively from an unquestionable foundation. There is no such foundation, even in "pure" philosophy (and certainly neither the principle of contradiction nor the conditions of "communication" could possibly fill that role). Mere decisionism is equally unacceptable, since it simply repeats what is: the Nazis are Nazis because they decided to be that, the same being true for both Christians and supporters of the Islamic Salvation Front. Everyone has "always already" decided to be something (if only a cynical, apathetic, spineless citizen), and if we don't go beyond that simple, tautological presentation of the facts, there is no reason for any political judgment.

But why *must there* be political judgment, why *must we* deliver such judgments? Why not cultivate our garden, or leave it all to "the people in the know"? There is no getting around two inaugural decisions or positions, susceptible of being defended by all sorts of more or less reasonable but not logically compelling arguments. There is the decision to do, rather than accept or endure. Then there is the decision to do this rather than that, the opting for one kind of regime rather than another. Those two decisions as well as the entire body of arguments aimed at justifying them presuppose the social-historical creation of a space and time in which political activity, in the broad sense defined above—as explicit aim and volition as to the institution of society, and readiness to account for and justify both—is already posited, so that revealed doctrine, the words of the ancestors, and so on have ceased to be acceptable reasons to do or to not do, to do this rather than that.

Downstream of this position, but downstream only, discussion, arguing, reasoning are possible and certainly needed. Provided it is understood that if we leave the field of the instrumental, the means-rational (in which hypothetico-deductive reasoning remains valid), such reasoning will be reasonable, as I said, but not compelling. Most of the time it will be enthymematic: *ex consequentibus vel repugnantibus*, as Quintilian would say. I can defend my political positions when confronted by someone who agrees that some consequences are superlatively desirable and others terribly detestable. But what person in her right mind would undertake to persuade a convinced Nietzschean of the excellence of democracy?

# Neither Resignation nor Archaism

*You didn't sign either of the two texts that have been circulated, taking a position on the Juppé plan.[1] Why?*

The first (the one proposed by *Esprit*) approved the Juppé plan, in spite of a few theoretical reservations, and was unacceptable to me. The second (known as the "Bourdieu list") was full of the traditional left-wing stereotyped lingo and references to "the Republic"—which Republic?—as though there were a purely "republican" solution to the huge problems presently raised. It was a mixture of archaism and escapism.

*So what do you think of the traditional left-wing positions on this social movement?*

Both the political left and the trade union organizations have again shown how empty they are. They have nothing to say about the substance of the issues. The Socialist Party, that dependable manager of the established system, demanded some vague negotiations. The heads of both unions, the CGT [Confédération Générale du Travail] and FO [Force Ouvrière], jumped onto the train once it had got moving, in an attempt to boost their image. Nothing new in that respect. What is new, on the other hand, and extremely important, is that we have witnessed the awakening of a social movement.

---

{A talk with Alexis Libaert and Philippe Petit, published in the weekly paper *L'Événement du jeudi*, December 21–27, 1995, under the title "Ni 'Esprit' ni Bourdieu: les intellos entre l'archaïsme et la fuite [Neither 'Esprit' nor Bourdieu: Intellectuals Are Torn between Archaism and Escapism]." *Esprit* is a left-wing journal.}

1. [In November 1995, Prime Minister Alain Juppé proposed a plan aimed at "reforming" the socialized medicine system to reduce its cost by increasing the financial contribution of users and setting a later age for civil servants' retirement, triggering a massive movement, predominantly of civil servants and workers in nationalized indus-

*An awakening or a return to older forms of struggle?*

Superficially, the demands were narrowly specific, and the movement seemed uninterested in the overall situation. But it was obvious, given the strikers' reactions and also the attitude of the majority of the population, that the heart of the struggle lay elsewhere: in a deep rejection of the existing state of affairs in general. The strikers were unable to express that rejection otherwise than by making specific demands. Since such demands don't take the overall situation into account, by definition, the outcome is necessarily a blind alley. Moreover, the strikers—students aside, and even they—did not succeed in creating forms of self-organization that would prevent a union takeover. For a long time now, I've been talking about the privatization of individuals, their withdrawal into the private sphere, their lack of interest in public affairs. That's the prevailing trend in contemporary societies. It isn't the only one; we aren't living in a dead, zombified society as yet. Last November and December's movements show that. Men and women are still prepared to act to defend their situation. But they come up against two tremendous obstacles. On the one hand, the double fraudulent bankruptcy of the communist and socialist "left" has produced profound discouragement and bewilderment that won't be easily surmounted. On the other hand, it's increasingly improbable that any reformed version of capitalism will survive. Just about everywhere, the system is going back on the partial reforms it had been obliged to concede over the last century, and its evolution (unbridled globalization under the sign of "neoliberalism") makes the persistence of highly differentiated national situations less and less possible. The resulting immensity, interdependence and complexity of issues make partial demands seem unrealistic and usually doom them to failure. The upshot is greater discouragement and more privatization.

*How do you account for the fact that workers in the private sector didn't join the civil servants?*

They sympathized, but there is a tremendous fear of unemployment and layoffs. Growing unemployment is now part of the logic of capitalist globalization, and the infinitesimal, ridiculous measures adopted by the French

---

tries, later joined by a student movement already in progress, with huge strikes and demonstrations. Under the pressure of the movement, widely approved by "public opinion" despite meager support from the media, including those purportedly on the left, Juppé withdrew his plan. Two groups of intellectuals issued papers taking opposite sides in the ongoing debate on the "reforms."—Trans.]

government won't change that. The ruling strata find it a good thing, actually. In the present phase, they prefer a large margin of the jobless to "discipline" employees. But the main point is that there's no reason for a well-managed firm to invest in France when it can go to China or elsewhere, where wages are a twentieth or a fortieth of the wages paid in France or in Europe in general. Now, once capital is free to go where it likes, thanks to the European Union among others, there is no curbing the process. With two or three exceptions, we may well be on our way to the desertification of the old industrialized countries—very much like what happened in the mining and steel-making regions of western Europe since 1960, but on an infinitely broader scale.

*You don't think the Maastricht Treaty can be a factor of social progress?*

As you know, I have always been an internationalist, and as such I favor the union of the peoples of Europe. But that has nothing to do with what is going on in the European Community. That union would only be truly meaningful, and moreover would only be possible, realistically, if it was political, first of all. Now it's clear that practically no-one wants a political union right now, neither the different peoples, nor the ruling oligarchies. Given that reality, they invented a false good idea, a lowly, technocratic trick, the monetary union. But how can a monetary union possibly function without a common economic policy? And who, other than a political authority, could impose a common economic policy? Actually, that's what is now being done, on the sly. The German determination to obtain economic and political hegemony in the long run is gradually taking shape. Europe has in fact been dominated by the German mark since 1980, and that state of affairs is being consolidated with the Maastricht arrangement. Mr. Trichet, who heads the Bank of France, prides himself on its independence—but it doesn't dare as much as blow its nose without checking with the Bundesbank. Which in turn is consistently following a policy whose sole orientation is the "stability of the value of its currency"; in short, a deflationist policy. Now if any capitalism is to work with zero inflation, it can do so only by producing unemployment.

*What would the solution be, in your opinion?*

There can be no solution without radical changes in the organization of society. But we can talk about that some other time, if you like.

# A Rising Tide of Significancy?

*In your 1993 discussion with Olivier Morel on "the rising tide of insignificancy," you offered a grim picture of French society. According to this analysis, France is not suffering an internal political crisis properly speaking; for, far from there being any debate or political conflict, there is a generalized consensus that dominates political life. To illustrate this point you called attention to the fact that there has been a steady decrease in strike days in France and that the demands of workers are usually corporatist. When you included this interview in your book* La Montée de l'insignifiance, *you added a brief note, written during the strikes of the students and the workers of November and December [1995], stating that whatever the ultimate outcome of the new social movement may be, it has an implicit significance that challenges this characterization. Later, in an interview conducted shortly after the strikes of the whole public sector that had virtually paralyzed France for over a month, you suggested that the movement was not fundamentally corporatist but, to the contrary, a radical rejection of things in general.[1] Does this new movement, along with your concomitant change in perspective, imply that you have a more optimistic analysis of French political life? Given that this was perhaps the most radical and popular protest movement in France since 1968,[2] would you now speak of a "rising tide of significancy"?*

---

[A previously unpublished interview conducted by Max Blechman, editor of the American anarchist periodical *Drunken Boat*, in April 1996, for an issue that never saw the light of day. The footnotes, except when bracketed, are Blechman's.—Trans.]

1. "Les intellos entre l'archaisme et la fuite," interview conducted by Philippe Petit, in *L'Événement du Jeudi*, December 21–27, 1995, 32: "But it is obvious, when one considers the reactions of the strikers as well as the attitude of the majority of the population, that at the heart of this struggle there is something else: a profound rejection of the state of affairs in general."

2. See, for example, Bernard Cassen, "Quand la société dit non," *Le Monde Diplomatique*, January 1996, 8: "Never, since 1968, has a movement evoked such . . . a quest for meaning."

No, that would be too rash; I stick to my terms. I added this note because
it seemed to me obvious that what had been going on before, in terms of
the waning of political and social conflict, could not be applied to this
period strictly speaking, precisely because this movement, though in appearance corporatist with a very narrow scope, was in fact the result of a
deep sense of dissatisfaction: "*On en a marre*," "we are fed up" with all this.
And all this was not just [neo-Gaullist Prime Minister] Juppé's attempt to
reform social security[3] or this and that and the other; it was the whole
system. This, I'm sure, is still there now, but I would not hurry to attach
a qualification to what happened in November and December and what's
happening now in terms of either "this was a last flame" or "this is a new
beginning." We have to see what will happen. Nothing has changed very
much. But there are signs that tend to show that something more than "a
last flame" was at work. These signs are, for instance, a revival of social
criticism, a revival of social critiques of the system; even considering the
attempts to revise Marx, and apart from the fashion/counter-fashion of
the movement, everyone realizes that the situation is at a dead end, and
that this dead end is unbearable. So for the time being I think we have to
keep our eyes open. I have spoken to some friends about beginning some
kind of bulletin or journal. I must add that my remarks on the waning of
the social and political conflict apply to all the rich countries, not just to
France.

*What would you qualify as important in this movement aside from the length of
the strikes, the wildcat initiatives, the sheer number of the strikers, the size of the
protests (two million two hundred thousand people taking the streets on the 12th
of December; again two million on the 16th, etc.)? Do you, for instance, consider
the student general assemblies, their occupation committees that spontaneously
developed in some fifty universities, their national coordination committee, and
the dialogue that emerged in December between striking students and striking
workers as constituting its most important break with Leftist movements in
France since 1968?*

Yes. But in this respect, apart from the students, the railway workers and
the others didn't go as far as in 1968, and that is another reason why I am

---

3. On the 15th of November 1995—during a period when student strikes and occu-
pations, ostensibly for improved studying conditions, were gaining national momen-
tum—Prime Minister Alain Juppé made a series of proposals to cut the expenses of the
social security system, to privatize the hospitals and the phone company, and to raise
the retirement age in the entire public sector, inspiring the latter to join the student
revolt.

cautious in my appreciation of the movement. There were not enough worker-organization committees worth speaking of in terms of the railway workers and the others, and these worker-organization committees were the only new forms of organization that have appeared since 1968. There were a series of delegates from different parts of the country attempting to formulate decisions on a national stage. The local general assemblies were a presupposition of that; they elected delegates, but the general assemblies were not the problem; the real question was, "What about the national level?" In previous struggles of the railway workers and Air France and others, coordination committees had been created to answer this question and to move forward, to solve this problem. In this way they were able to escape bureaucratic control of the movement. This has not happened in the movement of November and December, and this is another way of saying that the trade unions were not sufficiently challenged.

*In this respect the analysis of the trade unions of the '50s and '60s that you articulated in Socialisme ou Barbarie remains pertinent. The [Communist-led] CGT and the other trade unions followed the movement only to contain it and assure their place at the round-table of negotiations with the State. Would it be correct to say that as such you target the trade unions as a major force, or the major force, in preventing the strike of the public sector from becoming a general strike (extending to the private sphere), or in curtailing the autonomy of the movement?*

I do not "target" the unions; this is what they do; this is their business! It is as if you were to ask, "Are you tracing politicians to the capitalist system and the State?" Well, all right, but this is their business; the trade unions for over a century now have been based on the size of their demonstrations and the difficulty or incapacity of the workers' movement to manage its own affairs. The workers delegate their power to the union bureaucracy, and the same happens in America with the AFL-CIO. Of course, the role of the trade unions can be ambiguous, but one should not be astonished if on occasion the unions take on the role of stifling or suppressing or diverting the movement.[4] That's precisely their function in society.

---

4. By way of illustration, consider the following statement of an FO shop steward reported in *Le Monde*, December 18, 1995: "I am convinced that the confederal directors of the CGT and FO never wanted a general strike. Viannet and Blondel [heads, respectively, of the CGT and FO] shit in their pants at the idea. The movement was becoming too spontaneous, too autonomous. . . . [T]hey slammed on the brakes in an attempt to avoid our organizing strike committees in every neighborhood."

*How do you view a trade union such as SUD that is explicitly based on autoges-*
*tion (self-management, self-government) and is inspired by libertarian politics?*
*They specifically challenged the restrictive bureaucracy and the reformism of the*
*CGT [la Confédération Générale du Travail], FO [Force Ouvrière], and particu-*
*larly the CFDT [Confédération Française Démocratique du Travail], and saw*
*their ranks swell by the hundreds, during and after the strikes, mostly by railway*
*workers who decided to leave the traditional trade unions.[5] Two weeks ago during*
*the elections of union representatives at the SNCF [the public French railroad*
*company], SUD surprised everyone by gaining scores comparable to those of the*
*CFDT and FO. Are we witnessing a break with traditional trade unionism, or*
*do you believe that SUD is, by virtue of being a trade union, likely to fall eventu-*
*ally into the traditional role of being a bureaucratic intermediary between workers*
*and the State?*

It is obvious that the success of SUD represents the deep disappointment
workers feel toward the trade-union bureaucracy and especially the CFDT
bureaucracy. Now, as far as they adopt the traditional trade-union form,
one always has to wonder if they are not going to fall into the same traps
into which all the historical attempts to revive the trade-union movement
fell. Recall that one of the major points of the population during the movement was that they don't want another trade union. And once the movement was over they refused to develop the coordination committees. This
expresses the real problematic of the situation: if we keep on functioning
as a coordination committee, either it will transform into a trade union,
and then the trade union will again cause the same problems, or we remain
a coordination committee, and it will just decay (because people will not
go on gathering in meetings all over France, traveling six or twelve hours
on the road, if there is nothing tying them together any more, like a political movement). So there are lots of question marks here, and we must keep
our heads clear.

*You have taken your distance from active political engagement since the events of*
*May '68 and have increasingly devoted your time to theoretical work. I was*

---

5. [SUD (Solidaires, Unitaires, Démocratiques: supporting solidarity, unity, and
democracy) began in 1981 as a group of scattered independent unions and developed
considerably during the 1995 movement, when many workers quit the bureaucratized
unions, and especially the CFDT [Confédération Française Démocratique du Travail],
accused of sabotaging the strike. It crystallized as a national organization in 1998 with
the stated aim of challenging the corporatism of trade unionism and of resisting privatization in the French state economy.—Trans.] According to *Le Monde* (January 6, 1996),
"Its founders are inspired by the anarcho-syndicalism of the beginning of this century
. . . of a syndicalist movement that would achieve the project of social emancipation."

*therefore surprised to hear you say a moment ago that you are considering starting a bulletin. What is the incentive behind this new project and how would you describe it?*

The bulletin, or journal, is a kind of experiment. If it succeeds it will mean something, that there is a fire that is still alive. If there are very few responses, that too will be a sign, though that won't mean in and of itself that the project will stop.

*Was it the revitalization of a radical politics during the movement of last winter that inspired you to launch this project?*

No, the idea has been around since last spring. Considering how depressing things have become, people were saying, "Why don't we do something?" and perhaps they were already scenting the coming events of November and December.

*It seemed to me you were fairly isolated during the debates that have been called "the war of the intellectuals" in December. There were basically two camps that were defined during that period, those liberals who signed a statement published in* Esprit *critically supporting Juppé's social security reform (a position ironically shared by your former collaborator of Socialisme ou Barbarie, Claude Lefort),[6] and those close to Pierre Bourdieu, who signed a statement in* Le Monde *which was against the reform but remained uncritical of the unions and combined old-hat Marxism with vague republicanism. You refused to sign either statement,[7] but at the same time there was no "third camp" position that entered into public discussion. Who then do you expect to participate in such a project among the French public intellectuals of today?*

The project obviously will not appeal to those around Bourdieu or *Esprit*. As for Lefort, I have not worked with him since 1958.

*Yet after Lefort left S. ou B. you both collaborated again in the late '70s. . . .*

---

6. While the movement itself was going on, Lefort expressed his admiration for Nicole Notat (the president of the CFDT who supported the Juppé reforms, catalyzing a rupture in her own union) in "Les dogmes sont finis," *Le Monde*, January 4, 1996, 10.

7. [For Castoriadis' position at the time, see "Neither Resignation nor Archaism" in this volume.]

But that was purely on an intellectual level, because nothing else could be done then! We published two journals, as you know, *Textures* and then *Libre*, which were very theoretical. These journals had no connection whatsoever with any practical activity. They were certainly anti-establishment, but that is the most that could be said of them.

*And yet more specifically these journals did give voice to a theory of political autonomy and to a libertarian critique of the State that was nurtured by the anthropological work of Pierre Clastres, who was on the editorial committee of Libre. Now that Clastres is gone, and Lefort has essentially endorsed parliamentary politics, is there an intellectual milieu, or at all an intellectual environment, that can engage in such a theoretical adventure today?*

Maybe there is, but what we have in mind is not at all a theoretical project. What is missing today is not intellectual work but the ability of intellectuals to be in touch with what is actually going on at a deeper level of society, and this is what we are going to try to fight against.

*The two are separate?*

For me there is a separation between the two. . . .

*You therefore see little purpose in, for example, critiquing Habermas's criticisms of direct democracy, or creating a theoretical bridge between your ideal of a democratic polis and Hannah Arendt's, but want the bulletin to function exclusively as a grassroots forum?*

Nobody cares about Habermas's ideas on democracy; there are really no practical issues in his political philosophy.[8] Hannah Arendt is another

---

8. The relationship of Castoriadis' thought to that of Habermas has been the object of a number of studies since Habermas's 1985 text on Castoriadis, which was translated as "Excursus on Cornelius Castoriadis: The Imaginary Institution" and published in *The Philosophical Discourse on Modernity: Twelve Lectures*, trans. Frederick Lawrence (Cambridge, Mass.: MIT Press, 1987), 327–35 and 419 nn. 1–3; see also 318–26. For the differences between Castoriadis' conception of democracy and that of Habermas see, for example, Konstantinis Kavoulakos, "The Relationship of Realism and Utopianism in the Theories on Democracy of Jürgen Habermas and Cornelius Castoriadis," *Society and Nature* 2, no. 3 (1994): 69–97, and Andreas Kalyvas, "The Politics of Autonomy and the Challenge of Deliberation: Castoriadis contra Habermas," *Thesis Eleven* 64 (February 2001): 1–19. Castoriadis criticizes Habermas's analysis of democracy in "La démocratie comme procédure et comme régime" [in *La Montée de l'Insignifiance*].

thing, and we have a lot of common ground in this respect, but you know there is little difference between her thinking [at that time] and what S. ou B. was always saying. The real purpose of the bulletin is to address the difficulties that the radical movement faces now and how to clear the ground for its development.[9] We want to reject the Bourdieu approach and the *Esprit* approach, and to try to formulate proposals that may make a difference. The issue is not to create a new theoretical direction. Perhaps I am too presumptuous, but I could start a theoretical review any time I want. That is not the problem. The problem is to try to bridge the gap between all the developments and ideas which we have engineered over the last forty years, and the sense among people that these are far away and irrelevant to their concerns. That is the main question.

----

9. Castoriadis died on December 27, 1997, before exploring this idea of a "bulletin or journal" any further.

# A Singular Trajectory

*Your trajectory is a singular one, combining three dimensions: the will to act in the world through political, militant activity; thought, with philosophical activity; and interest in the psyche, expressed in psychoanalytic activity. How do you reconcile those three activities?*

I don't see any antinomy between those three activities. I'm not saying they are one and the same thing, or that one leads to the other, but still and all, they are intertwined. Philosophy and psychoanalysis, in particular, are closely linked. Psychoanalysis enables philosophy to visualize new fields, and philosophy is necessary, in the last analysis, for thinking about the foundations of psychoanalysis. The tie between psychoanalysis and politics is also very important. The idea isn't to transform patients—analysands—into militants; but the goal of psychoanalysis is to make individuals as autonomous as possible, just as the goal of politics is to make individuals and collectivities autonomous. Also, psychoanalysis sheds light on some aspects both of politics and of the difficulty eventually encountered in working and struggling for the collective project of an autonomous society composed of autonomous individuals.

*How do those three dimensions of the mind—the psyche, thought, and the will to act in the world—hold together? What is the articulation? Are they separate orders? How—if at all—does the transition occur, from one to the other?*

All three, as well as judgment, which we could also discuss, are powers, capabilities, of human beings. Although the subconscious and conscious mind, conscious thought, the will to act in the world are definitely distinct, nevertheless you can't say they aren't intimately related. Will is rooted in

{A talk with Lilia Moglia, on March 1, 1997. A Spanish version was published in *Página/12*, the supplement to *Radar* (Buenos Aires, Argentina).}

desire: a desire that has become conscious, thought-out, deliberate, accepted as will. Thought, on the other hand, depends on will, because you have to *want to* think. Thinking is neither mechanical nor passive. There is the will to elucidate the world of our experience. And that will is the requisite for philosophy.

*. . . Can you imagine one or several desirable anthropological types? Can we anticipate, roughly, what sort of anthropological types we suppose would act on our world, and help bring them into existence, as in self-realizing prophecies?*

Can I imagine a desirable anthropological type, capable of acting in the world? Yes, I certainly can. But what good would that do?

*The contemporary imaginary is capable, through its institutions, of inventing representations of the worst things, and in doing so, it often brings them into existence. Conversely, imagining the best possible things and proclaiming them, creating a representation of them, might reverse the process. Imagining a potential subject, a potential actor. . . .*

That actor can be imagined today, but I don't think that would be of any help. She would be a responsible, lucid individual, feeling responsible for what she says and does, attempting to think out what she undertakes and to act only *after* that thinking and deliberating. People of that anthropological type, if they existed, could also bring about a transformation of society, leading to an autonomous society. The question is whether contemporary humankind is still able to produce that anthropological type.

*If that meant a sufficient number of autonomous individuals was required to bring about a transformation of society, would such a transformation have to start by individuals transforming themselves?*

When I talk about the transformation of society I mean the transition, the radical change from present society to one that would be an autonomous collectivity, and that can be conceivable only as a collectivity composed of autonomous individuals. An autonomous collectivity is one whose attitude toward its own institutions is lucid, reflective and free, one that is not subservient to those institutions. One, therefore, which feels capable of changing its institutions when it feels the need or the desire to do so, of changing them with full knowledge of the facts, and considers it legitimate to do so. But a society of that sort is possible only provided the individuals partaking of it are autonomous as well. Of course we can always draw prophetic psycho-anthropological portraits: a novelist could do that, perhaps. But I couldn't say whether that might become a self-realizing prophecy. . . . I, at any rate, am not a prophet.

*. . . Two questions. The first has to do with the project of autonomy and the different dimensions of the mind we talked about before, the psyche, thought and will. Do you think the point of departure of a possible freedom is to be found primarily in one of the three? The second is: How, in your opinion, can we view the project of autonomy—with respect to individual values, on the one hand, and collective values, on the other—from the standpoint of that other dimension of the mind, which is the faculty of judgment?*

That is a very complex question. It's a fact that a free individual always partakes of a social-historical context; and within that social-historical context the individual is obviously born at a given point in history, in a place, with parents, with a language, all givens. That naturally forms a frame around the individual's autonomy. But when I talk about freedom, about individual autonomy, I don't mean some absolute or metaphysical freedom. I don't think one can think or do just anything simply because one has decided to do so. We will always be (among other things), the child of these times, as well as a man speaking this language rather than a different one, who has such and such a history, not another one. But with respect to those givens, an autonomous individual is capable of taking some distance. Take the example of Socrates and the Athenian who merely thinks like everyone else. They speak the same language and have the same experience of the same period, but Socrates is something other than a simple Athenian picked out of the crowd. Today too, there are individuals who can take their distance from their own heritage—that's what autonomy is. It means subjecting what one has received to a lucid, thoughtful examination, and saying to oneself: this I retain, that I don't.

*And freedom resides in that choice?*

Yes, and that examination can never be total. It can never modify everything we think, nor modify it all at once. It's an ongoing labor, and that labor is what I see as defining autonomy.

*. . . Let's talk about psychoanalytic work: there are schools, orthodoxies—sects almost—each advocating its approach, technique, method or path, sometimes fanatically. . . .*

Yes, but you can take a position on all that. For instance, in my own psychoanalytic work, I retain a conventional framework, but I have given the question a lot of thought, and I continue to do so. I think no better solution has been found so far. When it comes to interpreting, on the other hand, although I see myself as true to the spirit of Freud's method, I'm far from following to the letter everything he had to say about one subject or another. I think the theory needs considerable refreshing, which psychoanalysts haven't undertaken, and I try to work on that too. I'm a psychoanalyst because I happen to live in this particular society where psychoanalysis already exists, where Freud and his work already existed. But I did not become, and I try not to be, just one of the crowd of psychoanalysts. I try to think on my own and to transform that heritage if needed. Furthermore, I don't think it's possible to make that distinction, talking about the psyche, thought and will, and to wonder which is the point of departure. There certainly always is a point of departure, but it isn't located, first and foremost, in one of those three dimensions. After all, human beings, with all their inner contradictions and conflicts, are a totality, of sorts. All three are involved, therefore: the subconscious and the radical imagination as well as thinking, lucid reflection and will.

*You said, a moment ago, that you have to want to work on your psyche; you have to want to think. Does that mean that it's will that is the point of departure for that quest for freedom?*

Of course, but that will is also motivated by thought, and by desire. You have to desire to be free. If you don't have that desire you can't be free. But desiring it isn't enough; you have to do it; that is, you must advance a will, and implement a praxis, a reflective, deliberate praxis enabling the achievement of that freedom as the embodiment of a possibility inasmuch as it is desired.

*What would the nature and substance of that desire be?*

Desire is a deep-seated psychic force directed toward something, but which as such cannot account for or give a reason for what it aims at. Will, according to me, is sublimated desire. It is desire that has gone through elucidation, thanks to reflection. Moreover, I don't separate the role of judgment from that of thinking. Judgment is a decisive moment in thinking. Take individual thinking: if we set aside the legacy of history, the language, and the family in which people are born, the society in which they live, and so on, and consider the nucleus, which is to say the radical imagination, the creative imagination, then philosophizing is the creation, by the individual, of significations, but it is judgment as well. The radical imagination advances a number of things, which must be sifted out, filtered. That filter is judgment; and reflection plays a role as well. So does the ability to reason, which is not entirely acquired—it can't be learned by practicing it, although it may be refined by practice—and which is also essential for the coherent articulation of thought. Creation may occasionally occur in an incomplete form, or in fragments, or by a spurt of ideas. But philosophical reasoning requires reflection and judgment.

*Is judgment the locus of a conflict between conflicting wills?*

No, it is, among other things, a means of arbitrating between conflicting ideas. It is a faculty which enables us to "size something up," to appreciate whether it holds or not, whether it may be true or is clearly false. There is an ability to judge, which is an essential, irreducible faculty.

*After the death of God and for a while now, some so-called thinkers have constantly been celebrating the demise of all sorts of things, and especially of history, man, the subject, philosophy, ideologies, politics, work, art, and probably, if we prolong the series logically, we'll soon be able to inter currency as well. Against that rather somber background, what do you think of the paradox of the ethnocentric Western world, that I see as simultaneously ethnocidal and suicidal? Aren't we in a paradoxically mind-boggling, privileged situation of freedom, with the possibility of developing a new conception and a new foundation of the world, by reinstituting values and significations?*

. . . The West is ethnocentric, ethnocidal and suicidal, all at once, and that isn't a paradox. It is the fundamental antinomy of contemporary capitalism, which aims at the unlimited expansion of what is supposedly rational supposed control, but is actually a power-crazed delusion on the way to destroying the imaginary significations that enabled it to develop, as well as the natural terrain that provided the requisites for its expansion. And that imaginary signification leads to impotence, the very impotence of present society, in which no-one governs. Whereas they are proclaiming everywhere that globalization demands this and internationalization demands that, no government is capable of saying no, or of even attempting any opposition; it's like floodwaters, carrying everything in its wake. There is no control whatsoever there. It is urgent, right now, to manage to control the blind forces set in motion by the system, such as technoscience, the destruction of the environment, the craving for wealth and possessions, and so on.

. . . As for the "freedom" characterizing our situation, yes, there is a void upstream of it, because we aren't encumbered by strong social imaginary significations. A few do subsist, of course, and remain powerful: wealth, power, hierarchy, the star system. . . . But still and all, they are terribly worn out. From that standpoint, we are certainly in a situation—mind-boggling if you like—where we have abstract freedom, with the possibility of developing a new conception and a new foundation of the world. But the reinstitution of values and significations is necessarily the work of collectivities; it cannot be the work of an individual. The entire society must begin to act, to tend toward its transformation. If it begins to act, if it takes that direction, it will also create the significations and values attendant on that transformation.

*. . . Is a world containing many worlds conceivable? Is a plural whole, a multiple whole, a perpetually changing whole, conceivable? Also, with respect to the anthropological formations in a plural world, can we speak of a plural person, or a multiple person? . . . What about "human rights," in that case? Also, talking about psychological formations, Within one psyche, an individual consciousness, how can we imagine the mind? What would be the nature of the principle unifying the imaginary significations and affects of a plural subject?*

. . . I don't know what "plural person" means. I prefer to speak of an "open person." As for human rights, if you take the question from a general standpoint, it's a somewhat abstract expression; we don't really know what it covers. There is the Declaration, of course, but it isn't exhaustive; we don't know whether it should be extended, whether other rights should be established. Moreover, most of the rights it mentions are either formal or partial. For example, no declaration of human rights says that human beings have the right to participate in decisions concerning them. Whereas for me, one of the main political slogans should be: "No enforcement of decisions without participation in decision-making." That isn't what is going on. So-called representation is a farce; representatives don't represent the people; they represent an oligarchy. So the question of human rights must be rethought. I don't know what you mean when you ask about the nature of the principle unifying the imaginary significations of a plural subject. If we replace "plural subject" by "open subject," the answer resides in everything we have already said.

*Yes, of course. But if we aren't specific, it might seem that an open subject is an indeterminate individual.*

That's not so, any more than open thinking is indeterminate thinking. Indeterminate thinking remains inadequate thinking. An open subject is someone who is able to determine himself and who stays open to new determinations created by himself or received from others, be they friends or opponents. That's what an open subject is.

*A subject with the capacity of calling himself into question?*

Absolutely. But to call oneself into question, one must be someone. And in some sense, you have to be quite sure of yourself, not sure about your ideas, but courageous and convinced that you will be able to face up to having them challenged. That demands will and daring, of sorts, psychological and intellectual daring.

*. . . Speaking of the reign of currency, as someone who is completely ignorant, I would like to ask you a few questions. The globalization one hears about is simply the globalization of the financial market—and you have rightly called it a "planetary casino." It was made possible by the end of the bipolar world as well as by the revolution in telecommunications technology. But it seems to me that it also corresponds to the culmination of a process that has been accelerating over the last twenty-five years, one of the dematerialization of money and the arrival of temporal money, future-money, credit-money. Has the proverb "time is money" been turned around, into "money is time"? What do you think about that?*

Globalization is not only the fruit of the revolution in telecommunications technology. It is also, and above all, due to changes in production technology, thanks to which immense labor reserves, the manpower of Southeast and Eastern Asia and a few other countries, including some parts of Latin America, could be put to work for a pittance. We are all aware of the purely conventional, instituted nature of monetary signs. The dematerialization of money took the form of the conventionality of money in the modern world ever since banknotes were put in circulation. Those banknotes were theoretically convertible to gold, but the central banks would never have had enough gold to reimburse all the banknotes in circulation in the country had all the holders gone to them simultaneously and demanded gold in exchange. Currency has always been conventional. It is a fact that a new phase in that process has been reached at present. But that's mostly important for speculation, which is indeed totally unbridled nowadays. The major companies can send one hundred billion dollars across the Atlantic Ocean in a second. Transactions are instantaneous. From that standpoint, the planet has become a unified, virtual territory having nothing to do with the real territory. It's a planetary territory in which speculative activity never stops. It begins in Tokyo, at night—what is night for us—then goes on to Hong Kong, Bombay, Frankfurt, Paris and London, and ends in New York and Chicago. During that time, the value of the dollar, the pound, the franc, goods, shares, derivatives, and so forth, all fluctuate.

*Can that territory of financial flows become controllable? Can there be democracy there?*

No, it's an inseparable part of capitalism, and capitalism is incompatible with true democracy.

# Chronology and Bio-Bibliography

*Abbreviations*

For a better understanding of the context of Castoriadis' various publications, we have established a brief chronological frame of reference, including the main dates of public events, of events in the author's life, and of his publications. For a more complete bibliography, including other-language editions, readers are referred to the Internet site www.agoraint-ernational.org. The population and economic figures are of course not "precise" (some are the object of ongoing quarrels among specialists); the intent is to provide an order of magnitude.

CiL    *Crossroads in the Labyrinth* (1978). Trans. Martin H. Ryle and Kate Soper. Cambridge, Mass.: MIT Press, and Brighton, England: Harvester Press, 1984.

CL    *Les Carrefours du labyrinthe.* Paris: Seuil, 1978.

CMR    *Capitalisme moderne et révolution.* vol. 1: *L'impérialisme et la guerre.* Paris: UGE, "10/18," 1979; *vol. 2: Le mouvement révolutionnaire sous le capitalisme moderne.* Paris: UGE, "10/18," 1979.

CR    *The Castoriadis Reader.* Ed. David Ames Curtis. Malden, Mass.: Basil Blackwell, 1997.

CS    *Le Contenu du socialisme.* Paris: UGE, "10/18," 1979.

DDH    *Domaines de l'homme: Les carrefours du labyrinthe II.* Paris: Seuil, 1986.

EMO    *L'Expérience du mouvement ouvrier.* vol. 1: *Comment lutter.* Paris: UGE, "10/18," 1974. vol. 2: *Prolétariat et organisation.* Paris: UGE, "10/18," 1974.

FF    *Fait et à faire: Les carrefours du labyrinthe V.* Paris: Seuil, 1997.

FP    *Figures du pensable: Les carrefours du labyrinthe VI.* Paris: Seuil, 1999.

IIS    *L'Institution imaginaire de la société.* Paris: Seuil, 1975.

MI    *La Montée de l'insignifiance: Les carrefours du labyrinthe IV.* Paris: Seuil, 1996.

MM    *Le Monde morcelé: Les carrefours du labyrinthe III.* Paris: Seuil, 1990.

239

PPA    *Philosophy, Politics, Autonomy. Essays in Political Philosophy*, ed. David Ames Curtis. New York: Oxford University Press, 1991.

PSW    *Political and Social Writings. vol. 1: 1946–1955. From the Critique of Bureaucracy to the Positive Content of Socialism; vol. 2: 1955–1960. From the Workers' Struggle against Bureaucracy to Revolution in the Age of Modern Capitalism; vol. 3: 1961–1979. Recommencing the Revolution: From Socialism to the Autonomous Society.* Trans. and ed. David Ames Curtis. Minneapolis: University of Minnesota Press, 1988 and 1993 respectively.

SB    *La Société bureaucratique. vol. 1: Les rapports de production en Russie.* Paris: UGE, "10/18," 1973; *vol. 2: La révolution contre la bureaucratie.* Paris: UGE, "10/18," 1973.

SF    *La Société française.* Paris: UGE, "10/18," 1979.

S. ou B.    *Socialisme ou Barbarie. Organe de Critique et d'orientation révolutionnaire.* Paris, 1949–1965.

WIF    *World in Fragments: Writings on Politics, Society, Psychoanalysis, and the Imagination.* Trans. and ed. David Ames Curtis. Stanford, Calif.: Stanford University Press, 1997.

## *Chronology and Bio-Bibliography*

| Bio-Bibliographic events | World events |
| --- | --- |
| **1922**<br>March 11: Birth of Cornelius Castoriadis in Constantinople.<br>July: The Castoriadis family moves to Athens. | *April 3: Stalin becomes general secretary of the Russian CP; Aug.–Sept.: the Greek army is defeated in Anatolia; Aug.: failure of the general strike and factory occupations in Italy; Oct. 28: Mussolini's "march on Rome"; Dec. 30: founding of the USSR.*<br>*World population: 1,922,000,000; 18 cities with over one million inhabitants (the largest, London, has a population of 7.3 million).* |
| **1923** | *Oct. 21: failure of the communist uprising in Hamburg; Oct. 29: Ataturk becomes president of the Republic of Turkey; Nov. 9: Hitler attempts a putsch in Munich; Dec. 8: Trotsky denounces the "new course" in the USSR; Dec.: hyperinflation in Germany.* |
| **1924** | *Jan. 21: Lenin dies; Jan. 22: first Labour government in England; June 10: assassination of Italian socialist representative Matteoti; June–July: the 5th Congress of the Communist International (CI) demands the "Bolshevization" of Communist Parties; Nov. 3: the first radio news program is broadcast from the Eiffel Tower.* |

| Bio-Bibliographic events | World events |
|---|---|
| | *Stalin, Zinoviev and Kamenev form an alliance against Trotsky.*<br>*André Breton's* Surrealist manifesto. |
| 1925 | *"30th of May Movement" in Shanghai; Dec.: split between Zinoviev-Kamenev and Stalin, who allies with the "right" (Bukharin, Rykov, Tomski).*<br>*Wolfgang Pauli formulates the exclusion principle; Werner Heisenberg, the uncertainty principle.* |
| 1926 | *May 5–12: failure of the general strike in Great Britain; May 28: military coup d'état in Portugal; July: proclamation of the "united opposition" (Zinoviev, Kamenev, Trotsky); the CI forces the Chinese CP to disarm and to join forces with the Kuomintang.*<br>*Erwin Schrödinger founds wave mechanics; Paul M. Dirac evidences the physics of antiparticles; posthumous publication of Kafka's* The Castle. |
| 1927 | *April 12: onset of the massacre of communists by the Kuomintang in Shanghai; Aug. 22: execution of anarchists Sacco and Vanzetti in the United States; Dec. 11–13: an attempted insurrection is fiercely quashed in Canton, China; Dec.: the "left opposition" is excluded from the CP of the USSR.* |
| 1928 | *Oct.: beginning of the first five-year plan in Russia; July–Sept.: 6th Congress of the CI advances the policy of "class against class."* |
| 1929 | *Feb. 9: condemnation of the "right opposition" in Russia; Oct.: beginning of the forced collectivization in the countryside; Oct. 24: "Black Thursday"—the New York Stock Market collapses and the Great Depression begins.* |
| 1930 | *Oct.–Nov.: trial of the "industrialist party" in Moscow.* |
| 1931 | *March: trial of the "Mensheviks" in Moscow; Sept. 18: Japan invades Manchuria; April 14: proclamation of the Spanish Republic.* |
| 1932 | *July: unemployment figures for Germany: 5,400,000 officially unemployed, 5 million partially unemployed and 2 million unregistered jobless; Nov. 8: F. D. Roosevelt elected president of the United States; Dec.: beginning of the great famine provoked by Stalin in Ukraine (between 4 and 6 million deaths as of August 1933); introduction of the "internal passport" in the USSR.* |

| Bio-Bibliographic events | World events |
| --- | --- |
| **1933** | *Jan. 30: Hindenburg names Hitler chancellor; Feb. 27: burning of the Reichstag; March 4: inauguration of President F. D. Roosevelt, launching of the New Deal.* |
| **1934** | *Feb. 6: extreme-right rioting in Paris; Feb. 1–16: the socialist militia is crushed in Vienna; July 25: assassination of Austrian chancellor Dollfuss; Oct. 6–13: failure of the workers' insurrectional movement in the Asturias (Spain); Oct. 16: start of the Chinese Communists' "Long March" northward; Dec. 1: assassination of S. M. Kirov in Leningrad.* |
| **1935** | *Jan. 13: referendum in Saarland on whether to unite with Germany; Aug. 30–31: beginning of the "Stakhanovist" movement; Oct. 3: Italy invades Abyssinia.* Boris Suvarin's Stalin. |
| **1936** | *Feb. 16: victory of the Popular Front in Spain; April: dictatorship of General Metaxas in Greece; May: Popular Front government in France, strikes and occupations; June 7: "Matignon agreements" in France, introducing paid vacations and the 40-hour work week; June 12: publication of the "Stalinist" constitution, " the most democratic constitution in the world"; July 18: military uprising and beginning of the Spanish Civil War; Aug. 19–24: first great Moscow trial, against the Trotskyite-Zinovievite Terrorist Center (Kamenev and Zinoviev).* Keynes's General Theory . . . ; Charlie Chaplin's Modern Times. |
| **1937** <br> Castoriadis joins the Communist Youth Organization during his last year in high school. <br> Enters law school at Athens University. | *Jan. 23–30: trial of the "parallel center" (former Trotskyists) in Moscow; Jan.–March: strike with occupation at the General Motors factory in Flint, Mich.; July 7: onset of the Sino-Japanese War; May 3–6: the "May days"—the anti-Stalinist workers' insurrection in Barcelona is crushed; June: liquidation of the POUM (Partido Obrero de Unificación Marxista, or Workers' Party of Marxist Unification) in Republican Spain; Dec. 17: the Japanese army massacres tens of thousands of civilians in Nanking.* Trotsky's The Revolution Betrayed. |
| **1938** | *March 2–13: trial of the "block of rightists and Trotskyites" (Bukharin), last of the great Moscow trials; March 13: annexation of Austria by Germany; Sept. 29: the Munich Pact hands Czechoslovakia over to Germany; Sept.: founding of the 4th International (Trotskyist); Nov. 9–10:* Kristallnacht ("Night of broken glass") in Germany. |

| Bio-Bibliographic events | World events |
|---|---|
| **1939** | *March 16: Germany sets up the "protectorate of Bohemia and Moravia"; April 1: victory of Franco, ending the Spanish Civil War; Aug. 23: Nazi–Soviet Nonaggression Pact; Sept. 1: Poland is invaded, first by German then by Soviet troops; Sept. 3: England declares war on Germany, followed by France.* |
| **1940** | *March 5: execution, on Stalin's orders, of 25,000 Polish prisoners, some of whom are buried in the woods of Katyn; June 15: massive deporting of Balts following the occupation and annexation of the Baltic States by the USSR; June 14: German troops enter Paris; Aug. 20: Trotsky is assassinated in Mexico.* |
| **1941**<br>Castoriadis is the co-founder of the clandestine group and journal *Nea Epochi*, aimed at reforming the Greek CP from within. | *April 27: the German troops seize Athens; June 22: the German troops enter the Soviet Union; Dec. 7: the Japanese attack Pearl Harbor, beginning the war in the Pacific; Dec. 11: Germany and Italy declare war on the United States; Dec.: beginning of the systematic massacres of Jews in Poland and Russia.* |
| **1942**<br>Fall: Castoriadis joins the Trotskyist organization headed by Spiros Stinas, with whom he remained in contact until the death of the latter (in 1989).<br>Bachelor's degree in law.<br>Bachelor's degree in economics and social science. | *June 3–7: naval battle of Midway in the Pacific; Sept. 6: the German offensive is stopped at Stalingrad; Oct. 23: battle of El Alamein.* |
| **1943** | *Feb. 2: the Germany army surrenders in Stalingrad; May 15: the Communist International is "disbanded."* |
| **1944** | *Feb. 22: deportation of the Chechens and Ingushes; May 18–19: deportation of the Crimean Tatars; June 6: landing of the Allied troops in Normandy; July 22: Bretton Woods agreement; Oct. 5: General de Gaulle signs a ruling giving women the right to vote; Oct.: the Germans withdraw from Greece; Dec. 3: the Communist-led National Front attempts to seize power in Athens.* |
| **1945**<br>Dec. 29: Castoriadis arrives in France. | *Feb. 4–11: Yalta Conference with Churchill, Roosevelt, and Stalin; May 8: Germany surrenders (the war made about 50 million victims, including 16 million civilian victims in the USSR, and 6 million in Poland, 5 million of whom were Jews, victims of racial persecution); May 8–13: repression of nationalist riots in Setif (Algeria), causing thousands of deaths; June 26: signing of the Charter of the United Nations in San Francisco; Aug. 6* |

| Bio-Bibliographic events | World events |
|---|---|
| | *and 9: atomic bombs on Hiroshima and Nagasaki, killing 200,000 people immediately or within months; Aug. 14: Japan surrenders; Nov. 14: beginning of the Nuremberg trials; Nov. 21: the French Communists enter the de Gaulle government.* |
| **1946**<br>Creation of the "Chaulieu-Montal" (Castoriadis-Lefort) tendency within the (Trotskyist) PCI (Parti Communiste Internationaliste).<br>Aug.: "Sur le régime et contre la défense de l'URSS" ("On the regime and against supporting the USSR"), *Bull. Intérieur du PCI*, 31 (= *SB*, 1:63–72). | *Feb. 15: the first computer, ENIAC (Electronic Numerical Integrator and Computer), is put in operation at the University of Pennsylvania; June 21: Columbia Records announces the development of the first LP record; Aug. 21: Jdanov's report to the Union of Soviet Writers; Nov.: the French CP gets 28.6 percent of votes in the elections; Dec. 28: beginning of the war in Indochina.* |
| **1947** | *March–April: violent repression by France (about 100,000 dead) of the nationalist insurrection in Madagascar; April–May: Trotskyist militants launch a strike at the Renault factory in Boulogne-Billancourt; May 5: the French Communists are ejected from the government; June 5: speech advocating the Marshall Plan for reconstructing Europe; Aug. 15: independence of India and Pakistan; fighting between Hindus and Muslims makes hundreds of thousands of victims in the following months; Sept.: creation of the Communist Information Bureau (Kominform); Nov. 29: the U.N. approves the creation of a Jewish state in Palestine; Nov. 10: beginning of a wave of strikes in France, lasting until Dec. 10.* |
| **1948**<br>July: the "Chaulieu-Montal" tendency decides to break with the Trotskyist movement after the 5th Congress of the PCI.<br>Nov. 30: Castoriadis enters the OEEC (which became the OECD in 1960) as "administrator" (i.e., economist). | *Jan. 30: Gandhi is assassinated; Feb. 25: coup d'état in Czechoslovakia; April: split within the French CGT (Confédération Générale du Travail) union and creation of the (reformist) CGT-FO (Confédération Générale du Travail-Force Ouvrière); May 15: Ben-Gurion proclaims the birth of the State of Israel; June 24: beginning of the first blockade of the western zones of Berlin by the Soviet Union; June 28: Tito is denounced by the Kominform; Dec. 9: the General Assembly of the United Nations adopts a convention on genocide, ratified by the USSR in 1954.* |
| **1949**<br>"Socialisme ou Barbarie," *S. ou B.*, no. 1 (March 1949) (= *SB*, 1:139–83, and as "Socialism or Barbarism," in *PSW*, 1:76–106).<br>"Les rapports de production en Russie," *S. ou B.*, no. 2 (May 1949) (= *SB*, 1:205–81, and as "The Relations of Production in Russia," in *PSW*, 1:107–57). | *Jan. 1: a cease-fire ends the first conflict between India and Pakistan; Jan. 22: the Chinese Communists take Beijing; Jan. 24: start of the Kravchenko versus Les Lettres françaises trial; April 4: signing of the North Atlantic Treaty; May 12: end of the first blockade of Berlin; May 23: creation of the Federal Republic of Germany; July 14: explosion of the first Soviet atomic bomb; Sept.* |

| Bio-Bibliographic events | World events |
|---|---|
| | *16–24: trial of Laszlo Rajk, sentenced to death in Hungary; Sept. 15: Konrad Adenauer, Christian-Democrat, becomes chancellor of West Germany; Oct. 1: proclamation of the People's Republic of China; Oct. 7: proclamation of the German Democratic Republic.*<br>*George Orwell's 1984.* |
| **1950** | *Feb. 9: beginning of Senator Joseph McCarthy's anti-communist campaign; Oct. 21: the Dalai Lama leaves Tibet following its invasion by Chinese troops; June 25: the North Korean army crosses the 38th parallel; Dec. 28: China intervenes in the Korean war.* |
| **1951** | *April 5: death sentence for the Rosenbergs, accused of being Russian spies; May 12: first testing of the American H-bomb; May 23: Tibet becomes part of the People's Republic of China; Dec. 28: Korea is divided into two independent countries.* |
| **1952** | *May 28: violent demonstration of the French CP against the presence of General Ridgway; Nov. 1: American H-bomb; Nov. 20: Slanski trial in Prague.* |
| **1953**<br>"Sur la dynamique du capitalisme," *S. ou B.*, no. 12 (Aug.–Sept. 1953): 1–22; *S. ou B.*, no. 13 (Jan.–March 1954): 60–81. | *Jan. 13: the "assassins in white coats" affair and "anti-Zionist" campaign in the USSR; March 5: Stalin dies; April 27: Crick and Watson announce the discovery of the structure of DNA; June 17–19: workers revolt in East Berlin; onset of a wave of strikes and demonstrations in East Germany; June 19: the Rosenbergs are put to death; July: revolt in the Vorkuta gulags; July 25: signature of the Panmunjom armistice in Korea; Aug. 4: beginning of the civil servants' strike in France, a movement affecting several million workers over the month; Aug. 20: Soviet H-bomb.* |
| **1954** | *April 12: Bill Haley records* Rock around the Clock; *May 7: the French troops surrender at Dien Bien Phu; May 17: a U.S. Supreme Court decision declares segregation in schools unconstitutional; June: coup d'état organized by the CIA against president Arbenz in Guatemala; June 12: Pierre Mendès-France named prime minister of France; Nov. 1: a series of bombings mark the beginning of the Algerian War.*<br>*Marketing of the first transistor radio.* |

| Bio-Bibliographic events | World events |
|---|---|
| **1955**<br>"Sur le contenu du socialisme, I," *S. ou B.*, no. 17 (July 1955) (= *CS*, 67–102, and as "On the Content of Socialism, I," in *PSW*, 1:290–309). | *April 18: beginning of the Bandung Afro-Asian Conference, May 14: signature of the Warsaw Pact; June 20: beginning of major strikes in the Saint-Nazaire and Nantes region of France.* |
| **1956** | *Jan.: Mao Zedong launches the slogan "let a hundred flowers bloom . . ."; Jan. 31: Guy Mollet becomes prime minister of France; Feb. 14–25: 20th Congress of the CP of the Soviet Union; Khrushchev's secret report; March 12: the French parliament gives the government special powers in Algeria, with the support of the CP; March 20: independence of Tunisia; April 17: dissolution of the Kominform; June 28–29: workers riot in Poznan, Poland; Oct. 19: beginning of the "thaw" in Poland; Gomulka becomes general secretary of the CP; Oct. 20: the French intercept the plane carrying Algerian opponent Ben Bella; Oct. 23: demonstrations in Budapest; first intervention of the Russian army; beginning of the Hungarian workers' councils revolution; China backs the Russian intervention; Oct. 29: Israeli troops invade the Sinai; Nov. 3–4: Russian troops crush the Hungarian revolution; Nov. 5: French–British expedition in Port Said, Egypt; Nov. 6: the U.N. imposes a cease-fire in Suez; Dec. 9: the heads of the Central Workers' Council of Budapest are arrested.* |
| **1957**<br>"La révolution prolétarienne contre la bureaucratie," *S. ou B.*, no. 20 (Dec. 1956) (= *SB*, 2:267–337, and as "The Proletarian Revolution against the Bureaucracy," in *PSW*, 2:57–89).<br>"Sur le contenu du socialisme, II," *S. ou B.*, no. 22 (July 1957) (= *CS*, 103–221). | *March 25: signing of the Treaty of Rome; Sept. 23: race riots in several American cities; May: student movement in Beijing and in the provinces; Oct. 4: the USSR launches Sputnik I, the first artificial satellite; May 25: Mao puts an end to the "Hundred Flowers" movement; June 8: the student movement is crushed in China; July–Oct.: American military intervention in Lebanon.* |
| **1958**<br>"Sur le contenu du socialisme, III," *S. ou B.*, no. 23 (Jan. 1958) (= *EMO*, 2:9–88. and as "On the Content of Socialism, III," in *PSW*, 2:155–92). | *May 13: constitution of a "committee for public security" in Algiers, which issued an appeal to General de Gaulle; May 29: de Gaulle is appointed head of government by the National Assembly; Sept. 28: the Constitution of the 5th Republic is adopted by 79 percent of voters in metropolitan France; Oct. 29: John XXIII becomes pope following the death of Pius XII; Dec. 21: de Gaulle is elected president of France.* |

| Bio-Bibliographic events | World events |
|---|---|
| **1959**<br>"Proletariat et organisation," *S. ou B.*, no. 27 (April 1959), and *S. ou B.*, no. 28 (July 1959) (= *EMO*, 2:123–248, and as "Proletariat and Organization," in *PSW*, 2:193–222). | *Jan. 1: Fidel Castro enters Havana; the Common Market becomes effective; Jan. 8: Michel Debré is prime minister of France; March 1: beginning of the Tibetan rebellion, crushed by the Chinese army; March 17: the Dalai Lama flees to India.* |
| **1960**<br>Castoriadis named head of the Division of National Studies at the OECD.<br>"Le mouvement révolutionnaire sous le capitalisme moderne," *S. ou B.*, no. 31 (Dec. 1960), *S. ou B.*, no. 32 (April 1961), and *S. ou B.*, no. 33 (Dec. 1961) (= *CMR*, 2:47–203, and as "Modern Capitalism and Revolution," in *PSW*, 2:226–314). | *Jan. 1: the "new franc" is put into circulation; Jan. 1–Oct. 1: several African countries become independent; Feb. 13: explosion of the first French atomic bomb in the Sahara; March 21: Sharpeville massacre in South Africa; April 5: founding of the French PSU (Parti Socialiste Unifié); May 9: the sale of contraceptive pills is authorized in the United States; July 15: civil war in the Congo; Sept. 6: "Appeal of the 121" for the right to refuse to serve in the Algerian war; Oct. 19: beginning of the American blockade of Cuba; Nov. 9: Democrat J. F. Kennedy elected president of the United States; Dec. 20: beginning of a major wave of strikes in Belgium, lasting until Jan. 18.* |
| **1961**<br>Castoriadis is invited by the University Institute of European Studies in Turin, Italy, for a series of 25 lessons on the "Problems of balance and growth in the present-day European economy." | *Jan. 8: the contraceptive pill is marketed in France; Jan. 17: assassination of Patrice Lumumba in the Congo; April 11: start of the Eichmann trial in Jerusalem; April 17: failure of the U.S. anti-Castro Bay of Pigs landing in Cuba; April 21: first manned space flight by Russian Y. Gagarin; April 22–25: the generals' putsch in Algiers; Aug. 13: beginning of the building of the Berlin wall; Oct. 17–18: violent repression of a demonstration against the establishment of a curfew for Algerians in Paris; Dec. 11: the first American military advisers arrive in Saigon.* |
| **1962** | *Feb. 8: repression of the French left-wing demonstration against the OAS (fractious militaries for maintaining Algeria French) causes 8 deaths at the Charonne subway station; March 18: Évian agreements making Algeria independent; April 14: Georges Pompidou becomes French prime minister; June 1–2: strikes and rioting in Novotcherkassk (USSR); Sept. 20: border conflict between India and China; Oct. 11: beginning of Vatican II council; Oct. 22–Nov. 8: "missile crisis" in Cuba; Oct. 28: French referendum approves election of the president by universal suffrage; Nov. 21: cease-fire on the Chinese-Indian border.* |

| Bio-Bibliographic events | World events |
|---|---|
| **1963**<br>"Recommencer la révolution," *S. ou B.*, no. 35 (Jan. 1964) (= *EMO*, 2:307–65, and as "Recommencing the Revolution," in *PSW*, 3:27–55). | *June 3: death of John XXIII; June 21: Paul VI becomes pope; Aug. 28: Martin Luther King, Jr., leads a civil rights march on Washington, D.C.; Nov. 22: J. F. Kennedy is assassinated in Dallas.*<br>*Open Sino–Soviet conflict breaks out.* |
| **1964**<br>"Le rôle de l'idéologie bolchevique dans la naissance de la bureaucratie," *S. ou B.*, no. 35 (Jan. 1964) (= *EMO*, 2:385–416, and as "The Role of Bolshevik Ideology in the Birth of the Bureaucracy," in *PSW*, 3:89–105).<br>"Marxisme et théorie révolutionnaire," *S. ou B.*, nos. 36–40 (April 1964–June 1965) (= *IIS*, 13–230, and excerpts as "Marxism and Revolutionary Theory," in *CR*, 139–45). | *January: de Gaulle establishes diplomatic relations with Beijing; July 2: civil rights legislation in the U.S.; Aug. 5: beginning of bombing of North Vietnam; Sept. 14: beginning of the "Free Speech Movement" on the Berkeley campus of the University of California; Oct. 15: fall of Khrushchev; Brezhnev becomes general secretary of the Soviet CP; Oct. 16: the Labour Party, led by Harold Wilson, wins the elections in Great Britain; first Chinese nuclear bomb.* |
| **1965** | *Jan. 20: inauguration of Lyndon B. Johnson for a full term as president of the U.S.; Feb. 21: assassination of Malcolm X in the U.S.; April 28: the U.S. Marines land in the Dominican Republic; June 19: downfall of Ben Bella in Algeria; he is replaced by Houari Boumediene; Aug. 5: warfare between India and Pakistan (until Jan. 1966); Aug. 11–16: race riots in Watts, Los Angeles; Sept. 9: the new "Autonomous Region of Tibet" is amputated of its eastern and northeastern provinces; Oct. 1: after the failed attempted coup d'état by "progressive officers" in Indonesia, the repression led by general Suharto causes thousands of victims during the following months; Oct. 30: beginning of the Ben Barka affair; Nov. 24: General Mobutu takes power in the Congo; Dec. 8: end of the Vatican II council; Dec. 19: de Gaulle is reelected, becoming the first French president to be elected by universal suffrage.* |
| **1966** | *Feb. 10–14: trial and sentencing of writers Daniel and Siniavski in the USSR; March 9: France withdraws from the military command of NATO; April 9: the Vatican abandons the Index of prohibited books; May 18: beginning of the "Cultural Revolution" in China; July 2: first French nuclear test in the Pacific; Aug. 8: the Central Committee of the Chinese CP adopts the "16 points" of the "Cultural Revolution."* |

| Bio-Bibliographic events | World events |
|---|---|
| **1967** | *March 18: shipwreck of the oil tanker* Torrey Canyon *off Brittany, the first major oil spill; April 21: coup d'état of the colonels in Greece; May 30: beginning of the Biafra secession; June 5–10: Six-Day War between Israel and the Arab countries; Sept.: the Chinese government gains control again after the "Cultural Revolution"; Mao supports Zhou Enlai and the army; Oct. 9: death of Che Guevara; Nov. 30: first credit cards in France; Dec. 17: liberalization of contraception in France.* |
| **1968** Castoriadis is named director of the Directorate of Statistics, National Accounts and Growth Studies at the OECD. "La révolution anticipée" (= *SF*, 165–222, and as "The Anticipated Revolution," in *PSW*, 3:124–56). "Épilégomènes à une théorie de l'âme que l'on a pu présenter comme science" (= *CL*, 25–64, and as "Epilegomena to a Theory of the Soul Which Has Been Presented as a Science," in *CiL*, 3–45). | *Jan. 5: Dubcek is named general secretary of the Czechoslovakian CP; Jan. 30: beginning of the communists' Tet Offensive in Vietnam; March 22: occupation of the administration tower of the University of Nanterre, birth of the 22nd of March movement in France; April 4: assassination of Martin Luther King, Jr.; May 10–11: "night of the barricades" in the Latin Quarter; May 13: the Sorbonne is reopened and occupied; May 15: beginning of the factory occupation movement; May 20: about ten million strikers throughout France; May 25–27: "Grenelle agreements"; May 27: meeting of leftist parties in the Charléty stadium; May 30: speech by de Gaulle and massive Gaullist demonstration in Paris; June 5: assassination of Senator Robert Kennedy; June 23–30: massive victory of the Gaullist UDR party at the French legislative elections; Aug. 20: the Soviet tanks put an end to the "Prague Spring"; Aug. 23–24: massacre of students on Mexico City's Plaza of the Three Cultures.* |
| **1969** | *Jan. 20: Richard Nixon inaugurated president of the U.S.; Feb. 3: Yasser Arafat heads the PLO; March 18: beginning of American bombings of Cambodia; April 23: Nigerian troops seize Umuahia, putting an end to the Biafra war; April 28: de Gaulle resigns after losing a referendum; June 16: Georges Pompidou is elected president of France; June 26: Jacques Chaban-Delmas named French prime minister; July 11–13: the French SFIO (Section Française de l'Internationale Ouvrière) becomes the new Socialist Party; July 21: Neil Armstrong first human to walk on the moon; Aug. 17: Woodstock (New York) concert attended by 500,000 people; Sept. 1: Gaddafi's coup d'état in Libya; Willy Brandt becomes chancellor of West Germany; Sept. 29: first Chinese H-bomb; Nov. 14: 250,000* |

| Bio-Bibliographic events | World events |
|---|---|
| | *anti–Vietnam War demonstrators in front of the White House; Dec. 3: first heart transplant by Dr. Christiaan Barnard; Dec. 12: a bomb on piazza Fontana in Milan kills 16; beginning of the "strategy of tension" in Italy.* |
| | *Regimes calling themselves "Marxist-Leninist" in the Congo-Brazzaville and Somalia; the U.S. Department of Defense creates ARPANET, a network of 4 computers.* |
| **1970** Feb. 3: Castoriadis is named director of the Statistics, National Accounts, and Growth Studies Branch of the OECD. Oct. 15: Castoriadis is officially naturalized. Dec. 31: Castoriadis resigns from his position with the OECD. | *Jan. 12: end of the civil war in Nigeria; Sept. 4: Salvador Allende wins the elections in Chile; Sept. 6–27: civil war between Jordan and the Palestinians ("Black September"); Sept. 28: death of Egyptian President Gamal Abdel Nasser, replaced by Anwar El Sadat; Nov. 13: Assad's putsch in Syria; Dec.: workers revolt in the Baltic cities of Poland and downfall of Gomulka.* *Drought and famine in Ethiopia.* |
| **1971** "Le dicible et l'indicible" (= *CL*, 125–46, and as "The Sayable and the Unsayable," in *CiL*, 119–44). | *Jan. 25: Idi Amin Dada takes power in Uganda; March 2: secession of Bangladesh; repression by Pakistan sends millions of refugees in flight to India; April 5: Manifesto of the 323 in France, demanding freedom of abortion; June 11–13: François Mitterrand becomes general secretary of the French SP; Aug. 15: the United States announces that the convertibility of the dollar into gold is suspended; the dollar floats; Sept.: announcement of the death of Lin Biao; Oct. 25: China is admitted to the U.N.; Dec. 12: India victoriously conducts a lightning war, ending the Bangladesh conflict.* |
| **1972** Beginning of Castoriadis' participation (up to 1975) in the review *Textures* (with Marcel Gauchet, Jacques Lambinet, Claude Lefort, Robert Legros, and Marc Richir). "Introduction" to the republication of his writings in "10/18" (= *SB*, 1:11–61, and as "General Introduction" in *PSW*, 1:3–36). "Science moderne et interrogation philosophique" (= *CL*, 147–217, and as "Modern Science and Philosophical Interrogation," in *CiL*, 145–226). | *Jan. 30: "Bloody Sunday" in Londonderry, Northern Ireland; Feb. 21: Nixon-Mao talks in Beijing; March: first electronic mail; May–Oct.: massacre of Hutus (between 100,000 and 200,000 victims) by the Burundi army; May 22–30: signing of the SALT I agreements on the limitation of nuclear armaments; June 17: beginning of the Watergate scandal; June 27: French Socialist and Communist Parties sign a "common program for governing"; Aug. 4: Amin Dada decides to expel 40,000 members of Uganda's Asian minority; Sept. 5: killing of Israeli athletes at the Munich Olympic Games by a Palestinian terrorist commando, "Black September"; Dec. 17: Georges Marchais becomes secretary general of the French CP.* *Publication of the Club of Rome report (by D. I. Meadows et al.) on the limits of growth; 16,600 deaths in car accidents in France.* |

| Bio-Bibliographic events | World events |
|---|---|
| **1973**<br>Castoriadis begins psychoanalytic practice. "Technique" (= *CL*, 221–48, and as "Technique," in *CiL*, 229–59).<br>"La question de l'histoire du mouvement ouvrier" (= *EMO* 1:11–120, and as "The Question of the History of the Workers' Movement," in *PSW*, 3:157–206).<br>*La Société bureaucratique, 1: Les rapports de production en Russie.*<br>*La Société bureaucratique, 2: Les rapports de production en Russie.* | *Jan. 1: birth of the "Europe of Nine"; Jan. 27: Paris cease-fire agreements between the United States and North Vietnam; Feb. 13: A. Solzhenitsyn expelled from the USSR; June 19–Jan. 1974: workers at the LIP factory in Besançon, France, attempt self-management; Aug. 18: march on the Larzac (France) against the expansion of a military camp; Sept.: Enrico Berlinguer launches the idea of a "historic compromise" with the Christian Democrats; Sept. 11: coup d'état in Chile; assassination of President Allende; Oct. 6: Yom Kippur War between Israel and the Arab countries; ETA bombing in Madrid against Carrero Blanco, vice-president of the Spanish government; Dec. 22: OPEC decides to double the price of the barrel of oil.*<br>*Publication of Alexander Solzhenitsyn's* The Gulag Archipelago *in Russian, in Paris.* |
| **1974**<br>Castoriadis teaches economics at the Faculty of Nanterre from 1974 to 1976.<br>*L'Expérience du mouvement ouvrier, 1: Comment lutter.*<br>*L'Expérience du mouvement ouvrier, 2: Prolétariat et organisation.*<br>"Réflexions sur le 'développement' et la 'rationalité'" (= *DDH*, 131–74), report for the Figline Valdarno symposium titled "The Crisis in Development" (Sept. 13–17, 1974). | *Jan. 18: peace agreement between Israel and Egypt; April 2: death of Georges Pompidou; March–April: "Carnations Revolution" in Portugal, with strikes and occupations; May 16: India becomes a nuclear power; May 19: Valéry Giscard d'Estaing elected president of France; May 27: Jacques Chirac becomes prime minister; July 5: voting age drops to 18 in France; July 24: end of the dictatorship of the colonels in Greece; Aug. 9: threatened with impeachment, U.S. President Richard Nixon resigns and is succeded by Vice President Gerald Ford; Aug. 14: Turkey invades Cyprus; Sept. 12: Hailé Selassie, the last emperor of Ethiopia, is deposed by a "military council" led by Mengistu Haile Mariam; Nov. 28: the "Veil Act" legalizes voluntary interruption of pregnancy in France.* |
| **1975**<br>*L'Institution imaginaire de la société.*<br>"Valeur, égalité, justice, politique: de Marx à Aristote et d'Aristote à nous" (= *CL*, 249–315, and as "From Marx to Aristotle and from Aristotle to Us," in *CiL*, 260–339). | *April 17: the Khmer Rouge enter Phnom Penh (beginning of the massacres lasting until 1979 and causing about 2 million deaths); April 25: the SP and moderates win the elections in Portugal; April 30: Vietcong troops enter Saigon; May 21: beginning of the trial of the Baader-Meinhof group in West Germany; June 25: Mozambique becomes independent; Oct. 9: Andrei Sakharov receives the Nobel Peace Prize; Nov 11: independence and beginning of the civil war in Angola; Nov. 17: death of Franco; about 200,000 people massacred by the Indonesians in East Timor.*<br>*"Marxist-Leninist" regimes are established in Angola, Cape Verde, Guinea-Bissau and Mozambique; Helsinki Conference; beginning of the SS-20 missile program in the USSR.* |

| Bio-Bibliographic events | World events |
|---|---|
| **1976**<br>"L'exigence révolutionnaire" (= *CS*, 323–66, and as "The Revolutionary Exigency," in *PSW*, 3:227–49). | *Jan. 8: death of Zhou Enlai; Feb. 7: Hua Guofeng becomes prime minister of China; March 24: the army takes power in Argentina; April: demonstrations in Beijing against Mao and the "Gang of Four"; June 6: repression of black rioters in Soweto, South Africa; July 24: dioxin cloud over Seveso, Italy; Aug. 25: French premier J. Chirac resigns, replaced by R. Barre on Aug. 27; Sept. 9: death of Mao Zedong; Oct. 6: the "Gang of Four" is arrested; Nov. 2: Jimmy Carter elected president of the U.S.; Dec. 4: Bokassa becomes emperor of the Central African Republic; South Yemen becomes a "Marxist-Leninist" regime.*<br>*Apple markets the first personal computer.* |
| **1977**<br>Castoriadis is a member (until 1980) of the editorial committee of the journal *Libre* (with Miguel Abensour, Pierre Clastres, Marcel Gauchet, Claude Lefort, Maurice Luciani, and Krzysztof Pomian).<br>"Le régime social de la Russie" (= *DDH*, 175–200, and as "The Social Regime in Russia" in *CR*, 219–38). | *Jan. 1: Beijing and Washington establish diplomatic relations; Jan. 7: publication of the "Charter 77" by a group of Czechoslovakian intellectuals; Jan. 31: inauguration of Paris's Pompidou Center; July 21: Deng Xiaoping is reinstated in his functions; Sept.: break between the French CP and SP on the "updating" of the common program.* |
| **1978**<br>*Les Carrefours du labyrinthe.*<br>"La découverte de l'imagination" (= *DDH*, 327–63, and as "The Discovery of the Imagination," in *WIF*, 213–45).<br>"Transformation sociale et création culturelle" (= *CS*, 413–39, and as "Social Transformation and Cultural Creation," in *PSW*, 3:300–313). | *March 16: the Amoco-Cadiz discharges 100,000 tons of oil off the Brittany coast; May 9: assassination of Aldo Moro by the Red Brigades; July 14: A. Chtcharanski and A. Guinzbourg are condemned in the USSR; systematic recourse to psychiatry as a means of political repression; Sept. 17: Camp David Agreements signed between Egypt and Israel; Oct. 16: Karol Wojtyla becomes pope John Paul II; Nov. 19: the first dazibao challenging Mao and the "Gang of Four" is posted on the "Wall of Democracy"; beginning of the "Beijing Spring"; Dec. 6: new democratic constitution in Spain; Dec.: third plenum of the 11th Congress of the Chinese CP: beginning of economic reforms.* |
| **1979**<br>*Capitalisme moderne et révolution, I: l'impérialisme et la guerre.*<br>*Capitalisme moderne et révolution, II: Le mouvement révolutionnaire sous le capitalisme moderne.*<br>"Socialisme et société autonome" (= *CS*, 11–43, and as "Socialism and Autonomous Society" in *PSW*, 3:314–331).<br>*Le Contenu du socialisme.*<br>*La Société française.*<br>"Une interrogation sans fin" (= *DDH*, 241–60). | *Jan. 7: Vietnamese troops invade Cambodia; Jan. 14: human rights demonstrations in China; Feb. 1: Ayatollah Ruhollah Khomeini arrives in Teheran; Feb. 17: Chinese troops make an incursion into Vietnam; March 5: Hanoi announces a general mobilization and simultaneously Beijing announces the withdrawal of its troops; March 13: creation of the European monetary system; March 16: beginning of the repression of the "Beijing Spring"; March 26: Israel and Egypt sign a peace agreement; March 26–27: second "oil crisis"; March–June: height of the exodus of Viet-* |

| Bio-Bibliographic events | World events |
|---|---|
| 1979–1985: "La *polis* grecque et la création de la démocratie" (= *DDH*, 261–306); first version delivered as a lecture on Oct. 29, 1979, at a seminar led by Jürgen Habermas at the Max-Planck Institute in Starnberg, reworked for a course given in August 1982 at the University of São Paulo and in other talks, including a lecture, "The Greek *Polis* and the Creation of Democracy," read on April 15, 1982, during a Hannah Arendt Memorial Symposium in Political Philosophy organized by New York's New School for Social Research. | *namese boat people (150,000 people); April 1: proclamation of the Islamic Republic in Iran; April 11: Idi Amin Dada absconds; May 4: Margaret Thatcher becomes British prime minister; June 18: SALT II agreements between Carter and Brezhnev in Vienna; July 1: victory of the Sandinistas in Nicaragua; Oct. 16: Wei Jingsheng, one of the main leaders of the "Beijing Spring," receives a 15-year prison sentence; Nov. 5: seizure of hostages at the U.S. Embassy in Tehran; Sept.: downfall of Bokassa; Dec. 12: NATO makes a "double decision" to deploy Pershing 2 and cruise missiles; Dec. 27: beginning of the Soviet intervention in Afghanistan (between 1.5 and 2 million deaths as of 1992). First Walkman marketed by Sony.* |
| **1980** Castoriadis begins to teach at the École des hautes études en sciences sociales (up to June 1995). *De l'écologie à l'autonomie*, with Daniel Cohn-Bendit (Paris: Seuil). | *Jan.: Indira Gandhi wins the legislative elections in India; Jan. 22: Sakharov put under house arrest in Gorki; Aug. 2: 85 deaths in the neo-fascist bombing at the Bologna train station; Aug. 14: workers at the Gdansk shipyards go on strike; Sept. 22: beginning of the Iraq-Iran war; creation of the Solidarność trade union in Poland, Oct. 3: bombing of a Paris synagogue; Nov. 4: Ronald Reagan elected president of the U.S.* |
| **1981** *Devant la guerre: Les réalités* (Paris: Fayard). "La logique des magmas et la question de l'autonomie," contribution to the Cerisy symposium titled "L'auto-organisation" (June 10–17, 1981) (= *DDH*, 385–418, and as "The Logic of Magmas and the Question of Autonomy," in *CR*, 290–318). "Nature et valeur de l'égalité" (= *DDH*, 307–24, and as "The Nature and Value of Equality," in *PPA*, 124–42). Sept. 2–5: Castoriadis participates in a symposium on his work in Porto Alegre, Brazil. "L'imaginaire: la création dans le domaine social-historique" (= *DDH*, 219–37), based on "The Imaginary: Creation in the Social-Historical Domain," contribution to the Stanford University symposium titled "Disorder and Order" (Sept. 14–16, 1981). "Les destinées du totalitarisme" (= *DDH*, 201–18), based on a lecture, "The Destinies of Totalitarianism," delivered on Oct. 3, 1981, at an NYU symposium on the work of Hannah Arendt. | *Jan. 25: the "Gang of Four" condemned in China; Feb. 9: General Jaruzelski takes power in Poland; April 26: the French CP plummets at the first round of the presidential election, with 15.3 percent for its candidate, G. Marchais; May 10: Socialist François Mitterrand elected president of France; June 5: first scientific paper on the development of AIDS; June 24: in France, four Communist ministers participate in the Socialist government; June: Hu Yaobang, close to Deng, replaces Hua Guofeng; Sept. 17: abolition of the death penalty in France; Oct. 6: assassination of Egyptian President Sadat; Oct. 10: 300,000 pacifist demonstrators in Bonn, with the slogan "no American missiles, no Soviet SS-20s"; Oct. 30: over 2 million jobless in France; Dec. 13: General Jaruzelski proclaims martial law in Poland. IBM launches its first personal computer.* |

| Bio-Bibliographic events | World events |
| --- | --- |
| **1982**<br>"La crise des sociétés occidentales" (= *MI*, 11–26, and as "The Crisis in Modern Society" in *PSW*, 3:106–17).<br>"Institution de la société et religion" (= *DDH*, 364–84 and as "The Institution of Society and Religion," in *WIF*, 311–30). | *Jan.: the annual rate of inflation reaches 14 percent in France; Jan. 13: French workers win 5th week of paid holidays; April 2: Argentinian troops land in the Falkland Islands; April 25: Israel withdraws from the Sinai peninsula; May 21: surrender of the Argentinian army in the Falklands; June 6: Israel invades Lebanon; June 14: end of the military dictatorship in Argentina; Sept. 16–18: Sabra and Chatila massacre; Sept. 3: the Mafia assassinates General Dalla Chiesa in Sicily; Aug.: Mexico ceases its debt payments; Aug. 9: six deaths in a bomb attack on a restaurant in Paris's Jewish neighborhood; Oct. 8: Solidarność made illegal in Poland; Oct. 28: the Spanish Socialists win an absolute majority in the legislature; Nov. 10: Brezhnev dies; former KGB head Yuri Andropov becomes general secretary of the Soviet CP.*<br>*Beginning of the repression against the Indian peasants of Guatemala (tens of thousands of victims up to March 1994).* |
| **1983** | *Feb.: Nigeria decides to expel several million aliens; March 1: marketing of CDs in France; June 9: Margaret Thatcher's Conservative Party wins the absolute majority in Great Britain; April 29: the Argentinian government admits the death of 30,000 "missing" persons in Argentina; Dec. 3: the March for Equality organized by youths of North African origin arrives in Paris; Dec. 21: the French weekly* Le Canard enchaîné *reveals the "sniffer planes" scandal (1976–1979); Dec.: the first Pershing-2s are installed in Germany.*<br>*Beginning of the repression against animist and Christian groups in South Sudan: about 2 million victims over twenty years.* |
| **1984**<br>*Crossroads in the Labyrinth.*<br>"Temps et création" (= *MM*, 247–78), containing ideas first presented at the Cerisy symposium "Temps et devenir" (June 1983), later reworked for the Stanford University symposium "The Construction of Time" (February 1988) and published as "Time and Creation," in *Chronotypes: The Construction of Time* (Stanford, Calif.: Stanford University Press, 1991), 38–66. | *Feb. 9: death of Andropov; Feb. 12: beginning of the great British miners' strike; Feb. 13: Constantin Tchernenko becomes general secretary of the Soviet CP; June 5: massacre at the Sikh temple of Arimtsar; Oct. 31: assassination of Indira Gandhi; Nov. 6: U.S. President Ronald Reagan is reelected; Dec. 3: about 20,000 dead and 500,000 wounded following a toxic gas leak in a Union Carbide factory in Bhopal, India.* |

| Bio-Bibliographic events | World events |
|---|---|
| **1985** | *Jan. 19: the Pasteur Institute of Paris isolates the AIDS virus; Gorbachev becomes general secretary of the Soviet CP; July 19: French secret services attack the ecologist boat* Rainbow Warrior *in New Zealand; Nov. 21: mass demonstrations in Chile against the dictatorship.* *Drought and famine in Ethiopia.* |
| **1986** "Portée ontologique de l'histoire de la science" (= *DDH*, 419–55, and as "The Ontological Import of the History of Science," in *WIF*, 342–73). "L'état du sujet aujourd'hui" (= *MM*, 189–225, and as "The State of the Subject Today," in *WIF*, 137–71). *Domaines de l'homme (Les Carrefours du labyrinthe II).* | *Jan. 1: Spain and Portugal enter the European Community; downfall of Duvalier in Haiti; Feb. 25: Ferdinand Marcos flees the Philippines; Feb. 28: assassination of Olof Palme in Sweden; March 18: beginning of the "cohabitation" (of left and right) in France following the victory of the right at the legislative elections; April 26: explosion of a reactor at the Chernobyl nuclear plant, near Kiev; June 22: the Spanish Socialists again win an absolute majority in the legislature; Sept. 17: a bomb in front of a Paris department store kills 7; Nov. 25: "Irangate" scandal in the United States.* |
| **1987** *The Imaginary Institution of Society.* "Réflexions sur le racisme" (= *MM*, 25–38 and as "Reflections on Racism," in *WIF*, 19–31). "Voie sans issue ?" (= *MM*, 71–200, and as "Dead End?" in *PPA*, 243–75). "Psychanalyse et politique": lecture delivered on Oct. 25, 1987, during a Hannah Arendt symposium at New York's New School for Social Research (= *MM*, 141–54, and as "Psychoanalysis and Politics," in *CR*, 348–60). | *Jan. 16: Zhao Ziyang becomes general secretary of the Chinese CP; Jan. 27: Gorbachev launches* perestroika; *April 14: Soviet troops begin to leave Afghanistan; May 11–26: Klaus Barbie trial in Lyons, France; June 11: third consecutive victory of the British Conservatives; June 19: murderous attack by Basque group ETA in a Barcelona shopping center; Oct. 19: "Black Monday" on Wall Street and for stock markets everywhere; Dec. 12: beginning of the first* intifada *in the territories occupied by Israel.* |
| **1988** *Political and Social Writings, vol. 1.* *Political and Social Writings, vol. 2.* "Pouvoir, politique, autonomie" (= *MM*, 113–39, and as "Power, Politics, Autonomy," in *PPA*, 143–74). "Individu, société, rationalité, histoire" (= *MM*, 39–69, and as "Individual, Society, Rationality, History," in *PPA*, 47–80). "Imagination, imaginaire, réflexion" (1988–1991) (= *FF*, 227–81). | *May 8: Mitterrand reelected president of France; May 26: the Vietnamese government announces the withdrawal of its troops from Cambodia; Aug. 25: beginning of negotiations between Iraq and Iran to end the war; Nov. 8: George H. W. Bush elected president of U.S.; in France, the government led by Rocard creates a minimum income (RMI).* |
| **1989** "Fait et à faire" (= *FF*, 9–81), and as "Done and to Be Done," in *CR*, 361–417. "Anthropologie, philosophie, politique (= *MI*, 105–24). | *Feb. 14: fatwa by Ayatollah Khomeini sentencing writer Salman Rushdie to death for the publication of* The Satanic Verses; *March 8: the Chinese decree martial law in Lhasa; May 2: Arafat says the PLO Charter* |

| Bio-Bibliographic events | World events |
|---|---|
| | *calling for the destruction of the State of Israel is outdated; June 4: death of Ayatollah Khomeini; massacre on Tiananmen Square in Beijing; June 24: Jiang Zemin becomes general secretary of the Chinese CP; Nov. 9: the Berlin wall comes down; Dec. 14: the Christian-Democrats win the first free elections in Chile; Dec. 25: downfall and execution of Romanian dictator Nicolae Ceauşescu.* |
| **1990**<br>July 3–10: Symposium in Cerisy, France, titled "Institution-imaginaire-autonomie."<br>*La Société bureaucratique,* 2nd ed. (Paris: Bourgois).<br>*Le Monde morcelé (Les Carrefours du labyrinthe III).*<br>"Quelle démocratie ?" (= *FP,* 145–80, and as "What Democracy?" in *Figures of the Thinkable,* 118–50). | *Jan. 14: end of the Communist regime in Bulgaria; Feb. 11: Nelson Mandela freed after 28 years in prison; Feb. 26: the Sandinistas defeated in Nicaraguan elections; May 11– Aug. 23: Lithuania, Latvia, and Estonia proclaim their independence; Aug. 2: Iraq invades Kuwait; Oct. 2: reunification of Germany; Nov. 27: John Major replaces Margaret Thatcher as British prime minister; Nov. 9: Lech Walesa elected president of Poland.* |
| **1991**<br>*Philosophy, Politics, Autonomy: Essays in Political Philosophy.*<br>"Passion et connaissance" (= *FF,* 123–40). | *Jan. 17–Feb. 28: Gulf War; Jan. 21: victorious rebellion in Ethiopia; Mengistu flees to Zimbabwe; May 27: assassination of Rajiv Gandhi; June 12: Boris Yeltsin elected president of Russia; June 25: beginning of the wars in Yugoslavia, following the declaration of independence of Slovenia and Croatia; Aug. 19–21: failure of an attempted coup d'état in the Soviet Union; Oct. 30: beginning of the Near Eastern peace conference in Madrid; Dec. 8: Russia, Ukraine, and Byelorussia create the Commonwealth of Independent States (CIS); Nov.: siege of the Croatian city of Vukovar by the Serb forces; Dec. 10: adoption of the Maastricht Treaty for the European Union; Dec. 21: end of the Soviet Union; Aug.: French frigates sold to Taiwan; Dec. 26: the Algerian FIS (Islamic Salvation Front, or ISF) wins the legislative elections.<br>The international property market collapses.* |
| **1992**<br>"La construction du monde dans la psychose" (= *FF,* 109–22 and as "The Construction of the World in Psychosis," in *WIF,* 196–210). | *Jan. 11: coup d'état in Algeria, with the elections called off, beginning the low-level civil war that caused between 100,000 and 200,000 deaths up to 2002; April 6: beginning of the siege of Sarajevo; June 14: end of the "Rio Summit"; June 29: assassination of Algerian president Boudiaf; July 17: independence of Slovakia; July 20: "Black Monday on the stock markets; Dec. 9: U.S. Marines land in Somalia; Dec. 20: Slobodan Milošević reelected president of Serbia.* |

| Bio-Bibliographic events | World events |
|---|---|
| | *Approval of the projected Three Gorges Dam on the Yangtze River, requiring the relocation of over one million people.* |
| **1993**<br>*Political and Social Writings*, vol. 3.<br>"Psychanalyse et philosophie" (1993–1996)<br>( = *FF*, 141–54 and as "Psychoanalysis and Philosophy," in *CR*, 348–60). | *Jan. 1: the Maastricht treaty goes into effect; Jan. 20: Bill Clinton inaugurated President of U.S.; Feb. 26: bombing of New York's World Trade Center; March 28: the French left is defeated in the legislative elections; March 29: E. Balladur is prime minister of France; May 24: independence of Eritrea; June 6: fourth consecutive electoral victory for Spanish Socialists; Sept. 13: peace agreement between Israel and the Palestinians; Sept. 21: Yeltsin dissolves the Russian parliament; Oct. 3–4: Russian troops crush the parliamentary rebellion; Nov. 18: free-trade agreement (NAFTA) between the United States, Canada, and Mexico.* |
| **1994**<br>"La démocratie comme procédure et comme régime" ( = *MI*, 221–41). | *Jan. 1: beginning of the peasant revolt in Chiapas, Mexico; March 27: Silvio Berlusconi wins the Italian elections; April 6: beginning of the massacre of Tutsis and moderate Hutus in Rwanda, making close to a million victims; May 4: signature of the Arafat-Rabin agreement on Palestinian "self-government"; May 10: Mandela becomes president of South Africa; July 13–Sept. 13: balseros crisis in Cuba; Oct. 16: fourth consecutive electoral victory of Helmut Kohl in Germany; Dec. 9: beginning of peace negotiations in Northern Ireland; Dec.: financial crisis in Mexico; Republicans win control of both houses of the U.S. Congress.* |
| **1995**<br>1995–1996: "Les racines psychiques et sociales de la haine" ( = *FP*, 183–96, and as "The Psychical and Social Roots of Hate," in *Figures of the Thinkable*, 153–64). | *Jan. 1: Austria, Finland and Sweden join the European Union; Jan. 19: Russian troops take the presidential palace in Chechenya; April 19: Oklahoma City (U.S.) bombing; May 7: Jacques Chirac elected president of France; July: over 7,000 people massacred by the Bosnian Serbs in Srebrenica; March 2: stockbroker Nick Leeson arrested; the Barings, a British commercial bank, is ruined; Nov. 4: Yitzhak Rabin assassinated in Tel Aviv; Nov. 21: peace agreement among Serbia, Croatia, and Bosnia; Nov. 24: Japanese banks have advanced 100 billion euros in bad loans; Nov. 24– Dec. 27: strikes in France in protest against the "Juppé plan" for reforming the socialized medicine system.* |
| **1996**<br>*La Montée de l'insignifiance (Les Carrefours du labyrinthe IV).* | *March 3: the right wins the elections in Spain; April 21: left-center victory in Italy; May 3: Chisso, a Chinese chemical firm, admits its responsibility in the 1,200 deaths caused by* |

| Bio-Bibliographic events | World events |
|---|---|
| | *mercury pollution, since 1932, near the Japanese port of Minamata; May: Chirac announces the end of conscription in France; May 29: Benjamin Netanyahu becomes Israeli prime minister; July 3: Boris Yeltsin reelected president of Russia; Sept. 6: for the first time in France, an asbestos victim is allowed to file suit against John Doe; Oct. 9: some elected officials in the Paris area denounce systematic corruption in the awarding of government contracts.* |
| **1997** *The Castoriadis Reader.* *World in Fragments: Writings on Politics, Society, Psychoanalysis, and the Imagination.* *Fait et à faire (Les Carrefours du labyrinthe V).* "La 'rationalité' du capitalisme" (= *FP*, 65–92, and as "The Rationality of Capitalism," in *Figures of the Thinkable*, 47–70). Dec. 26: death of Cornelius Castoriadis, in Paris. | *Jan. 20: U.S. President Bill Clinton inaugurated for second term; Feb. 19: death of Deng Xiaoping; Feb.: repression following anti-Chinese rioting among the Uighur population of the Xinjiang region; Feb. 4: Milosevic acknowledges the victory of the opposition in the Nov. 1996 Serbian elections; Feb. 22: scientists announce the cloning of a ewe, Dolly, in Roslin, Scotland; March 12: the French Congressional financial commission assesses the cost to the nation of the Crédit Lyonnais Bank scandal at 20 billion euros; May 2: Labour leader Tony Blair becomes British prime minister after 18 years of Conservative rule; May 12: first peace agreement in Chechnya after 3 years of conflict; June: beginning of the financial crisis of the "new Asian economies"; the French right is defeated at the legislative elections and Lionel Jospin becomes prime minister; June 30: Hong Kong returned to China; Sept.–Oct.: several hundreds of thousands of acres of forest burn down in Indonesia; Oct. 8: in North Korea, Kim Jong-Il replaces his father, Kim Il-Sung; Dec. 3: China, the United States, and Russia refuse to sign the treaty on anti-personnel weapons, in Ottawa; Dec. 30: killings in Algeria: 400 dead.* |

## Posthumous Publications of Works by Cornelius Castoriadis

### IN FRENCH

**1998**   *Post-scriptum sur l'insignifiance. Entretiens avec Daniel Mermet.* La Tour-d'Aigues: Éditions de l'Aube.

**1999**   *Dialogue.* La Tour-d'Aigues: Éditions de l'Aube.
*Figures du pensable (Les Carrefours du labyrinthe VI).* Paris: Seuil.
*Sur* Le Politique *de Platon.* Paris: Seuil.

**2002**   *Sujet et vérité dans le monde social-historique. Séminaires 1986–1987 (La Création humaine, 1).* Paris: Seuil.

2004   *Ce qui fait la Grèce 1. D'Homère à Héraclite. Séminaires 1982–1983 (La Création humaine, 2).* Paris: Seuil.

2005   *Une Société à la dérive. Entretiens et débats 1974–1997.* Paris: Seuil.

2007   *Fenêtre sur le chaos.* Paris: Seuil.

2008   *La Cité et les lois. Ce qui fait la Grèce 2. Séminaires 1983–1984 (La Création humaine, 3).* Paris: Seuil.

## In English

2002   *On Plato's* Statesman. Stanford, Calif.: Stanford University Press.

2007   *Figures of the Thinkable.* Trans. Helen Arnold. Stanford, Calif.: Stanford University Press.